Silent Justice

The Clarence Thomas Story

Silent Justice

The Clarence Thomas Story

John Greenya

BARRICADE
BOOKS

Fort Lee • New Jersey

Published by Barricade Books Inc.
185 Bridge Plaza North
Suite 308-A
Ft. Lee, NJ 07024

First Printing
Printed in the United States

Library of Congress Cataloging-in-Publication Data
Greenya, John
    Silent justice: the Clarence Thomas story / John
    Greenya.
        p. cm.
    ISBN: 1-56980-209-2
    1. Thomas, Clarence, 1948- 2. United States. Supreme
    Court--Biography. 3. Judges--United States--Biography.
    I Title.

KF8745.T48 G 74 2001
347.73'2634--dc21
[B]
                                            2001043055

To Denise

Contents

9:45 a.m., Friday, October 11th, 1991

While the fitful overflow crowd waited in the Caucus room of the Old Senate Office Building for Clarence Thomas to appear and be questioned about the charges brought by Anita Hill, the nominee, his wife Virginia, Sally Danforth, and her husband Senator John Danforth, waited in the Senator's small office. At the Senator's request, the four of them shoe-horned their way into the office's tiny bathroom. As they stood there, shoulder-to-shoulder, Danforth pushed the button on a tape recorder, and the familiar strains of "Onward Christian Soldiers" filled the air as they held hands and sang along. Clarence Thomas, Supreme Court nominee, closed his eyes and tapped his feet to the music. After a while, Danforth stopped the tape, put his hands on Thomas's shoulders, and said, "Go forth in the name of Christ, trusting in the power of the Holy Spirit."

Several miles away, at home in his den, Bary Maddox, the owner of Graffiti, the audio-video store where Clarence Thomas used to rent adult videos, sat transfixed. He was in a quandary. Having always liked Thomas, and excited that a customer of his had been nominated for the Supreme Court of the United States, he wondered what Thomas would say when asked if he had ever discussed pornographic videos with Anita Hill, as she had charged.

That evening, when Thomas answered that question by saying, in effect, how dare you ask me such a question, Maddox—still in front of his television set and still transfixed—turned to his wife and said, sadly, "That's a non-denial denial. He just lied."

Introduction

Clarence Thomas: Enigma Redux

"The person you see is Clarence Thomas."

–U.S. Supreme Court
nominee Clarence Thomas
September, 1991

Writing about Clarence Thomas is not easy. That is, getting at the *real* Clarence Thomas is not easy. For one thing, nobody is neutral on the subject. Mention that you are writing a book about Clarence Thomas and no one says, "Ho, hum" or "Who's that again?" or, dismissively, "Oh, really?" In over 30 years of writing and publishing more than a dozen books, I have never written about or with anyone whose very name produces such opposite reactions, all of them strongly held. People either love Clarence Thomas or they hate him. It's as simple as that.

For example, at the beginning of the project, when friends and acquaintances would ask what I was doing and I'd say I was writing a book about Clarence Thomas, the reaction was always immediate and, quite often, visceral.

Those who knew him would immediately mention his friendliness, his openness, his intelligence, and his sense of humor, in particular his "big, booming laugh." Those who knew of him and admired him would speak of his rise to great heights from most humble beginnings. Some would cite his philosophical and political positions, such as his well-known stand against affirmative action, and others some of his judicial opinions or other writings they admired. In almost every instance, their admiration was unqualified.

What *was* qualified, however, was the degree of their willingness to cooperate. When I asked if they would consent to being interviewed about Justice Thomas, the response from his supporters was almost always couched in terms of whether or not he was "cooperating" with me. Did he know I was writing a book about him? Yes. Had he agreed to see me and be interviewed for the book? No. "Well, in that case, I'm afraid I can't...." For example, the director of public affairs at one of the institutions of higher learning from which Clarence Thomas had graduated was candid enough to tell me that the fact that he would not grant me an interview would "affect the degree of cooperation we would be willing to give you." (But then, weeks later, she reversed herself and cooperated fully.)

After a while, it became evident that one of the main reasons why many of these people would not talk to me was that they were following his lead, or thought they were. Whether that was true or not, they felt that because he would not talk to the media, neither should they.

People who opposed Justice Thomas were, on the other hand, only too willing to talk about him, and in many cases quite scurrilously. One liberal writer friend, on hearing the name of my subject, burst out with, "Ah, Scalia's bitch!"

An actor friend from California responded immediately to my phone message that I was doing an "unbiased" book on Clarence Thomas—actually, I think I'd said "unauthorized," but it makes no difference now—by firing off an e-mail accusing me, basically, of selling out everything that is good and true (and liberal) in this country: "I hear you're setting about to write an 'unbiased' bio of Clarence Thomas. Is this the same Supreme Court Justice who, in answering a question about his silence on the bench during the Bush/Gore voting case, declared that he was 'afraid to talk as a young man in grade school.' Whoa! Bending over backwards to make *him* sound like a reasonable jurist may cause you to be looking far up your own hind quarter. Best of luck." And then, just in case the first part hadn't been insulting enough, he added, "For my own amusement: who's footing the bill for this project?…"

Most surprising in its vehemence was an e-mail message from a lawyer friend who'd worked in the Department of Justice under President Gerald Ford's Attorney General Edward Levi. (I later learned he thought I had said I was going to help Thomas with an autobiographical book.)

> I wouldn't touch the topic with a barge poll. If you lie down with dogs you get up with fleas. Thomas is so repellent and evil, so grossly unqualified to touch the hem of Thurgood Marshall's garment, so disgraceful, that you can only lose—personally and professionally—by going anywhere near him.…Thomas's life was put under a microscope during the confirmation process. Since then he has disappeared inside a black hole. What more could anyone possibly learn, or want to learn, from (or about) such a reptilian creature?

Other than that, Mrs. Lincoln, how did you like the play?

Many comments from people opposed to Thomas were cloaked in humor. One man, a distinguished trial lawyer who tried his first case before Thomas was born, said, "My theory is that Clarence Thomas is a ventriloquist, and that the puppet is Scalia!" That was followed by a suggestion on how to open the book:

You begin with five to ten pages on the intellectual stature and major judicial opinions of Antonin Scalia, followed by two to three paragraphs on the same subjects for Clarence Thomas. The fact that God could put those two men on the same Supreme Court only proves he has a sense of humor!

The heat with which many of the anti-Thomas people expressed their opposition was matched by that of his supporters, especially those who knew the justice personally. One man, a Washington lawyer now in private practice but with a string of important government assignments behind him, asked me in to "chat" before deciding if he would agree to be interviewed on the record. Although he never did agree to be interviewed, the "chat" lasted over two hours, during which he raised a number of intriguing points. Having known Clarence Thomas for three decades, he sees him as the undeserving victim of a left-wing conspiracy, in much the same way as First Lady Hillary Clinton saw her husband as a target of the right.

Citing David Brock (*The Real Anita Hill*) as an author who has expressed, in print, the same view of Thomas-as-victim, he blames what he terms the "iron triangle," made up of several key Democratic senators, a larger group of high-level Senate aides (whom he calls the Shadow Senate), and the media—all of whom he believes to be excessively liberal. It was this group, he feels, that ganged up on Thomas and almost cost him the nomination. He believes the fight, with all its attendant notoriety, cost Thomas dearly, especially in the arena of public opinion. In fact, had that not happened, "Clarence Thomas would be the most important African-American in the country today, and that includes Colin Powell."

The lawyer cites another book that he feels is helpful— along with a knowledge of the Justice's Horatio Alger, up-by-his-own-bootstraps life story—in understanding "where Clarence is coming from." Its title is *Our Kind of People:*

Inside America's Black Upper Class, and it was published in 1999 by Harper Collins. Its author is Lawrence Otis Graham, graduate of Princeton University and Harvard Law School and today a writer and television commentator. Graham's book purports to pull back the veil on the world of the black upper class and explain its "obsession with the right schools, families, social clubs, and skin complexion." According to Thomas's lawyer friend, the fact that this world has always been closed to Clarence Thomas is one of the explanations why he has, to this day and despite the heights to which he has risen, so much anger.

Clearly, this attitude is not a figment of Justice Thomas's imagination. Author Graham quotes a well-placed black friend from Washington, D.C. as saying that while upper class African-Americans in the nation's capital accepted the late (Democratic) Commerce Secretary Ron Brown into their select company, they've never given either Thomas or Colin Powell a similar welcome.

> I ask if it's because of their political party affiliation, even though I know that a significant number of the old guard hold onto their Republican status. My friend shakes his head. "No, they have nothing against Republicans."
>
> "Then what is the distinction?" I ask. "Why would black Washington accept outsiders like Ron Brown and reject a Supreme Court justice and a serious presidential contender who enjoys national popularity?"
>
> "Sometimes it's an issue of who demonstrates black pride," my friend explains, as he shares some of the assessments that his parents and their friends—all old guard insiders—have made about people like Powell and Thomas. "They don't like people who are too black, like Jesse Jackson, but they also don't like people who seem to avoid embracing black people and black institutions."

Whether this rap on Thomas (or Powell) is fair is probably now beside the point, as it is highly doubtful that were the justice and his wife invited to join any of these groups they would do so. In a city in which the social pecking order is very clearly defined—and a Supreme Court justice and spouse rank *way* up there—Clarence Thomas and Virginia Lamp Thomas seem not in the least interested. For his part, well before his 1987 marriage to Lamp, Thomas was known for marching to a different drummer. It is probably safe to say that he is the only member of the U.S. Supreme Court to drive a Corvette—or a Chevy Camaro IROC muscle car before that—or, speaking of muscle, to have been an avid weight lifter for more than 25 years. And it is probably even safer to say that the Thomases are the only Supreme Court couple raising a youngster, having adopted his seven-year-old grandnephew in 1997. (When Clarence Thomas gave the American Enterprise Institute's prestigious Boyer lecture in 2001, after acknowledging the reigning dignitaries in proper order, he added, "and my buddy Mark.")

Given these regular-guy, almost blue-collar, roots, one might expect that Thomas would be the voice of the common man on the highest court in the land.

Indeed, at the time of his nomination, his patron and mentor Senator John Danforth predicted, "He will be the people's justice. He understands the ordinary citizen through the disadvantages of his own experience." But given his votes, and certain of his written opinions, that does not appear to be the case. However, with the exception of his education, following the expectations of others, especially the stereotypical expectations of others, has always been a sore point for Thomas.

Take religion, for example. Born a Baptist, young Clarence became a Roman Catholic at the behest of his grandfather. He followed that faith so seriously that for a while he studied to become a priest, after which he transferred to a Catholic college where he was taught by Jesuits. However, on the day after graduation he was married for the first time in an Episcopal church. Years later, after he married his second wife in a Catholic ceremony, they began to worship at a fundamentalist church where some of the members actually spoke in tongues. About five years ago, succumbing to the gentle pressure of a Jesuit priest who had been the president of his college and that of his Supreme Court colleague Antonin Scalia, he again returned to the Catholic faith and is now, it is said, more devout than ever.

Politically, he has moved from middle-of-the-road Democrat to liberal Democrat to Republican to moderate Republican to conservative—some would say very conservative—Republican. Some would also say that had he not made that final transition, he would not be sitting on the U.S. Supreme Court today.

But it has been in the area of civil rights where Clarence Thomas has been most noticeably different. He didn't just *oppose* such concepts as quotas and racial set-asides, and affirmative action in general, he made his name by opposing them. In a high-profile speech, he dissed his own sister for having been on welfare and included her children as well (one of whom would produce "my buddy Mark"). On the way up, he took shots, again in public, at such revered figures as Martin Luther King, Jr. and Thurgood Marshall, as well as Rev. Jesse Jackson. He quoted, admiringly, the writings of conservatives, both black and white, who were well-known for their lack of sympathy for "the struggle."

According to former Senator Paul Simon, civil rights pioneer Rosa Parks was so annoyed at Thomas's referring, in his opening statement to the Senate Judiciary Committee on the occasion of his nomination to the Supreme Court, to herself and to Dr. King, that she told Simon in the hallway, "With what he stands for, he shouldn't be permitted to use Martin Luther King's name that way!"

And the late Carl Rowan, a great friend of Marshall's, wrote, "Over forty years I had heard Marshall curse, in a hundred ways, 'the goddamn black sell-outs.' I had no doubt what he was saying about Clarence Thomas.... He had in one moment of sudden candor said, when the vote confirming Thomas was final, 'We've gone from chicken salad to chicken shit.'"

Yet for all this animosity, if that is not too *weak* a word, that Thomas seems to generate so easily, it is not at all difficult to find people who, on a personal level, feel just the opposite. And they are by no means all conservatives. Take, for example, Sylvia Neal, former associate dean at the University of Chicago Law School, who says she is "as far to the left as one can get." Ms. Neil assisted a group of law students who'd invited Thomas to judge their moot court competition. "As a special request, he asked that we invite some neighborhood children—the university being in Hyde Park where there are a number of inner-city neighborhoods—so that we can meet with them. We did so, and he spent well over an hour with these children, and asked them to follow up with him about their homework and whether they had any questions, and I know he followed up with them. It was a very, very warm experience. *And* he insisted there be no 'PR,'—it wasn't done for the cameras or to make his name better known in the community. He really did it in order to mentor these children."

A personal story of a very different sort is told about one of Thomas's first law clerks, a young man who was only halfway through his term with the Justice when his wife took deathly ill. When he called to tell Thomas's secretary that he was at the hospital—and why—and asked that she inform the justice that he would not be in chambers the next day, the woman gave him Thomas's home number in suburban Virginia, and insisted he call his boss himself. To the astonishment (and eternal gratitude) of the young law clerk, Supreme Court Justice Thomas showed up at the hospital as fast as his car could get him there, still dressed in his jogging clothes.

Perhaps the public perception of Clarence Thomas would be somewhat different if he were not so silent, or, to put it another way, if his silence were not so general and his public appearances so selective. Thomas speaks frequently, and often to young people, but thus far—in his first decade on the high court—it has seldom (if ever) been at venues known to be liberal. (In the past, he has gone so far as to refer to his legal alma mater, Yale, as a "mistake on my résumé" but then, as one of his former clerks points out, "They still don't have a picture of him up in the law school. You'd think if one of your graduates makes it to the Supreme Court you'd at least put up his picture.") But he's spoken, sometimes more than once, at places like Pat Robertson's Regent University, and he helped open Ave Maria Law School in Grand Rapids, Michigan, the conservative Catholic law school founded (and funded with $50 million) by Tom Monahan, who also founded the Domino's Pizza empire.

He routinely denies media requests for interviews (but then so do almost all of the Supremes, as the less-reverent media like to call them). When I started this book, I wrote and requested an interview, being careful to mention, as references, two stalwart Republican conservatives whom I have worked with or written about in the past, Henry Hyde and Kenneth Starr, but that did not help. Justice Thomas, through the Court's office of public information, said no. And some months later, he also said no when Lyle Stuart, the publisher of this book, having read several of the early chapters, wrote and asked if he would care to read the finished manuscript in order to catch errors of fact. Neither of these denials surprised anyone who knew the Justice and his ways. Nonetheless, when just the right (pun intended) spirit moves him, Clarence Thomas will cooperate, as he did when he and his wife appeared on the cover of *People* magazine not long after his contentious confirmation battle. Or when he officiated at the wedding of Rush Limbaugh.

For the most part, however, he remains silent. And of this silence the most conspicuous, and most confusing, is his silence on the bench. In an interview for this book, I asked former U.S. Attorney General Griffin Bell why, in his opinion, Justice Thomas has asked almost no questions during oral argument in his ten years on the Supreme Court.

Bell, himself a former U.S. District Court judge and fellow Georgian who, despite being a Democrat, helped convince then-Senator Sam Nunn of Georgia to support Thomas's nomination, explained, "I've always suspicioned that it was because he felt hurt at the hearings. He was so bruised and battered in the hearings that it had the effect on him of causing him to be withdrawn. I went through a very tough confirmation proceeding myself, and I know what it does to you. And he went through something worse than I did, far worse, and I would think that he thinks he was about as unfairly treated as anybody could have been. And I think so too, but I'm biased about it. In fact, I think the confirmation process is the worst abuse of due process in this country."

What about Justice Thomas's explanation that he's silent because of his embarrassment at having grown up in Georgia speaking a dialect known as Gullah? Bell, whose Southern accent is heavier than Thomas's says, "If that would be a good reason not to speak, I couldn't speak myself! I never have understood why he doesn't ask questions. He *should* ask questions, at least occasionally."

The key word is "hurt." To this day, the post-confirmation writings and public speeches of Clarence Thomas often dwell on thoughts of courage and integrity and loyalty, and are couched in terms that often sound more militaristic than jurisprudential. As one veteran trial lawyer said, somewhat inelegantly, in reference to a Thomas appearance and speech, "It's like a *scab*, like a wound that he won't let heal because he keeps picking at it. You can tell it still bothers him a lot."

At a panel discussion sponsored by the Black Law Students Association at American University Law School in March of 2001 entitled "Clarence Thomas After 10 Years," one of the panelists had some blunt advice for the Justice on this very point. Borrowing a line that former District of Columbia Mayor Marion Barry once directed at his critics, he said, "Get over it." At this moment, however, the chances that the Justice will accept this advice do not appear to be great. When Thomas spoke to the American Enterprise Institute, also in March 2001, his tone often verged on the truculent, and one would not have been at all surprised if he too, like the late Timothy McVeigh, had used the last lines of "Invictus"—"I am the master of my fate/I am the captain of my soul."

It was in part a reprise of the tone and tenor of his remarks to the National Bar Association, an organization composed of black lawyers and judges, in Memphis in 1988 in which he had strung together a litany of complaints, such as, "Unlike the unfortunate practice or custom in Washington and in much of the country, the court is a model of civility...." and, "Though being underestimated has its advantages, the stench of racial inferiority still confounds my olfactory nerves," and "I, for one, have been singled out for particularly bilious and venomous assaults…[because of]…a deeper antecedent offense: I have no right to think the way I do because I'm black."

Very near the end, Clarence Thomas asked, as one of a series of rhetorical questions, "…isn't it time to move on? Isn't it time to realize that being angry with me solves no problems?"

Isn't it just possible that Justice Thomas could benefit, along with everyone else, if he heeded his own advice? But if he did, then he might no longer be an enigma.

Section I
Up From...Almost Nothing

Chapter One

One night in the spring of 1945, a young civil rights lawyer by the name of Thurgood Marshall, on a swing through Southern states trying cases and gathering information that would culminate, a decade later, in the landmark desegregation decision of *Brown v. The Board of Education of Topeka, Kansas*, stopped briefly in Pin Point, Georgia, and spoke at the Brotherhood of Friendship Society meeting hall. It is highly unlikely that anyone in the audience that night, as impressed as they must have been by the passion of this fiery advocate, would have predicted that two decades later he would become the first African-American named to the United States Supreme Court. What none of them could have known, and would never have been so foolish as to predict, was that in March of 1948, in a one-story, one-room wooden shack just down the dirt road from the meeting hall, by the three-room school house and the seafood packing plant and across from the Sweet Fields of Eden Church, would be born a male child who would grow up to become the *second* African-American named to the United States Supreme Court. Some things are just too far fetched.

Even though it was located but seven miles from Savannah, in terms of style and grace the Pin Point, Georgia, of the 1940s and 1950s was light years away from its big city neighbor to the west. With a population of 500, Pin Point was more hamlet than town, more drive-past than drive-in. The thought that this little bump in the road could be the birthplace of a child who would rise to become a justice of the United States Supreme Court—a *black* child who would rise to become a justice of the United States Supreme Court—was inconceivable. The distance from here to there, or, as the justice himself would grow fond of saying, from the outhouse to the courthouse, was simply too great. A black child from Pin Point, Georgia, becoming a member of the U.S. Supreme Court? It simply couldn't happen. Except that it did.

* * * *

For Clarence Thomas, the seven-pound infant brought into the world by a midwife on the night of June 23, 1948, the child destined to inherit the chair, if not follow in the footsteps, of Thurgood Marshall, Pin Point was his whole world, at least in the beginning. The household into which Clarence Thomas was born consisted of his mother, Leola, his sister Emma Mae, and, for a short while, his father, a farmer known simply as M.C. Thomas. When Clarence was two, his mother gave birth to her third child, a son she named Myers after her father, Myers Anderson, a man whose influence would loom large in the future of Clarence Thomas.

Poor and hard-scrabble as it was, Pin Point was not without its attractive aspects. Warm weather brought a profusion of flowers common to the low country, such as azaleas, giant hydrangeas, watermelon flowers, and magnolias. The streets may have been little more than dirt roads, but they led to the ocean and the salt marshes, where even children as poor as the three Thomases could enjoy trolling for crabs at the water's edge or tossing a ball made from an old stocking stuffed with Spanish Moss that grew on so many of the area's multitudinous trees.

Few of the houses, most of which had been set above the watery soil on cinder blocks or large, sawed-off, tree-trunk sections, had more than one room, and there were no amenities such as shades for the single bulbs that gave them what little light they had after dark. The house in which Clarence Thomas was born, and in which he lived for the first five years of his life, like almost all of the others, had no indoor plumbing and certainly no indoor toilet. Water came from a pump in the yard, and the outhouse was a shared affair, servicing the needs of several adjacent families as well as their own. Another common sight behind each dwelling was a small vegetable garden, or patch, from which came healthy fare to go along with the staples of shrimp and fish. Both inside and outside the simple dwellings, neatness was evident. As the most famous former resident of Pin Point would say many years later, "We were poor but proud. I keep hearing this connection between disorder and poverty. You didn't see any disorder."

The house in which Thomas spent his first years (it was actually the house of his aunt, Annie Graham) was next door to Varn & Son, the crab and oyster packing plant where his mother worked, and where she was known to be the fastest of the fast. As she told one of her son Clarence's first biographers, "I could do seventy-five pounds if I sat there all day. When I was pregnant with Clarence, I would go home and

25

lie down for a while, then I'd go back and still beat them all." She also recounted the time she and other crab and oyster pickers, who were paid five cents a pound, threatened to go out on strike for more money: "We were going to strike for 10 cents, but when the man came in no one said a word. They knew I was the one to shoot my mouth off, so they all looked at me and I spoke up and we got it. It's no wonder where Clarence got it from to speak his mind."

Poor as they were—*everyone* in Pin Point was poor— the Thomas family got by, barely, on the wages of Leola and the somewhat sporadic earnings of M.C. But when Clarence was two years old, there was a major alteration in his world. His father, who had never been the most faithful of men, had impregnated his latest girlfriend, and when Leola confronted him and asked what he planned to do about it, M.C. solved the problem by taking off for Philadelphia and abandoning the family just months before the birth of his second son, Myers. For all intents and purposes, he would never again be a factor in Clarence's life, at least not a positive one.

With her wages from the plant, and whatever else Leola could pick up working as a maid in nearby Savannah, the family made do. While the total family income was probably below what was considered subsistence level at the time in rural Georgia, life, at least for a child, was not without some saving graces. As preschoolers, the three Thomas children made the dusty streets and the waters' edges their playgrounds. One biographer would later write in a book that was part of a series on distinguished African-Americans, "If the children were lucky enough to find an abandoned tire, they climbed into it and gleefully rolled down the road. A discarded bicycle wheel provided hours of entertainment; they made it roll along by using a stick or a bent hangar, and when they tired of that, they took out the spokes and flung the wheel through the air with backspin, so that it landed in the dust and rolled back to them. They made trains from soda cans and fashioned skatemobiles from old skate wheels and stray pieces of wood."

In a speech he gave to a conservative religious group (The Acton Institute for the Study of Religion and Liberty) five years after becoming a member of the Supreme Court, Clarence Thomas talked about those early days: "Almost a decade ago I heard a minister say that we were money-poor and values-rich in our youth. That is certainly true of my youth, though I did not know that we were money-poor until I was told so during my college years. Indeed, as long as we had food on the table, a roof over our heads, and clothes on our backs, we were money-rich. In all those years I didn't hear a single complaint about what we didn't have. Sure, we were told as kids we couldn't have this or that toy, because there was no money for it. But this was not offered as a complaint, but rather as a realistic assessment of our financial position as a family. Not getting what we wanted when we wanted it (or at all) didn't mean we were money-poor."

Four years later, in a speech to a similar group (The John M. Ashbrook Center for Public Affairs, part of Ashland University in Ashland, Ohio), he touched on the same theme. Referring to the current day, he said that in contrast to the "positive environment" in which he'd grown up, "What we're doing [nowadays] is inundating these kids with negatives. Everything is negative. You can't do this, you can't do that. And then we allow the neighborhoods in which they live to be in chaos. I grew up in a neighborhood that wasn't considered a great neighborhood, but it was peaceful. It was conducive to survival. And the people were just good upstanding people. We weren't assaulted when we went to school. We weren't in fear for our lives. You could walk to the library. It was poor and lots of people grew up like that. For the life of me, I don't understand why those of us who say we are so passionate about little kids can't see that they can't grow up in these environments."

In 1954, the year Thurgood Marshall and his team of dedicated civil rights lawyers won the *Brown* case, Clarence Thomas started first grade. It was also the year he got his first pair of shoes, along with some hand-me-down clothes from a local church. From 1950, when his father left the family, until 1955, young Clarence had been living a relatively carefree life. Because it was a safe family-oriented community, Clarence and his siblings, especially his younger brother Myers, were allowed a good deal of freedom to roam the immediate neighborhood. In time, Leola Thomas gave up her job at the crab and oyster packing plant and went off to work as a cleaning woman or maid in nearby Savannah. The boys, left in the care of their aunt, who also led a hard life, had even less supervision.

One day in 1955, when Clarence and Emma Mae were in school and their aunt was at work, Myers, who was supposed to be staying with and under the care of an uncle, wandered back into Aunt Annie's little ramshackle house. Somehow, a flimsy curtain touched the red-hot wood stove, and within minutes the tarpaper shack was engulfed in flames and soon destroyed completely.

New arrangements had to be made in a hurry, and once the dust, if not the ashes, had settled, Clarence and Myers were living in Savannah with their mother, and Emma Mae was back in Pin Point with Aunt Annie.

Home for Leola and her two growing boys was one room in a crowded tenement building on a busy block in a black commercial area. The kitchen, such as it was, had to be shared with the three other families that lived in the run-down building. Again, there was no indoor toilet. In fact, the old-fashioned privy in the backyard was often unusable. Leola made but 10 or 15 dollars a week, and one room was all she could afford. That winter—the first to follow the historic Supreme Court decision in the *Brown* desegregation case—she enrolled Clarence in first grade, afternoon session only, in the Florence School, an all-black public school where, he later admitted, he spent most of the time staring out the window. Before long young Clarence Thomas would discover the joys of reading, but whoever it was who lit the lamp of his love for learning, it was not anyone in the Florence School.

Clarence lost more than his boyish innocence in the move to Savannah. He also lost his unawareness of racial prejudice. Tiny little Pin Point had so few public buildings there was no need to segregate its facilities, but in Savannah, the signs were everywhere. "Room for Rent, White Only." "White Faucet." "White Entrance." "Whites Only Need Apply." Even the library, which Clarence looked upon with awe, was for white readers only. He would have to use the Carnegie Library in the "colored section." It was not just a different world, it was the real world.

One thing that did not change was the amount of freedom he and his younger brother Myers enjoyed. With their mother working all day, and no Aunt Annie or older sister to check on their whereabouts, they roamed the streets of their black Savannah neighborhood almost at will. While their mother worried about this state of affairs, there was little she could do about it. Her fears, however, reached a point where she was forced to seek the help of her own father, a stern man with whom she did not have a close relationship.

Dictionaries should carry a picture of Myers Anderson alongside the definitions of the words "self-made" and "industrious." Even though he was not able to attend school past the third grade, he was a man of sharp intelligence, fierce pride, and gargantuan work habits. Had he lived today, he'd be called an entrepreneur. Among his early businesses were an ice delivery route and a wood delivery route. When he invested in a machine to make cinder blocks, he didn't just sell the product, he used it to build three small houses; one became his own dwelling and the others were "rent houses." His most successful venture was his home heating-oil delivery business which prospered in part because Myers was willing to get up every morning at 3:30 and get down to the wholesaler to buy his day's supply. Along with a friend, he started a black nightclub that became so popular—and profitable—that the landlord took it away from him. While other proud African-Americans of his generation might have become bitter as a result of such a setback, it only made Myers Anderson work harder. And when he attempted to get a license for his fuel delivery business, it was denied, and he was advised to get a white man to front for him. Again, Myers shouldered the rebuff and went his own way, just as he did when he was told that because of his race he could not take the test to become a certified electrician even though he had the requisite knowledge and experience and had, in fact, already wired the premises in question (his three houses) himself.

Still seething 30 years later, Clarence Thomas told an interviewer: "My grandfather had an opportunity to make a lot of money during the building boom after the Korean War and World War II, but he couldn't get the license. A black person could not obtain an electrician's license. So what they would do is wire an entire house and then pay maybe $100 to a white electrician to connect the wire from the post to the box—about a two-minute job."

Savannah, Georgia, in the 1940s and 1950s was ruled by *Plessy v. Ferguson* (and in some pockets *Dred Scott*), and not by the rationale of the *Brown* decision.

The reason that Leola Thomas and her father were not close was the long-standing tension over the fact that he had never married her mother. The two had met in a rural area quite a way from Savannah, and after Leola was born, Myers had, in effect, sent mother and child off to Pin Point and Aunt Annie. He then married another woman, and they moved to Savannah where he began his steady climb up the economic ladder. Leola was forced to grow up a fatherless child, a scar she still bore as a young adult beginning her own family. But now, in 1955, she had hit a very rough patch, and, worried what might happen to her two rambunctious sons, she finally turned to her father for help.

Myers Anderson represented more than just a better alternative, more than simply a safe haven. He was a rock. In addition to owning his own business, he was a man of property. But, even more important as far as the future of his two young grandsons was concerned, he was a man of principle and probity. If they moved into his house and came under his care and discipline, they would stand a very good chance of growing up to become real men.

Knowing this, Leola swallowed her pride and asked her father to take her children. She would continue to live in Savannah and provide whatever help she could. But Myers, Sr. said no. Fortunately for Clarence and Myers, Jr., their step-grandmother was a kind woman. Tina and Myers had never had children of their own, and most of the people who knew the families would have understood, given Tina's age and situation, if she'd resisted the idea of bringing two rough-and-tumble boys into her comfortable and orderly environment. But Christina (or simply Tina or Teenie) Anderson felt just the opposite way. She not only believed that Myers had an obligation to help his daughter and his grandchildren, but actively encouraged him to do so.

Eventually, Myers agreed, but not entirely. He would take the two boys, and he would raise them as he saw fit, but the girl, Emma Mae, would have to go back to Aunt Annie in Pin Point. With the possible exception of Emma Mae, it was a good deal for everyone concerned, especially Clarence and little Myers. Instead of one room in a crowded tenement building, they now lived in a house with six rooms, a real kitchen out of which came three good meals every single

31

day, and an *indoor* toilet that worked all the time.

The most important change, however, was that they now had, for the first time in their young lives, a male role model. So great would be the influence of Myers Anderson on Clarence Thomas that one of the first items the younger man took with him in 1991 to his chambers at the U.S. Supreme Court was a bronze bust of his grandfather. Across its base was inscribed one of Myers's favorite aphorisms: "Old Man Can't is dead. I helped bury him."

Unlike many older people who favor such expressions, Myers Anderson lived them in his daily life. Like the military officer who would never order his men to do a difficult task that he would not do himself, Myers practiced what he preached. Years later, in his speeches, Clarence Thomas would include another of his grandfather's favorites, one that was designed to rid the boys of any ideas of ever skipping school: "He would tell us, 'If you die, I'll take you to school for two days to make sure you're not faking.'" Then, revealing a hint of his characteristic sense of humor, Thomas would add, "I often wondered if the other students would object to a dead person being in the classroom."

In addition to his belief in a strong work ethic, Myers also had a strong religious belief, having converted from the Baptist faith to Catholicism as an adult. For himself, he saw the Church as his ultimate salvation; for his grandsons, he saw it as their immediate educational salvation. Thus Clarence and Myers, Jr. soon found themselves enrolled in St. Benedict the Moor, a Catholic grade school. The school was staffed by Irish nuns, members of a branch of the brown-robed Franciscan order that had been started in the early 1900s specifically to educate poor African-American children. So strong was the influence of the Irish nuns on the young African-American students that some of the children eventually began to speak with a brogue. Welcome as the nuns were to the parents of their charges, they were considered meddling outsiders by many white adults, especially the more bigoted ones. The KKK, who always called them the "Nigger nuns," once parked an empty hearse in front of their convent as a not-too-subtle warning.

Between the nuns and his grandfather, young Clarence Thomas learned both the meaning and the practice of discipline. Dressed in his school uniform of blue pants, blue sweater, white shirt, and dark tie and shoes, he marched off to St. Benedict's and a much more rigid and difficult educational environment than he was used to. At first there were some adjustment problems—his second grade nun gave him three Ds, but they were the last Ds he was ever to see on a report card. Once he got with the program, Clarence Thomas excelled. Clearly, he was motivated by more than fear of his grandfather's belt. He didn't just learn to read; he learned to love reading. He also took part in a wide variety of school activities, both secular and religious, becoming a crossing guard, an altar boy, and holding class office. The one thing about which he had no doubt was the sincerity of the nuns' desire that he go as far in life as he could possibly go—and that he get there on his own efforts and merit. "They made us believe we were the equal of anybody," he would repeat years later, "and they gave us the same tests the white schools took. They refused to let us buy into the notion that we could never do well, despite all the stereotypes of inferiority around us."

Many years later, he told a primary school graduating class: "One of the rewards I received when I graduated from the eighth grade was a knock on my head from Sister Mary Virgilius—well, it was a love tap, and it was simply to remind me that I was pretty lazy, and I was. . . .

"The nuns kept expectations high, but they also provided us with a firm love, and they had a conviction that indeed we could do—and they saw to it that we did it."

Seeing to it that he did "it"—an abstraction that covered

a lot of ground—was also a chief aim of Clarence's grandfather. It was clear from the day they moved in with him and Tina that Myers Anderson had no intention of letting Clarence and his brother continue their lay-about ways. Come Saturday morning, if they weren't out of bed by 7:00, he'd be in the backyard yelling through their window, "Laziness is for the rich. Y'all think you're rich?"

The boys had work to do everyday. Whether it was chores around the house or help with the heating-oil deliveries, they worked before school and from the time they got home to dinner time and then again after that. As a reward for his diligence and good grades, if it was still before nine o'clock when the work was finished, Clarence would be allowed to run down to the Carnegie Library. Years later, when asked about his formative years, he would seldom fail to remember, and praise, what he called simply, "the librarians at the segregated library at Carnegie." After a while, his family learned that when Clarence couldn't be found, the first place to look for him would be the Carnegie Library on East Henry Street.

Just because school was closed in the summer, that did not mean Clarence and Myers, Jr. were out of work, or "idle," one of their grandfather's favorite no-words. In 1957, Myers Anderson bought 72 acres of farmland outside of Savannah, and immediately put the boys to work transforming it into yet another productive possession. Years later, Clarence would recall his first impression of what would become "the farm:" "[He] said he had work for us to do, so, as usual, we piled into the 1951 Pontiac and rode. He took us to a field that had lain fallow for years and had grown up. He drove down the remnants of an old road. We made our way across the field to an old oak tree. He looked at it, surveyed it, paced pensively and announced that we could build a house there.... Five months later we were finishing the steps of the house that we built."

Clarence and Myers, Jr. would spend their summers at

the farm from then on, working the fields, tending the cows, and all the other tasks associated with farm work. They often helped their grandfather pitch in to assist in the building or rebuilding of simple houses for neighbors, and, as a result, the future Supreme Court justice developed more than a rudimentary skill as a carpenter (and to this day relaxes by doing such work around his own home).

Clarence's love of reading didn't take a summer vacation. One of the Carnegie librarians worked out an arrangement whereby each week she would choose an armful of books she knew he would like and give them to a friend of his who attended the same church (Myers and Tina would bring the boys in from the farm for mass each Sunday at a church in Savannah.)

Clarence's taste in books was always rather eclectic. Beginning with the complete *oeuvre* of Dr. Seuss, he worked his way up to C. S. Forester's Horatio Hornblower novels by way of westerns and books on sports. Always a good athlete himself, his early heroes were Boston Celtic guard Bob Cousy—whom many basketball authorities still rank the best (and flashiest) ballhandler ever to play the game—and track and Dallas Cowboys football star Bob Hayes. (Decades later in Washington, when political and philosophical opponents of Clarence Thomas learned he favored the Cowboys, rather than the hometown Redskins, it was viewed, and written about, as additional proof of what they saw as his purposely perverse personality.)

Of this period, he once said in a speech, "Nobody I knew, nobody in my neighborhood, read. I just started reading because I read about things I liked."

As for the Hornblower books, he recalled, "I didn't like the water myself, but reading about how they handled the ships during storms, and all their adventures out on the ocean, it was like you got on this magic carpet and zoomed off to another world. You could go anyplace, do anything, dream and imagine. It took me out of that segregated library in the segregated South."

Many years later, in what would become in effect his stump speech, Clarence Thomas would look back and evaluate the impact of his grandfather (and his grandmother) on his life. It went something like this: "Of course I thought my grandparents were too rigid, and their expectations were too high. I also thought they were mean at times. But one of their often-stated goals was to raise us so that we could stand on 'our own two feet.' This was not their social policy, it was their family policy—for their family and not those nameless families that politicians love to whine about. The most compassionate thing they did for us was to teach us to fend for ourselves, and to do that in an openly hostile environment. In fact, the hostility made learning the lesson that much more urgent. It meant the difference between freedom and incarceration, life and death, alcoholism and sobriety."

Having made that point, Thomas the speaker would then attach what had become, over the years and what he strongly felt to be his travails, his singular message, his conservative touchstone: "We were raised to survive in spite of the dark, oppressive cloud of governmentally sanctioned bigotry. Self-sufficiency and spiritual and emotional strength were our tools to carve out and secure freedom. Those who attempt to capture the daily counseling, oversight, common sense, and vision of my grandparents in a governmental program are engaging in sheer folly."

That statement was a reiteration of what he had said earlier: "I grew up under state-enforced segregation, which is as close to totalitarianism as I would like to get." The home he'd grown up in was, he said, "...strong, stable, and conservative. In fact, it was far more conservative than many who fashion themselves conservatives today. God was central. School, discipline, hard work, and knowing right from wrong were of the highest priority. Crime, welfare, slothfulness, and alcohol were enemies. But these were not issues to be debated by keen intellectuals, bellowed about by rousing orators or dissected by pollsters and researchers. They were a way of life: they marked the path of survival and the escape route from squalor."

Chapter Two

It wasn't as if Clarence Thomas, entering his teenage years, was unaware of bigotry and racism. No African-American growing up where he did could have been. In fact, he and his brother had been witness to several incidents involving their grandparents that left such a mark that years later Clarence would come back to them, again and again, in speeches and interviews. In one case, he and his brother were working in a field on their grandparents' farm when a white woman pulled up in a Buick Electra and asked for directions. Within earshot of the youths, she addressed their grandfather as "Miles, boy."

Years later, Clarence would tell a magazine writer that when the woman said that, "...you could see him seethe. He looked around and saw his little kids there. You could see him seethe. People say what kind of manhood does it take to yell back and get mad, but what must it have taken for him not only to take the insult but the stares from his kids seeing him called a boy. The most significant things," regarding civil rights, "were things that I saw day-to-day, not the protests downtown or in Washington."

Another searing incident happened when Myers, Sr., discovering that he was about to run out of gas, pulled in to a white filling station. Tina had an urgent need to use a restroom, so Clarence's grandfather asked the owner if his wife could use the facilities, only to be told that they had no "colored" restroom. Myers told the man he could keep his gasoline, and, proudly, drove off. He was fortunate enough to find another station before his car ran out of gas or his wife ran out of patience.

Young Clarence Thomas was aware of that kind of prejudice and inhumane treatment, and he was also aware of what he would later call garden-variety racism. In 1987, two years before he became a federal appellate judge, he told Juan Williams, whose *Atlantic Monthly* article was one of the first in-depth looks at this relatively new phenomenon in Washington, a black conservative, that African-American acquaintances in Savannah knew him as "ABC—America's Blackest Child." This was a reference to the fact that he was very dark complected and had nappy hair and thick lips, physical characteristics opposite those of the socially accepted, light-skinned, wavy-haired young people whose features were closer to those of Caucasians than their fellow blacks. He reminded his interviewer that, "for someone to call you black in the sixties meant serious business."

That background of understanding, significant as it was, still did not prepare Clarence Thomas for meeting racial prejudice head-on and in a place where he least expected it—a Catholic seminary. It was bad enough that this could happen in a seminary, but it was worse that it happened in two of them.

The first seminary was called St. John Vianney Minor Seminary (the "minor" indicating it was a high school level for younger boys who might go on to become priests.) When Clarence was in the tenth grade, his grandfather decided—unilaterally, Myers' standard way of making decisions—that the older of his two grandsons, the one who did so well in school and made him so proud that he bragged about his grades at the local chapter of the NAACP—should become a priest. So, after Clarence had finished two years of high school at Pius X, an all-black Catholic school in Savannah, Myers took him out and enrolled him in the all-white St. John's, which was located 10 miles from Savannah in a place with the wonderful name of the Isle of Hope.

Becoming a Catholic priest requires a solid foundation in Latin, and as Clarence had not taken that subject in his first two years at Pius X High School, his new school required him to repeat his sophomore year. Most teenagers would have been devastated by the "loss" of a school year, especially one they had completed successfully, but not Clarence Thomas. "It was the best thing that ever happened to me," he later wrote, "[and] it gave me a year to be older than my classmates, and to repeat some subjects like geometry." He also viewed it as an opportunity to spend more time on English, which he considered one of his weaker subjects. Later, using that same reason, he chose it as his college major.

Actually, Clarence Thomas had no weak subjects, at least not in the sense that most high school students would use that term. A prodigious worker, he routinely brought home very high grades. Indeed, the caption under his senior year picture in the St. John's yearbook was, "Blew that test: Only a 98." But academics are only half of the high school experience, the other being social and extracurricular life.

As a seminary student, Thomas found the prohibition against dating and "fraternizing" with girls more of a relief than a problem. When he tried—at the suggestion of the school—to induce his friend and former classmate Lester Johnson to transfer to St. John Vianney, Johnson's first objection was to the absence of girls, not the fact that if he did so it would immediately double the number of African-Americans in the school. Young Clarence's answer, that if he wanted to he could see girls on the occasional weekend back home, did little to counter his friend's complaint. It also indicated that Thomas, who'd led a very sheltered life, exhibited very little, if any, interest in girls at that point in his life, which was fine, considering his vocation.

Unbothered by the absence of the opposite sex, the young seminarian was very bothered by the presence of racism and overt bigotry, especially in a school that had been founded to train young men for the priesthood in a faith whose creed embodied love for one's neighbor. In his sophomore yearbook, a fellow student wrote, "Keep on trying, Clarence. Some day you'll be as good as us." As the only other black student in the school had already dropped out, Clarence Thomas had no trouble understanding who "us" referred to. According to his later writings, these years within the bosom of bigotry left an indelible mark on his spirit—and in his memory. A friend he had made at law school in the early 1970s says that having had to face what might be termed Christian bigotry was "the first thing Clarence would tell you about himself."

On the extracurricular side, Clarence Thomas shone. As an athlete, he had no peer. He was the quarterback in football, the captain and leading scorer on the basketball team, and a multi-event man in track. He was described in the school paper as being "faster than a speedy spitball" and "more powerful than home brew." He was active in the drama department, playing small roles in such chestnuts as *The King and I* and *Mr. Roberts*. He not only wrote for the school paper, he was its co-editor. In one column, following civil disturbances in the aftermath of the 1964 Civil Rights Act's passage, he wrote, "I think races would fare better if extremists would crawl back into their holes and let the people whom this will really affect do a little thinking for themselves, rather than follow the Judas goats of society into the slaughter pens of destruction." (A fondness for colorful rhetoric would become a mainstay of his writing and, especially, his speechifying. In a speech to the conservative American Enterprise Institute almost 40 years later, then Supreme Court Justice Thomas used phrases such as: "...judges can be buffeted by strong winds that tear them away from the basic principles they have sworn to safeguard;" "...A judge must attempt to keep at bay those passions, interests, and emotions that beset every frail human being;" "In my humble opinion, those who come to engage in debates of consequence, and who challenge accepted wisdom, should expect to be treated badly. Nonetheless, they must stand undaunted. That is required. And, that should be expected, for it is bravery that is required to secure freedom;" and, "It does no good to argue ideas with those who will respond as brutes. Works of genius have often been smashed and burned, and geniuses have sometimes been treated no better."

For any of the white seminarians, these academic, athletic, and social accomplishments would have been more than enough, but for Clarence Thomas they had begun to ring hollow. Expecting that his faith and his determination to become a priest would carry him through on a cloud lined with happiness, he found instead that he was beset by a number of unforeseen problems, almost all of which had to do with race.

Of this period in the life of the future Supreme Court Justice, Juan Williams wrote, "...Thomas was in a state of crisis. He had never been around so many whites. Now he was living with them. He saw how many more possessions they had, how the other boys commanded respect as seminarians in a town where he was at best ignored.... Most devastating of all were the racist jokes and slights that Thomas's fellow seminarians made at his expense. Myers Anderson had held the church up as a moral and ethical model. But, Thomas told me, 'After lights out, someone would yell, "Smile, Clarence, so we can see you." The statement wasn't the bad part, it was no one saying, "Shut up."' On Thursday afternoons, when students went to town with their friends, Thomas was left alone. Movie theaters were still segregated; to eat at a restaurant with classmates would have created a stir."

One problem that had to do with race had nothing to do with white people. It was the attitude among his fellow African-Americans that when it came to skin color, the lighter the better. As Norman Macht (apparently the only biographer to whom Thomas granted access) writes: "Clarence's dilemma was far from unique. Brenda Tapia, who enrolled in Washington's Howard University, a predominately black school, to escape the white racism of the South, had a similar experience. 'I was the wrong shade of black,' she said. 'At Howard, if you were not light, bright, pretty near white and sitting on your hair, you were likely to experience a lot of prejudice [from other blacks].... I got into a thing about hating black people, and that is a pretty difficult place to be. When you hate white people and you hate black people you get kind of lonely.'"

Macht says Clarence Thomas, despite his youth, met this crucial problem head on: "...the double-barreled derision [from blacks and whites alike] did not create hatred in Clarence. Instead, it reinforced his focus on his own inner resources and integrity.... As he later recalled, he decided 'then and there at the ripe old age of 16 that it was better to be respected than liked. Popularity is unpredictable and vacillating. Respect is constant.'" (Not all commentators, especially later ones, agree with Norman Macht. The suggestion of a form or degree of self-hatred has been raised and written about so frequently that Thomas himself often brings it up in his speeches, the better to knock it down, apparently.)

The idea of black self-segregation based on shades of darkness is by no means an old-fashioned or passé idea. As recently as 2000, a book on that very subject opened with the following bit of (unattributed) blank verse:

> Bryant Gumbel is, but Bill Cosby isn't.
> Lena Horne is, but Whitney Houston isn't.
> Andrew Young is, but Jesse Jackson isn't.
> And neither is Maya Angelou, Alice Walker,
> Clarence Thomas, or Quincy Jones.
> And even though both of them try extremely
> hard, neither Diana Ross nor Robin Givens
> will ever be.

The book—*Our Kind of People* by Lawrence Otis Graham, a Harvard-trained lawyer—has rankled African-Americans, especially those of the middle and upper classes, from the day it first appeared in bookstores. In part, this negative reaction stems from the author's fondness for blind quotes of a rather scurrilous nature. For example, in making his point that neither Secretary of State Colin Powell nor Supreme Court Justice Clarence Thomas are acceptable to the black social elite of Washington, D.C., Graham writes: "'Powell and Thomas,' says a Washington Boulé [a prominent black social club affiliated with the Sigma Pi Phi fraternity] 'have almost nothing to do with black people in this town. They don't join our groups and don't attend black events unless they are the featured speakers. And being married to some low-class white woman from God knows where,' adds the Boulé member's wife, 'is hardly going to help Clarence Thomas make a transition into our community. He doesn't like us and we don't like him.'"

As much as these and other problems bothered the young Clarence Thomas, he kept his complaints to himself, and did what would become one of his trademarks—he worked hard. Myers, Sr. called it "keeping your nose to the grindstone." And, he continued to tend to his inner landscape by reading, reading, and more reading. Like innumerable boarding-school students before him, he waited until lights out and then used a flashlight to continue reading, under the covers. Dr. Seuss and the novels of Horatio Alger gave way to *Gone With the Wind* (he tried to read 50 pages each night) and Richard Wright's classic *Native Son*. Years later, Thomas would write that this book in particular "really woke me up," and that its author, who became one of his lifelong favorites, "captured a lot of the feelings that I have inside that you learn how to suppress."

If Clarence was becoming disenchanted with the idea of the priesthood as his future, he didn't mention it with any frequency, and certainly not to his grandfather, who loved the idea of his sober and studious grandson as a man of the cloth. Myers Anderson's faith was simple and uncomplicated, and although Clarence would on occasion discuss with his grandfather certain of the ideas he was encountering in class (such as natural law, a concept that would appeal to him his entire life), there were no grand clashes of a theological or philosophical nature. Like other thoughtful young men, regardless of race, Clarence found that his main problem with Catholicism stemmed from Catholics themselves, not from the doctrine. Chief among these was the idea that young men of faith could be as racist and bigoted as their heathen counterparts.

His discontent was evidenced during his last pre-college summer, that of 1967. Clarence and a white classmate with whom he had become friendly were hired by St. John's as counselors at a camp on the school grounds. Each day began with a salute to the American flag and a lusty chorus of the pledge of allegiance, but when they got to the words "liberty and justice for all," both Clarence and his classmate would quietly add "sometimes." Years later, Thomas recalled, "It was our way of acknowledging that the ideal was not the reality for many people."

Despite these misgivings, when his grandfather suggested, upon Clarence's graduation from St. John Vianney Minor Seminary, that the young man continue his studies for the priesthood at a seminary in the Midwest, Clarence did not object. Thus he found himself, in the fall of 1967, as a "novice," a first-year student of the priesthood at the Immaculate Conception Seminary in Missouri. It did not turn out to be the religious experience he most likely anticipated. In fact, it cost him not only his calling, but almost his faith itself.

Once again, Clarence Thomas resembled an island of black in a sea of white. And once again, he found himself among Southern bigots. Discovering anti-Christian racial attitudes among his high school classmates had been bad enough, but to find them also prevalent here, on the level of secondary education, struck him as much worse. In seven or so years these young men would be ordained as Catholic priests, the representatives of Christ on earth, yet they seemed little different in their racial attitudes than the average white youth on the streets of Savannah.

A decade and a half later, recalling his experience at both the seminaries he attended, Thomas would tell an audience, "Not a day passed that I was not pricked by prejudice." But, he said, in another speech, "I was determined not to see every slight or criticism as discrimination or bigotry. Once you get into the habit of doing that, you disempower yourself. Your attitude becomes, no matter what I do, discrimination will prevent me from doing well. I knew bigotry, but I refused to attribute everything to that."

When he came home for Christmas vacation, he laid out

his doubts and fears to his parish priest and to his grandmother (though not his grandfather, who still spoke with great pride of Clarence becoming a priest). Still, after the break, he returned, determined to make a go of it. Quitting in the face of adversity was not part of his makeup.

Eventually, however, his resolve was tested up to and beyond the breaking point. He had gotten used to seeing white classmates cross the street when they saw him coming toward them, but in early April of 1968, something happened that so sickened him that he knew he had to leave. It was the 4th, the day of the shooting of Dr. Martin Luther King, Jr. The news had just come over the radio, Thomas would later recall, "...and I was following this white seminarian up a flight of stairs, and I overheard him say, 'That's good. I hope the son-of-a-bitch dies.' I knew I couldn't stay in that so-called Christian environment any longer."

Clarence also knew that his grandfather would be upset by his decision to leave (and he was), but the atmosphere had become too much for him. He later said, "I had given my word, but after major soul-searching, I regretfully concluded it was the right decision for me."

Thirty years later, in a controversial speech to the National Bar Association, the prestigious group of black lawyers, some of whose members had asked that his invitation to speak to their annual convention be rescinded, he made specific reference to those days of shame and anger:

> I am sure that each of us has his or her memories of that terrible day in 1968. For me it was the final straw in the struggle to retain my vocation to become a Catholic priest. Suddenly, this cataclysmic event ripped me from the moorings of my grandparents, my youth and my faith and catapulted me headlong into the abyss that Richard Wright seemed to describe years earlier.
>
> It was this event that shattered my faith in my reli-

gion and my country. I had spent the mid-60s as a successful student in a virtually white environment. I had learned Latin, physics and chemistry. I had accepted the loneliness that came with being "the integrator," the first and the only. But this event, this trauma, I could not take, especially when one of my fellow seminarians, not knowing I was standing behind him, declared that he hoped the SOB died. This was a man of God, mortally stricken by an assassin's bullet, and one preparing for the priesthood had wished evil on him.

The life I had dreamed of so often during those hot summers on the farm in Georgia or during what seemed like endless hours on the oil truck with my grandfather expired as Dr. King expired.

As so many of you do, I know exactly where I was when I heard the news. It was a low moment in our nation's history and a demarcation between hope and hopelessness for many of us.

According to Jane Mayer and Jill Abramson, co-authors of the 1994 Thomas biography *Strange Justice*: "After he left the seminary, Thomas never told his mother the Martin Luther King story. 'I just felt he didn't want to go,' she recalled. Nor did other classmates remember it exactly as Thomas told it. A close friend at conception, Tom O'Brien, recalled that, a month or two before the end of the term, Thomas came to him teary-eyed and simply said he was leaving because he had run into 'too many rednecks.'" The authors then go on, immediately, to state one of the main themes of their book, "But while the details varied—possibly depending on how comfortable he felt with his audience—the underlying theme did not. Well before Anita Hill testified against him, his sense of being treated unfairly by the world had become the leitmotif of his life story."

In an unintentionally ironic reversal of one of Dr. King's

most famous phrases, Clarence Thomas was free at last from the world of the seminary. That summer, while working in a paper bag factory, he thought about going to Savannah State, a small black school where he already knew a number of students, but, once again, someone in the Catholic Church had other ideas for him. He didn't know it, but he was about to replicate the action indicated by the title of Willie Morris's popular book of that era and go *North Toward Home.*

One has to wonder what might have become of Clarence Thomas had he transferred to a traditional all-black college or university. According to Juan Williams (in the by-now-famous *Atlantic Monthly* interview): "Thomas remembers a 'self-hate' stage where 'you hate yourself for being part of a group that's gotten the hell kicked out of them.' He tried to fit in. He avoided every form of stereotypical behavior attributed to blacks. He took pains to speak perfectly—not in slang, not loudly. He stressed academic achievement. But acceptance did not come. When he left the seminary, he held a conviction he has carried since: there is nothing a black man can do to be accepted by whites. Consequently, despite his anger at segregation, he does not automatically grant that integration is good for black people."

Williams, who had interviewed the future judge over a five year period before writing his 1987 article, continued, "Thomas wants to know in every instance what integration means for blacks. If it means losing the alternative of going to their own schools, running their own businesses, then he doesn't like it. He has too many scars from episodes in which, in the name of integration, he was the only black. Today he says, 'The whole push to assimilate simply does not make sense to me.'"

Those feelings—much closer to the teachings of Booker T. Washington than those of W.E.B. Dubois—would have to percolate on the back burner for a while. Another authority figure, this one white, from Clarence Thomas's past had something in mind for his college years, and it wasn't Savannah State.

The first time young Clarence sat in a classroom of Sister Mary Carmine was at Pius X High School which he'd attended for two years before switching to the minor seminary. But their paths crossed soon after that because she also taught (chemistry) at St. John's, and the mutual admiration society begun at Pius X continued at St. John's. In fact, it was Sister Mary Carmine who, having spotted Clarence early on as a promising student who could use a nudge in the right direction, had given him the battered but still usable typewriter with which he eventually mastered the world of QWERTY.

When she heard that Clarence had left the seminary, she sent for him. It was not a summons he would take lightly. When they met, she told him in forceful tones that he could make it in the great world outside of Savannah, Georgia, and its racial enclaves. He was good enough, she assured him, to make the grade at any of the white schools, even the elite. But she wasn't quite ready to see him in the full grasp of the secular world. The school she had in mind for him was the very Catholic, and very well-respected Holy Cross College, a Jesuit institution in Worcester, Massachusetts.

"The tenacious Sister Mary Carmine was not about to abandon the cause of Clarence Thomas," writes Norman Macht, the biographer with whom Thomas cooperated on the former's 1995 book. "[S]he believed [him] capable of more than he envisioned for himself.... Throughout the summer of 1968, she urged Thomas to send for the application forms, but he was not interested. He applied to the University of Missouri and was accepted.

"Undaunted, Sister Mary Carmine wrote to one of her former students, Bob DeShay, who was at Holy Cross, and asked him to send the forms to Thomas. Then she kept after Thomas until he reluctantly filled them out. He was accepted;

he still did not want to go to a 'white' school—there would be only six blacks in his class—but he was no match for the iron will of the determined Franciscan sister. So, in September, he boarded a train north, carrying $100 stashed in his shoes, a box of Tina's fried chicken, and a head filled with doubts and uncertainties."

Chapter Three

Higher Educations

W hen Clarence Thomas was nine, his grandfather took the family to Philadelphia and New York to visit relatives. Although struck, as any boy of his age and background would have been, by the enormity of these huge cities, one of his most prominent memories of that trip was his grandfather's anger at learning a relative was on welfare. How anybody who was well enough to work could be on the dole was beyond the ken of Myers Anderson, Sr., who was fond of saying, "Man ain't got no business on welfare as long as he can work." Young Clarence, schooled in self-reliance by his grandfather and a succession of nuns, grew to share that attitude.

Given that brief introduction to the country's most heavily populated region, he was not necessarily intimidated as the train bore him northward, through the old, pre-airport transportation infrastructures of Richmond, Washington, Baltimore, Philadelphia, Newark, New York, and half a dozen other cities before it reached Worcester, the last stop before Boston, 40 miles to the east.

Worcester was a factory town that had seen better days. And while shabby genteel can be charming in the South, in the North it is more often simply depressing. But the College of Holy Cross was a different matter. Situated on a hill overlooking the city, it had (and still has) a lovely campus featuring main buildings done in the Greek Revival style. To Clarence Thomas, a serious-minded young man who'd never met a library he didn't like (as long as it wasn't segregated), it was a serene and lovely place. Already convinced he would never really fit in, he knew nonetheless that it was a place he could enjoy, and, he felt, one in which he could do well.

"We got here at the same time, Clarence and I," says Fr. Joe Fahey, a Jesuit priest. "He'd just transferred in as a sophomore, having had a year at that seminary in Missouri, and I was a young priest. I could tell right away that he had something special. He was bright and, as I soon learned, industrious, and direct. He didn't speak up a lot, but when he did, people listened. Although I wasn't his teacher, he'd come by from time to time, and we'd just talk. We would discuss the war—Vietnam was really heating up then—and other topics of the day. I always enjoyed seeing him."

According to Fr. Fahey, one of the other topics they discussed was civil rights. Fr. Fahey had marched with Dr. Martin Luther King, Jr., which must have impressed the future jurist, and he had been part of the Holy Cross faction that pushed to find and admit more black students under a relatively new policy known as affirmative action. The Jesuit says Clarence Thomas had strong views about the country's record of black suppression, but a certain ambivalence when it came to that new policy.

"We had these open fora where students could get up and speak," Fr. Fahey recalls, "and from time to time Clarence would speak up. He didn't do so very often. But when he did I was always struck by his honesty and his forthrightness. I remember one time when a white student—a nice, well-meaning kid—got up and asked the few blacks in the group, 'What is it you want?'

"I'll never forget Clarence's response. He said, 'You got, I ain't; you got, I want.'"

In truth, Clarence Thomas didn't have much time for rap sessions, no matter how serious the topic (unless they were held late at night in the dorm, after the day's work was over) because his scholarship was anything but a "full ride." Consequently, he worked in the dining hall, an experience that would cause him to empathize with waiters and kitchen help for years to come. One white classmate, who also went on to become a lawyer, recalls the time Thomas, then on the federal appellate bench, invited him to a judicial conference. When the white lawyer arrived, at first he couldn't find his friend and host, but then: "I heard a familiar booming laugh, and there was Clarence, shooting the breeze with one of the waiters he'd met when the man had served him the night before."

Thomas was by no means a one-dimensional "grind" at Holy Cross. In addition to school work and part-time employment, he volunteered for community service, helping serve breakfast to impoverished black youths in Worcester.

He also remained physically active, playing intramural football and basketball and was a sprinter on the track team. Like Fr. Fahey, Fr. John Brooks, then the vice-president and later the president of Holy Cross, came to know Thomas well. Of the young man's indoctrination to the college, he says, "It had to be hard coming up as a black from the South and into the northeastern community with a heavy population from Boston. But he didn't let it throw him at all."

In fact, the young Clarence Thomas didn't let much of anything throw him. Fr. Joe Fahey remembers a self-confident and quiet but not withdrawn youth who was good with people and loved to laugh. He was particularly quiet in the classroom, preferring to let other students ask the questions, a distant foreshadowing of the way he would conduct himself on the highest bench in the land. Of the college years, biographer Norman Macht writes, "Thomas sat in the back and rarely asked a question. Although he wanted to be judged by his work and not for doing well 'for a black man,' his silence in class derived from a different problem. 'One reason for my being inconspicuous was that I had difficulty speaking proper English,' he later said, 'I would think about the right way to phrase a question while I was trying to say it, and trip over myself. Some people thought I had a stuttering problem. So I remained quiet.'"

Macht goes on to say that in order to overcome this problem, Thomas deliberately chose English as his major—"...because he knew that speaking correctly and being able to express himself clearly and effectively would be essential to success in whatever he did." (As the question of Thomas's silence on the Supreme Court had not yet arisen in 1994 when he wrote his book, author Macht does not address it.)

The possibility that affirmative action produced, in effect, a double standard for evaluating the achievements of African-Americans was already troubling Clarence Thomas during his college years. He was particularly bothered by affirmative action programs that accepted and pushed forward blacks who did not have the proper qualifications. He later told *The New York Times* that while he was at Holy Cross he personally witnessed the "destruction" of many black students who had been accepted despite being unqualified. "It was wrong for those kids and it was wrong to give that kind of false hope." He much preferred the attitude of the older generation, which, he said, knew "...intu-

56

itively that it was better to be educated without knowing where it would lead them than to be uneducated." While hardly the attitude of those in the forefront of the civil rights movement, it should not have been a surprise coming from a youth raised by Myers Anderson, who was forever reminding Clarence and his brother that as far as he had gotten and as much as he had achieved, he could have done even more had he been educated. And in addition to his grandfather's homilies and exhortations, Clarence had been self-nourished on an early diet of Horatio Alger and a later one of Ayn Rand, and in college he was introduced to, and swiftly became enamored of, the novels of Richard Wright with their strong message of black self-sufficiency.

Along with hundreds of thousands of other young black men in the 1960s, Thomas let his hair grow until it qualified as a legitimate Afro, sported a goatee, and took to wearing fatigues and combat boots. He also wore, says Fr. Fahey, "those bib overalls. I think it was supposed to show his sympathy with the poor." Thomas didn't just spout slogans; he read and studied works by Malcolm X, as well as Booker T. Washington. He claimed a degree of solidarity with the Black Panthers (the kitchen in which he worked as a volunteer was one of their projects), and he helped found the Black Students Union, serving a term as its treasurer before losing a close race for president. Of this period, one biographer wrote, "He was neither a firebrand leader nor a blind follower, but an independent thinker and a voice of moderation."

Other commentators would read the same personal data and come up with less flattering appraisals, such as the conclusion that he was a deeply conflicted young man with a lot of anger at a system that let him in the door, only to remind him, over and over, that it was a side door and not the front.

In 1984, reminiscing about his years at Holy Cross, he told the alumni magazine that in his first year he felt as if he were in "a cold, isolated foreign country" where he was "the black spot on the white horse." He said that he almost quit at the start of his second year. "I had my trunk all packed. I had decided that it was true, what the other blacks had been saying, that Holy Cross was a crusher, that it would break your spirit."

Fr. John Brooks, the Jesuit who was then the vice-president and would later become the president of the college, and a man Thomas would thank publicly over the years, intervened. Just as Myers Anderson Sr. would have done, had his grandson the nerve to tell him what he was seriously contemplating doing, Fr. Brooks persuaded the disheartened student to stick it out.

In his junior year at Holy Cross, Thomas put his idea of solidarity on the line when he took part in a protest. In support of a handful of their fellow black students who claimed they'd been unfairly disciplined for their part in a rally against military recruitment on campus, almost all the 20 or so Holy Cross blacks walked off campus.

Thirty years later, in 2001, Fr. Joseph LaBran, who then worked at Holy Cross, still has a vivid recollection of what he says was generally known as the "black walk-out:" "I got down there early that day and I witnessed the whole thing. In the crowd of say 70 to 80 people, there were a number of members of SDS, Students for a Democratic Society, and some of them got a little out of hand. There really wasn't any violence, but they linked arms and there was a lot of shoving and pushing on both sides, and they succeeded in getting the recruiters, who were from General Electric, to leave the campus.

"The next day, the assistant dean of students, a Jesuit who'd been a chief in the Navy, posted a set of rules, beginning with the statement, 'Holy Cross Is An Open Campus,' and alongside that he put up a list of 20 names, including about half a dozen black students. It was completely out of proportion as far as the blacks were concerned. A crowd gathered, and some of the students confronted him over the inclusion of these names, wondering how he could have chosen these particular people.

"One of the black students—it may have been Ted Wells [who went on to Harvard in a joint graduate program of law and business, and is today one of the leading trial lawyers in the country]—asked, 'What norm did you use?'

"The response of the assistant dean of students was rather unfortunate. He said, 'We went through the mug book,' meaning he'd looked at pictures of all the students and focused on the blacks. With that, all of the blacks, except for one quiet student, and including Clarence, walked out."

The next day, at a hastily called trustees meeting, Fr. LaBran stood up and said, "We've got to get those kids back or we'll have to close the school. We can't treat our students that way."

Into the breach stepped Fr. John Brooks, who agreed to approach the students, mollify them by explaining the school was in fact on their side, and bring them back, all of which he did.

"Nothing happened to me personally" Clarence Thomas later recalled, "but my friends were being treated unfairly, so I stood up for them and we all walked off campus."

It didn't take long for second thoughts to catch up with him. "I asked myself, 'I have a straight-A average. Why am I walking out? And how do I explain what I am doing to my grandfather, to whom education means everything, if I am suspended from school too?' I was very happy when Father Brooks helped to resolve the problem and allowed us all to return."

By this point it was clear that well before he reached the age of majority, Clarence Thomas could and did think for himself. What was not so clear was the reason why. In their biography of Thomas, Jane Mayer and Jill Abramson quote a classmate of Thomas's who recalls that there were always four views on any issue: "the left, the right, the center, and Thomas's." Some friends from those days also suggested that Thomas *liked* to be different, to take different positions, especially those not normally associated with African-Americans, just for the sake of being different. And, they say, not only was he often out on a limb all by himself, but he seemed to enjoy that position.

The two authors cite the example of the time Holy Cross's black students voted in favor of establishing an all-black dorm, or, at least, an all-black corridor of a formerly integrated dorm. Clarence Thomas, they say, was the only African-American who voted against the idea. One of his reasons bothered the black students, and another bothered *everyone*. The first was that if African-Americans wanted to live by themselves, then they should transfer to an all-black school; the second was that "...he didn't want to live among blacks because he didn't want to make it easy for whites to avoid him."

The separate dormitory section for African-Americans was in fact set up, and the students moved in, Thomas among them. But he insisted on bringing his white room-mate with him. Given such in-your-face actions, perhaps it shouldn't surprise anyone that Thomas would tell an interviewer, 15 years later, "I don't fit in with whites, and I don't fit in with blacks." Mayer and Abramson write, "He suggested that his experience at the forefront of integration had contributed to this isolation. But as his behavior at college suggests, Thomas sought out isolated positions well before he had a coherent philosophy."

One of the strongest influences upon Thomas during his first years in college was Malcolm X, the fiery black leader whose autobiography was assigned reading for all newcomers to Holy Cross in 1968. He was much taken with its tenet of black self-reliance in both personal and business affairs. He so liked the following passage that he memorized it: "As other ethnic groups have done, let the black people, whenever possible, patronize their own kind, hire their own kind and start in those ways to build up the black race's ability to do for itself."

The picture that emerges from reading and from talking to friends and former classmates of Thomas's 25 to 30 years later is of a very hard-working young man with an independent streak who had yet to make up his mind about a number of important issues, but who, at the same time, very much disliked having anyone presume to know what he thought—or, more importantly to him, *ought* to think—about anything. To paraphrase what he would say, many years later, to a group of black lawyers who'd opposed his nomination to the highest court, "I am my own man." (The title of his speech was: "I am a man, a black man, an American.")

According to most accounts, he was very much his own man at Holy Cross. It seemed to him that he would be making a mistake if, during his college years, he set up a color barrier to friendship. For one thing, it wouldn't be very pragmatic: "If one is at Holy Cross," he wrote some years later, "he should profit from the experience by learning to associate with and understand the white majority."

He made friends at his own pace, and as his busy schedule allowed. One good friend was John Siraco, the white student who became the roommate Thomas insisted on bringing with him (and his Malcolm X poster) to the "black-only" dorm.

For a number of reasons, Clarence Thomas was not a party animal. For one thing, he preferred to use his limited free time as study time. He was determined to get good grades (and he did, graduating with a 3.7 GPA) as a way of climbing whatever career ladder he might eventually choose to climb, and he was at least equally determined to show the Holy Cross community not just that he could do it, but that he, Clarence Thomas of Pin Point, Georgia, unlike many of the other 20 or so black students on campus in his class, had never *needed* affirmative action in the first place.

Another reason why Clarence was no party animal was that it was not in his nature (much as he might have wished it was). Like the rest of the student body, he was the product of his environment, but his environment—about as different from that of the norm as it was possible to be—was hardly conducive to easy relationships with "the guys," not to mention the opposite sex. Except for a few years at the beginning of grade school and a year and a half in high school, Clarence had not gone to class with girls. And until he went to Holy Cross, where there were also no girls for his first two years, he had been in a deeply religious atmosphere, where even thinking of girls could, under certain conditions, be deemed sinful. In fact, given that background, it would have been most unusual had he been at ease with, and to any great degree successful with, the opposite sex.

This is not to say that he was not good company, especially for other males, white as well as black. People who "knew him when" remember Thomas with what certainly seems like genuine fondness, as did, by all accounts, the late Gil Hardy, an African-American who went to both Holy Cross and Yale Law School with the future Supreme Court justice. Other black friends, such as Russell Frisby, Lester Johnson, and Edward P. Jones, while professing close friendships with him, also note his unease with girls and women. It was clear to them that he was by no means a feminist, and may even have been its opposite. One friend (Frisby) is on record as saying he thinks Thomas felt "women's groups were benefiting at the expense of minorities."

Whether Thomas's early (and in his mind unpleasant) experience with affirmative action was the cause of his turning against it with such vehemence in later years or whether there may have been an even deeper reason buried somewhere in his psyche will probably never be known. Tony Califa, a law school classmate who was also admitted under affirmative action guidelines but says he never felt "looked down upon" for it, suggested a reason to Mayer and Abramson: "It's hard to say whether Clarence ever truly had any real self-esteem. I'd have to say no. Mine came from my grandparents. But in his case, I think his grandfather taught him ethics and discipline, but nothing beyond that. I always knew I would be successful before I was. But Clarence was the other way around. He always had to prove it, and even then I'm not sure he believed it."

The next scene in the first act of the drama that would see Clarence Thomas move from Pin Point, Georgia, to the highest court in the land was about to take place as his college years drew to a close. But first there was an addition to the cast. Prior to going co-ed in 1972, Holy Cross experimented with the concept by bringing in girls from nearby Catholic girl's schools. One of these students was a quiet, shy, and relatively light-skinned African-American girl who was part Japanese. Her name was Kathy Ambush, and very quickly she and Clarence became an "item."

Kathy's world was a revelation to Clarence Thomas. Her family was middle class—her father was a dental technician in Worcester—and also decidedly functional, it was the mirror opposite of Thomas's birth "family." While he must have known that such families existed, it had to be his first intimate connection with one of them. Within days of their meeting, he and Kathy were inseparable, at least to the extent that a student as busy and hard working as Clarence Thomas could be.

While this wonderful change in his social life was taking place, Clarence, like so many young Americans his age, was trying to decide what to do with his immediate future.

Thanks to the looming specter of the war in Vietnam, Uncle Sam had plans for any and all of them who did not have plans of their own. For this, and several other reasons, Clarence began to think about law school.

When Fr. Joe Fahey got word of this possibility, he sent for Thomas, who told him which schools he was applying to. "They were very good schools," the priest recalls, "but they were not what I, as a New Englander, thought of as the top echelon, meaning Harvard and Yale. He asked me, 'Do you think I can do it?' meaning get into and succeed in law school, and I said, 'Yes, I do, but why not shoot for the moon?'"

The young priest told the college senior that while he thought his choices were good schools, they weren't, in the priest's opinion, the best. But, more importantly, he told him he believed he was definitely good enough to get into the better schools and that if he did, it would give him not only a superior legal education but would also afford him the opportunity to meet people who could "open doors" for him in the future.

"To that, Clarence said, 'Let me think about it,'" says Fr. Fahey. "I did, and several weeks later he came back with recommendation letters to Harvard and Yale in his hand. 'Here,' he said, 'Since this was your idea, you should write these letters.' I was only too happy to do so, and he was accepted by both schools and chose Yale. Now I don't mean to suggest I was the only one who encouraged and helped him, because there were others who did, Fr. Brooks for one. But I've always been proud of the part I played."

The other important second-act scene took place immediately following his graduation. On June 4, 1971, Clarence Thomas graduated from Holy Cross College. On June 5, in an *Episcopal*, not a Catholic, church in Worcester, Massachusetts, he married Kathy Ambush. For someone with such deep roots in the church of Rome to marry "outside the church," while still an unusual occurrence, was allowed under the reforms in the Catholic religion following Vatican II.

* * * *

On February 13, 2001, United States Supreme Court Justice Clarence Thomas gave the prestigious Boyer Lecture at the American Enterprise Institute, the capital city's leading conservative think tank. He was introduced by a former member of the Yale Law School faculty, Judge Robert H. Bork (whose own nomination to the U.S. Supreme Court in 1987 had been defeated after a very bitter partisan fight). The following is what Judge Bork had to say, in part, in introducing Clarence Thomas:

> Tonight we do honor to a man who lists his hometown as Pin Point, Georgia. You can believe that if you want to. To me it seems highly dubious. I think it's a public relations gimmick. Kind of like Honest Abe the rail-splitter. Or Jimmy Carter, the man from Plains. Or, come to think of it, the man from Hope who has recently left us—or semi-left us.
>
> Speaking of the man from Hope, there is an interesting contrast between him and our honoree. Both the man from Hope and Hillary were students of mine when I taught at the Yale Law School. Well, I no longer say they were my students. I say they were in the room...some of the time. By sad contrast, Clarence Thomas never took a course I offered.
>
> Some professors might be sensitive about that, if they lack self-confidence. But I say, let it pass, let it pass. Why he couldn't have taken just one measly course, I don't know. After all, I taught three every year. But let it pass. It's not as though he didn't take every other business-related course in the school. But let it pass.

He has never even tried to explain this extraordinary behavior to me. But by now, as you can see, I have forgotten all about it. If he had taken just one course, people would not be calling me a failed professor today. But let it pass, let it pass.

Once he'd finished ribbing Justice Thomas, Judge Bork went on to relate what was apparently his first impression of AEI's honoree.

The future Justice Thomas appeared on the steps of the Yale Law School fresh from his career as a radical activist at Holy Cross. So that there should be no misunderstanding, he sported an Afro and, if a contemporary witness now also at AEI is to be believed, the student Thomas put up in his study an assortment of flags calculated to offend people of all political persuasions. The truth is that his radicalism was a manifestation of a sturdy independence of mind and spirit that refused to accept the slogans and shibboleths of any faction. That spirit has carried him through to today, and to the Justice he has become. Not that he now offends everyone, just the right people. The rest of us love him....

While Judge Bork may have been exercising some literary license when he described Clarence Thomas as a radical activist in 1971, he was right on the money when he said Thomas took "every other business-related course in the school." As Juan Williams wrote in 1987, based on the information Thomas had provided him in the series of interviews they'd done over the previous five years, "At Yale, Thomas avoided his professors and sat in the back of the classroom. He did not want to be identified as a black student—one who perhaps had been admitted and must be coddled precisely because he was black. He shunned courses on civil rights, instead studying tax law, legal accounting, antitrust law, and property law. He remembers feeling 'the monkey was on my back' because classmates believed that he and the dozen or so other blacks in his class were there to satisfy the school's social-policy goals, not because of their academic qualifications. Nevertheless, Thomas thrived academically. Sitting in the back of the classroom and working anonymously in the library, he earned good grades. He was less impressed by the hard-edged minutiae of the law than by the notion that he was competing successfully with the best white minds. Yale gave him renewed confidence even as he was, in effect, hiding his face to avoid calling attention to his race. He felt alienated from a system that was trying to open itself to him, and became more of a loner than he had been before."

As might be expected, Thomas did not agree with all the conclusions Juan Williams drew from their sessions. A year after the article appeared in *The Atlantic*, he told an interviewer for the conservative publication *Reason*, that he disagreed with Williams's statement that he was a black nationalist, "I think Juan stopped short—he got halfway to the destination and got off the train. He is certainly an excellent writer and a good person, but I'm not a nationalist...."

Williams was right, however, about the degree to which Thomas kept himself out of the limelight in law school. For one thing, it was a hard and certainly very demanding curriculum, and for another Thomas was married.

He and Kathy had had a child, a son they named Jamal Adeen, in February of 1973, and with finances always a serious concern, he had a lot on his plate. As indicated by Juan Williams, and underlined years later by Judge Robert Bork, Thomas concentrated on courses dealing with the law's relationship to business, not individuals.

Twenty years later, when President George Bush named Clarence Thomas to the nation's highest court, the media made a mad dash into the past to report on the various stages of the nominee's life. One of the best jobs was done by *U.S. News & World Report*: "Some of Thomas's opposition to race-preference programs stems from his experiences at Yale, where he saw affirmative action helping many more middle-class blacks than poor blacks like himself. He was always strapped for money—wearing workman's overalls and shirts worn through at the elbows—and he grew close to classmates from similarly poor backgrounds: Frank Washington, the son of a laborer, and Harry Singleton, whose mother cleaned houses. 'The notion of being responsible for your own place in life was a dominant theme for all three of us,' says Washington, now a cable-TV executive in California. Above all, Yale reinforced Thomas's belief that affirmative action taints every black's achievement and robs him of respect. As he told *Washington Post* reporter Juan Williams in 1980, 'You had to prove yourself every day because the presumption was that you were dumb and didn't deserve to be there on merit.'"

Of that period in his life, Thomas later said, "At that age, you actually think you can go out and change the world. I wanted to right some wrongs that I saw in Savannah, some specific wrongs with respect to my grandfather and what he was able to do with his life, as well as the overall wrongs that I saw as a child there." And in 1991, at a law school commencement, he said, "...my reason for going to law school in the first place was to return to Savannah to assist in righting the wrongs which I felt existed there throughout my childhood." But if that was in fact his goal, Thomas did not prepare for it by taking civil rights courses, or by active involvement in black causes. Still more of a liberal than anything else—he voted for George McGovern in 1972, opposed the war in Vietnam, and smoked the occasional joint—he spent his first law school summer working for the Legal Assistance Association in New Haven. But he turned down the opportunity to help

Yale attract more black law students, even though he knew the attrition rate was as bad or worse there than it had been at Holy Cross. He was increasingly bothered by the fact that the so-called quotas were not helping those who needed help the most.

As he told Juan Williams, "If quotas help you, fine. If they make your life wonderful, fine. If they get you a BMW or Mercedes, say that is why you want quotas. Man, quotas are for the black middle class. But look at what's happening to the masses. Those are my people. They are just where they were before any of these policies."

He followed that inclination in the summer after his second year of law school, returning to Savannah to work for Hill, Jones and Farrington, the city's first integrated law firm, as one of the recipients of a fellowship designed for students who wanted to work on racial issues. According to Jane Mayer and Jill Abramson, who devote more time to Thomas's college and law school years than do the other biographers, he was not an easy fit. "In the friendly milieu of the law firm, Thomas appeared somewhat aloof, going his own way in small ways and large. Colleagues recall him working alone and with great intensity in the firm's law library, sometimes drumming his feet on the floor so noisily he had to be asked to stop."

The co-authors also note his resistance to routine socializing, stating that he refused the free lunches at the city's best restaurants offered by the firm as part of the wooing process. Name partner Bobby Hill suggested that Thomas did this because he disliked, and was uncomfortable being around, both "...his white and lighter-skinned black colleagues, most of whom were better off than he." They quote Hill as saying, 'We had two [whites] in the firm at the time, and they often came to the lunches with us. I think that's why he went off on his own.' Instead, he said, Thomas brought his own lunch, usually Spam. 'I gave him a hard

69

time about that Spam,' recalled Hill." (In later years, Clarence would regularly credit Hill, who died in 2000, as a mentor and major influence on his life.)

During his final year in law school, Thomas found himself in a position that was both similar to and at the same time very different from that of his classmates, especially his white classmates. On the one hand, he was about to graduate from one of the most prestigious law schools in the country, and in that sense he stood out. But he also stood out because of his blackness, and because he and other blacks who had made it through three years of Yale Law School were expected to seek "help my people" types of legal positions. Thomas found it demeaning that a firm would look at him as a kind of civil rights window dressing. While that may have been why he went to law school in the first place, he didn't want prospective legal employers to think that was the only kind of law he could learn how to practice. And that did seem to be what they were doing.

Increasingly in years to come, law firms would actively pursue graduates who were members of minority groups, but in 1974 that was not yet the case, especially not for blacks. Frank Washington, a black classmate of Thomas's, told Mayer and Abramson that he had applied to 40 law firms and received only one offer—which was one more than Clarence Thomas had received.

Clarence was more than just annoyed and disappointed by his experiences in applying for jobs with firms in Atlanta, a city that was already beginning to pat itself on the back for its improved racial climate. "Prospective employers dismissed our grades and diplomas," he said later, "assuming we got both primarily because of preferential treatment. No matter how well we had done on exams, our grades were suspect." He said he felt his interviewers were more interested in what he had done in the eighth grade than in law school, as if that advanced degree were, somehow, not real.

Then one day Clarence Thomas happened to look on the job board at the law school and saw the notice of an opening on the staff of the attorney general of the state of Missouri, John C. Danforth. Promising low pay and hard work, but with no mention of civil rights or *pro bono* cases, it would turn out to be (except for the low pay part) just what he'd been looking for.

In his 1994 book, *Resurrection*, John Danforth, by then a United States senator, recalls his first meeting with Clarence Thomas. "I first met him in the law school faculty lounge when he was a third year law student at Yale, interviewing for a position in the Missouri attorney general's office. I promised him more work and less pay than anyone else in his class, and he has often reminded me that I was true to my word. He came to Jefferson City and did the work of my office and did it well. For me, Clarence Thomas was no idealized dream of rags to riches; he was a person whom I got to know seventeen years before his nomination and whom I had known ever since.... It was not the legend of Clarence Thomas, the poor kid from Pin Point, that inspired my loyalty. It was the reality of Clarence Thomas here and now."

Of his first boss, Clarence Thomas would later say, "Danforth was a good guy. He ignored the hell out of me."

Section II
To The Bench
1974-1988

Chapter Four

"The best thing that happened to me was that I couldn't get a job out of Yale."

–Clarence Thomas

That was Justice Thomas's answer to the question "After Yale, then what?" asked him by a student at Regent University's Robertson School of Government in 1998. Thomas is almost always open and at ease with young people, especially young people from conservative religious institutions, and this instance was no exception. When it was later printed in one of the school's publications (*NeoPolitique*), it was labeled "A Casual Conversation With Justice Clarence Thomas."

Thomas went on to say that not being able to find a job after he'd finished law school "...was good because...as some doors close, other doors open.... I wanted to go to Atlanta; I wanted to go to Savannah at one point, but that didn't work out. I wanted to go to Washington, D.C., and

73

quite frankly, couldn't get a job. A young attorney general came along and said, 'Join me in Jefferson City, Missouri.' I said, 'Where?' And it was not much pay and I had family obligations and a lot of student loans. And I went out to Jefferson City, Missouri [and] what was very difficult financially, turned out to be the most magnificent job because there was so much work, and the people's attitudes were so straightforward and honest that there was no way I could be discriminated against in [Missouri]. On September 14 I was sworn in as a member of the Missouri bar, and on September 17, I stood before the Missouri Supreme Court for my first argument.... The job turned out to be with Senator Danforth, then Attorney General Danforth [who] turned out to be one of the most honest and decent human beings ever, just a wonderful man."

Thomas, who described his assistant attorney general position as "a perfect job," gives full credit for that situation to Danforth, the man who would become his career mentor. "I think it's interesting that he recruited me. First, he said he was not going to say that he knew what it meant to be black, without money, from the South. He didn't have any of those problems. He was one of the heirs of the Danforth fortune—the Ralston Purina fortune—and had a wonderful life. The second thing he said was, 'Clarence, there's plenty of room at the top.' Of course, then I was still cynical and negative.... I said, 'that's easy for him to say.' And it turns out that less than 20 years later...in October, 1991, sitting on the Supreme Court, you realize beyond belief, that he was absolutely right."

Working for John Danforth was both an extension and, ultimately, an expansion of Clarence Thomas's connection with strong figures, usually, but not always, male, who were devout adherents to a Christian faith. In the beginning there had been his grandfather and the nuns at St. Benedict's, in particular Sister Virgilius, and then several priests at Holy

Cross (Fr. Brooks and Fr. Fahey, among others). There seems not to have been any strong religious figures in his life during his law school days, but there are some plausible reasons for this. For one thing, Yale, unlike all the other schools Thomas had attended for the last decade and a half, was a secular institution; for another, Thomas had married outside the Catholic Church, meaning he'd wed Kathy Ambush in the church of her denomination, Episcopalianism, and this may well have added to his sense of removal from a Catholic sphere of influence.

John Danforth, however, was different. Also a Yale law graduate, he was not a secular humanist, but rather an extremely devout Christian, in his case also the Episcopal branch. In addition to his law degree, he had an earned degree from the Yale divinity school. An heir to the immense Ralston Purina fortune, had John Danforth wanted to, he could have sat back and done nothing more strenuous than clip dividend coupons for the rest of his life. Instead, he put his beliefs into practice in his daily life. Even as a young lawyer on Wall Street, he did charitable works on a regular basis, such as helping cancer patients in his free time.

He had entered politics in the epochal year of 1968, the year that saw the murders of Dr. Martin Luther King, Jr. and Robert Kennedy, as well as race riots in any number of cities and political (and police) riots in Chicago during the Democratic convention. According to Jane Mayer and Jill Abramson, "As a moderate, Danforth committed himself to providing more opportunity to those without his advantages. Lacking close ties to St. Louis's black community, he decided to search for the best and brightest young aides in the country, paying special attention to minorities and the underprivileged. It was on one such scouting trip in 1974 that he visited his alma mater, Yale Law School.

"In Danforth's eyes, Clarence Thomas displayed a number of admirable traits. Although he was not ranked near the top of his class, his triumph over poverty and discrimination suggested that he was a disciplined, strong-willed person and made for an impressive life story. And although Danforth was a Republican in Missouri and Thomas a Democrat from Georgia, Thomas's former aspiration to become a priest appealed to Danforth's deeply religious nature, especially given Thomas's statement that he had abandoned the path to the priesthood after encountering too much bigotry at the seminary in Danforth's own state. For a patrician bent on making racial amends, Thomas was in many ways the prefect recruit."

When Clarence Thomas and his family arrived in Missouri in the fall of 1974, it must have seemed to him like reincarnation, so different was his situation than that of the last time he'd been in the Show Me state. Six years earlier, a callow youth of 19 or 20, he'd led a sheltered life of religious yearning, only to have what he'd thought were his life plans destroyed by the inescapable presence of racial bigotry in his daily life. Upon his return, he was a married man with a family, the graduate of a fine Jesuit college in the East and of one of the country's best law schools. From the dorm rooms of Immaculate Conception Seminary to the offices of Missouri's attorney general was a leap that, six years before, he could not have imagined making. For all its up-by-your-bootstraps impressiveness, however, Clarence Thomas's job as an assistant attorney general in the state of Missouri was hardly the sort of position that would cause envious comments from his former law school classmates. And there is evidence to suggest that he himself was well aware of that fact.

His job interviews prior to reading Danforth's notice on the Yale Law School bulletin board had not been to his liking. Interviewer after interviewer either assumed he wanted to work for the greater good of the African-American population or told him he would have that opportunity, expecting him to react positively to the news. In Capitol Games,

76

their 1992 book on the Thomas-Hill controversy, Timothy Phelps and Helen Winternitz relate one such interview: "Thomas recalled being interviewed by a partner in one of the [major Atlanta] firms, who had graduated from an obscure law school and whose office was full of Confederate artifacts, asking him about his grades in grammar school." From Atlanta to Washington, D.C., Thomas found much the same thing: assurances that he would be given lots of time to do *pro bono* work. That was not the way to get his attention. As he told Juan Williams in 1987, "I went to law school to be a lawyer, not a social worker. If I want to be a social worker I'll do it on my own time." And the writer Edward P. Jones (author of the well-received collection of short stories *Lost in the City*), an African-American Holy Cross graduate who'd been a year behind Thomas and had also been recruited as part of the school's affirmative action push in the late 1960s, recalled in a 2001 interview for this book that Clarence Thomas, shortly before he left Holy Cross, was not talking about using his law degree to do good works. "I can still see him coming out of an elevator in the basement of Fenwick Hall, and saying to the guy he was with, another black student, maybe Ted Wells, 'I am so tired of being poor.'" Most of Thomas's biographers mention that when he moved into his first office as an assistant attorney general in Missouri, he replaced his Malcolm X poster with one of a Rolls-Royce automobile. But it is just as likely that this was not an example of avarice, but of the young lawyer's often-quirky sense of humor.

Jones's recollection, however, does not square with what Justice Thomas told the student interviewer for *NeoPolitique* in 1998. He said, "I made a decision when I was in the early part of my career not to ever work for money....I would never take a job for money, never switch jobs for money...so often we think, 'I can make 15% or 20% more if I move over here.' But that would mean either that I wasn't working for something that was meaningful to me, or if I was working on something meaningful, that it was for sale. There was a price tag on it. And I've kept true to that. I will not work for people I cannot look up to. I would rather starve than do that. One favorite saying is, 'You don't criticize the person who is putting food on your plate.' And if I was going to work for someone about whom I was going to be critical, then I would prefer simply to leave. The positive side is that if you really feel strongly about someone, you really put in the extra effort."

Leaving aside the question of Clarence Thomas's exact motivation and frame of mind when he accepted the job in "Jeff City" (years later, during an interview, he commented as an aside, "If you ever want to be deprogrammed from any kind of cult, go to Jeff City."), it is clear that he felt quite strongly about John Danforth and thus did put in the extra effort.

In his book on Thomas, Norman Macht begins his chapter on the Jefferson City experience by introducing another young lawyer, this one white, by the name of Clifford Faddis, who worked for the Department of Revenue. He and Thomas became friends, often playing basketball with other young men from the attorney general's office or watching sports on television. Faddis told Macht, "What stood out in my mind about Thomas was his integrity. We talked about changes we would like to see in the system, but he never spoke ill of it, never complained, never expressed anger. He was always positive about how hard we had to work to succeed and how we should all—black and white—learn to live together. And he never swore."

No one disputes the part about working hard, but people who knew Thomas at the time, either in college or law school or both, laugh out loud at the final comment. "Please," said Edward Jones, "we all knew Clarence had a real trashy mouth. He and Gil Hardy [who'd gone to Holy

Cross and Yale law with Thomas, and who died in a diving accident in 1989] in particular, used to talk just terrible to one another. But it was no big deal. A lot of black guys talked like that, and nobody thought less of them for it. But there was no doubt that Clarence was one of the premier foul talkers. A favorite saying of his was, 'Suck a straw out of my ass.' He was forever saying that. In fact, the authors of that book [*Strange Justice*] mentioned that expression when we were making the ABC documentary, and named their source. I was glad they didn't ask me, because I would have had to say, yes, he did use that expression a lot."

Gordon Davis, another Holy Cross graduate who went to school with Thomas and Jones, and also an African-American recruited under the school's active affirmative action program, agrees. Interviewed for this book in 2001, he said, "We kept in touch for the first ten years or so after Holy Cross and then I lost contact. I was just so surprised by the changes in him, because when he was in college he was a liberal, maybe even a civil rights activist. I guess the only reason I'd have to contact him now would be to see if he could make his views credible. I'd *love* to debate him.

"As for his language, a lot of us talked kind of raunchy at that period in our lives, but Clarence was one of the worst. At times he'd say some really gross things. I don't know what would come over him. But when it came out in the confirmation hearings about the gross language and the pubic hair in the Coke during the confirmation hearings, it was no surprise to me. That's how he talked."

In *Resurrection*, John Danforth writes of Clarence Thomas that "When he worked on my staff...he delighted in speaking his mind and taking strong positions, yet he did not speak with anger, only with intensity and spirit."

Obviously, a young man is going to speak differently in the company of his close male friends than he does when he is around his boss and his older professional colleagues. But the comments of people like Gordon Davis and Edward Jones suggest that in the case of Clarence Thomas, the gap between the two may have been greater than the norm.

Whatever the case, there is no dispute over the fact that Clarence Thomas plunged headlong into life in Jeff City. He and Kathy, and their son Jamal who was born in 1973, lived in a small flat down the street from a state penitentiary building. Kathy Thomas, who'd interrupted her education to get married to the future Supreme Court justice, went back to school to get her degree, enrolling at the all-black Lincoln University. For a family of three with large student loan balances to repay, Thomas's yearly salary of $10,800 did not leave them with much at the end of the month, or allow for entertaining to any great degree. But they were happy at being together again, Thomas having gone ahead of Kathy and Jamal in the summer to study for the Missouri bar exam. (Because he had so little money, he was given room and board by Margaret Bush Wilson, a local black activist who would later become an NAACP chairperson. Some years later, Thomas would recall that when he left at the end of the summer, he asked what he owed her, and she told him, "Just along the way, help someone who is in your position." Wilson, who always spoke highly of the young Thomas she knew, did tell one interviewer years later that at the time "He was already beginning to sound like a conservative, but one with an open mind.")

He passed the bar and was admitted to practice on September 14, 1974. On September 17, another assistant attorney general led him into a courtroom where a criminal case was about to begin, told the judge that Thomas was a newly minted lawyer, and left him there to fend for himself (and the government). Thomas recalls, "I thought I was going to die."

As it turned out, and, apparently, to Thomas's liking, actual trials were few and far between. John Danforth had promised to work him hard, but not to give him "civil rights" cases, and he was as good as his word on both accounts. The only criminal cases he handled for the first half year or so were appellate cases, a type of practice that does not involve juries. Most of the legal work he did for the State of Missouri involved tax or corporate work, specialties he'd prepared himself for by opting to take extra courses in these areas during law school. In what was perhaps his "greatest victory" as a young assistant attorney general, Clarence Thomas successfully argued a case that affirmed the state's right to ban vanity license plates, then much favored by Missouri VIPs. It was the kind of in-your-face win over the "haves" that he particularly liked. As for memorable events on the loss side of the ledger, there was his attempt to convince the Missouri Supreme Court to tax profits made on pinball machines.

Thomas dressed up his first (shared) office as a government lawyer, a public servant, with his Rolls-Royce poster and a Georgia state flag, which many people, to Thomas's delight, mistook for a confederate flag. He also delighted in having fun with, or at the expense of, one of his first office mates, a shy and reserved young Missourian by the name of John Ashcroft. Later both governor of the state and a U.S. Senator from Missouri for one term, in 2001 Ashcroft was named Attorney General of the United States by incoming President George W. Bush. Supreme Court Justice Clarence Thomas administered the oath of office. Mayer and Abramson write: "According to Andy Rothschild, now an attorney in St. Louis but then a friend and fellow lawyer, Thomas liked to taunt another member of the office, who was prim and painfully shy, by making outrageous, gross, and at times off-color remarks. 'Clarence was loud and boisterous, kind of the office clown. He couldn't help but needle the guy—he just liked to get under his skin,' Rothschild recalled.... A tightly-wound, strait-laced teetotaler who was the son of a fundamentalist minister and who was himself a gospel singer and songwriter, Ashcroft was easily flustered by Thomas, according to a second colleague who also remembered such episodes. This apparently encouraged Thomas to goad him even further."

It was at about this time that the political views of Clarence Thomas began to solidify, which meant that they changed considerably from what they'd been when he was a young college student in the liberal northeast six years earlier. In a step that would chart the course of his future at least as much as his choice of profession, he became, officially, a Republican. Some people say his decision was a way of saying thank you to John Danforth, others that it was simply a natural outgrowth of the way his thinking had been progressing as he entered his mid-to-late twenties, and still others that it was a purely pragmatic "career move" based solely on self-interest and advancement. Most likely, it was a combination of all three.

Clarence Martin, a black lawyer in Savannah who met Thomas when they both worked for the same Savannah law firm one law school summer, says that when he visited Thomas In Jefferson City shortly after he'd switched his party affiliation. "I saw a change in Clarence then. He said, 'The Republicans are going places in the next ten years, and I'm going to attach my wagon to their star.'" But, Martin continues, "In many ways he was already conservative in his social views, and he really admired Danforth." When Martin asked him how he could become a Republican, he says his friend's answer was, "Blacks need to be on both sides, and these people are the power."

Fletcher Farrington, a partner in the firm where both Thomas and Martin had worked in 1972, told Mayer and Abramson he believed Thomas switched parties to advance his own career, not because of any deep-seated, heartfelt philosophical reasons: "He told me he talked to the Democrats first, but they weren't particularly interested in him. Then he went to the Republicans, and they embraced him. I don't want to say that Clarence was a complete opportunist, but to some extent his politics were shaped by his opportunities...his ambition was not to make a particular change in society but to go as far as he could go."

On this point, the authors of *Strange Justice* also quote the late Bobby Hill, the activist civil rights lawyer and Farrington partner who had been so helpful to the young Clarence Thomas. "You can't tell me that it wasn't just about getting ahead, because, ideologically, from me to Danforth is a long way. You're talking two extremes. I'm a liberal civil rights lawyer, and he's a Republican patrician. Thomas didn't care if he was hitching himself to a good star or not. The only thing he cared about is the one thing that the two of us had in common: we were both rising."

When Thomas was asked, by the *NeoPolitique* interviewer in 1998, about the change in his political affiliation, it led to an interesting exchange.

Q. How did you go from a McGovern liberal...

A. I was never a liberal.

Q. What were you?

A. I was a radical.

Q. You were radical, o.k. How did you go from being a radical—in terms of your ideology and philosophy? What did you read, who did you talk to? How did you develop your thinking?

A. I read all the German philosophers: a lot of us were into relativism, nihilism, existentialism... but then when I got to the Attorney General's office I started to read more economics, and Tom Sowell was actually the one. When I read *Race and Economics*, it really moved me back to an approach that was consistent with my own predisposition and my own background. And over the years then I read others—Hayek, Paul Johnson, there's a whole range of people. I've been through the Ayn Rand period. People who think intrigue me....My wife and I were recently in England [and] we spent an hour with Maggie, Lady Thatcher, and the thing that I found intriguing about it was how well read she is. And the thing that I find intriguing about so many people in leadership positions is how they think about things. She was pulling books off her shelf that were underlined, highlighted, and thought through. Reading is critical if you're serious. I'm irritated with people who don't want to do the heavy lifting, but they want results [thinking] let somebody else do the heavy lifting.

For decades now, Thomas has been crediting the conservative black economist and thinker Thomas Sowell with opening his eyes to the reality of life in America for a black man. This is how he explained it to *Reason* magazine editor Bill Kauffman in 1988 Kauffman asked Thomas, on first encountering Sowell, did he agree with him right away or did he "think he was nuts?"

Thomas replied, "I think initially I thought he was nuts. I was just starting Yale Law School, and someone had given me *Black Education: Myths and Tragedies*, [and said] 'You've got to read this crazy book. This guy is out of his mind.' I picked it up and flipped through it. It really went against all the things we'd been indoctrinated to believe about the radical movement and the peace movement when we were in college. So I threw it in the trash.

"I went on my merry way, challenging all sorts of things but not really aligning myself with anybody or any idea. I went out to Jefferson City, Missouri—if you ever want to be deprogrammed from any kind of cult, go to Jeff City—and I just rethought everything. A friend of mine, I'll never forget it, called me up and said, 'Clarence, there's another black guy out here who is as crazy as you are. He has the same ideas that you have. There are two of you! I can't remember his name,' he said, 'it's Sowl or Sool or Sail or something.' I said, 'Oh my goodness.' He said, 'I've got the review of a book that he just wrote.' So I immediately dropped everything I was doing and got the review of his book, *The Economics of Politics and Race*. It was like pouring half a glass of water on the desert. I just soaked it up. Then I tried to get a hold of him. I called UCLA [and] nobody knew where he was, so I didn't contact him. A friend of mine noticed that he was speaking at Washington University [in St. Louis], so I left work and went over there. He was really great. I went up to him and begged him to sign my book. Then he moved to Stanford, and I bugged him. I know I bugged the man. When I got to Washington I used to hold court every morning with some of the other black staff assistants and give lectures about these things."

The reaction to his Sowellian proselytizing was, says Thomas, "mixed...there were some people who when they saw me tried to evade me—at 12:15 they were trying to catch a 12:00 plane! At any rate, I consider him not only an intellectual mentor, but my salvation as far as thinking through these issues. I thought I was absolutely insane. His book was manna from heaven."

Thomas referred to Sowell in his now-famous address to the National Bar Association in Memphis in 1998, telling that largely hostile audience, in a slightly altered version, "Ironically, many of the people who are critics today were among those we called 'half-steppers,' who had been co-opted by 'the man' because they were part of the system that oppressed us. When the revolution came, all of the so-called Negroes needed to be dealt with. It is interesting to remember that someone gave me a copy of Prof. Thomas Sowell's book, *Education, Myths and Tragedies*, in which he predicted much of what has happened to blacks and education. I threw it in the trash, unread, declaring that he was not a black man since no black could take the positions that he had taken, whatever they were, since I had only heard his views were not those of a black man. I was also upset to hear of a black conservative in Virginia named Jay Parker. How could a black man call himself a conservative? In a twist of fate, they both are dear friends today, and the youthful wrath I visited upon them is now being visited upon me, though without the youth. What goes around does indeed come around."

James (Jay) Parker would turn out to be something of a lightning rod in the early 1980s when Thomas began to climb the Reagan administration ladder. While Sowell was an intellectual economist and an author-teacher, Parker was first and foremost a political activist. A very early Goldwarterite, he was to conservatism what Jane Fonda (then) was to liberalism. In their book, Phelps and Winternitz call him, "...a zealot, a radical in the conservative cause."

They continue, "He fervently believed that no level of government, from the federal to the state to the local, had any business providing food, clothing or housing to anyone, no matter how poor or desperate. Private charitable groups should do that work, he said, and to his credit his own resumé boasted a long list of such endeavors. He was also dead set against affirmative action."

Back In 1977, Thomas found himself without a mentor when John Danforth moved to Washington as Missouri's new junior senator. But while Danforth may have been out of sight, he still had Clarence Thomas in mind. When Thomas told him he wanted to leave the attorney general's staff, mainly to make more money, Danforth not only understood, he went to bat for Thomas, helping him secure a legal position in the St. Louis office of the giant Monsanto Chemical

Corporation. Once again, before accepting the job, Thomas made it clear he was not going to be the house black, working only on civil rights and related matters. Assured that would not be the case, he took the job. He did Environmental Protection Agency work and product liability cases, and by all accounts did well if not brilliantly. (One former supervisor said, "In a staff of extremely competent and bright lawyers, Clarence Thomas could and did hold his own," a positive, if not ringing, endorsement for a young lawyer.)

He was pleased with the increase in salary, from $11,000 to $20,000, and as usual fit in well, his easy-going personality enabling him to mix with his co-workers, the great majority of whom were white, at both professional and social affairs. If he was seething with ambition to move on to bigger and better things, it was not a dream he shared with many other people. Nonetheless, when John Danforth called and told him he had another job for him, this one in Washington on his senate staff, Clarence Thomas wasted no time in saying yes.

For yet one more time, Thomas made his acceptance of the job conditional on its not being a "black slot," a position in which he would deal solely with civil rights and other racial issues. And once again John Danforth agreed. Thomas had developed some expertise—or at least some experience—in environmental matters and also in the energy field, and it was these areas on which Thomas worked for Senator Danforth as a legislative assistant from 1979 to 1981.

It was, in fact, during this time that Thomas first learned of Jay Parker. One of Thomas's coworkers in Danforth's office gave him a copy of Parker's magazine, *The Lincoln Review*. Thomas was so taken with its contents that he picked up the phone and called Parker, telling him, "I like what you've got to say." The bond that was quickly forged is still strong.

According to Mayer and Abramson, while Thomas

joined a group of black professional Hill staffers, he was not particularly active. They quote Robert Harris, another member of the group, as saying of Clarence Thomas, "…there was an element of [his] not wanting to be that closely connected with something so identifiably black." They also relate the experience of Jon Sawyer, a reporter in the Washington bureau of *The St. Louis Post-Dispatch*, who told them of his astonishment when, one day at lunch, Clarence Thomas, the still-new Senate staffer told him that "the spot he wanted was nothing less than a seat on the U.S. Supreme Court."

Hubris? Hype? Humor? In an interview for this book, Sawyer amended that quote by saying that at the time he thought Thomas, whom he had interviewed several times and always found pleasant and forthcoming, was kidding, though with hindsight he now wonders to what degree. If Thomas was serious, it indicates a most timely prescience, for in 1979 or early 1980, few if any political prognosticators were on record as seeing bright futures for black conservatives. But as Thomas may or may not have foreseen, there was a major figure on the horizon who would dominate American politics for at least the next decade.

His name was Ronald Wilson Reagan. And he, or his legacy, would make Clarence Thomas, one way or another, a household name.

Chapter Five
Washington I, From the Hill to the DOE

...you have to remember I was thrown on this scene. After we got back from the Fairmont Conference in 1980, it was the first time I'd had any articles written about me. All of a sudden my views, or at least the journalistic synopses of views are in a major paper, the Washington Post. *I wasn't used to this kind of thing. I never ran for office. I never raised my hand in college. And suddenly my name is in the paper. And to hear the things they said about me— Carl Rowan and some of the others. It does affect you. But it is so bad and so offbase that you just have to shake your head. Winston Churchill was asked, why did you become prime minister? He said, 'Ambition.' Well, why did you stay so long? He said, 'Anger.' That's one of the reasons why I went back up for reconfirmation. You're not going to run me out of town. I'm going to stay right here. If I'm not reconfirmed, I'll drive a truck. I'll work in a gas station. I'll work at McDonald's....*

–Clarence Thomas
Reason *magazine, 1987*

If reading Thomas Sowell was, as Clarence Thomas has said, his "Road to Damascus" experience, then attending the Fairmont Conference was his first visit to Mecca. But before he made that trip he had become well acquainted with another "country," the land of Jay Parker.

While Sowell's main tenets of black self-sufficiency and avoidance (at all costs) of "victimization mentality" resonated deeply within the still-young Clarence Thomas, Jay Parker's political conservatism seemed to motivate him more strongly at this point in his life. One could hardly have had better conservative credentials than those of Parker. He'd worked in the Draft Goldwater movement five years before the famously conservative Arizona Senator became his party's nominee in 1964. Five years later he was the first black on the board of directors of Young Americans for Freedom. So extreme were some of Parker's views that during the 1980s he was a (very well) paid lobbyist for South Africa, a connection that would be brought up and used against Thomas during his Supreme Court nomination hearings.

While it has never been shown that Thomas had anything but disdain for South Africa's policy of racial apartheid, he nonetheless developed and sustained a closeness to Parker. Indeed, Supreme Court Justice Thomas praised him publicly, along with Sowell, in his Boyer lecture at the American Enterprise Institute in 2001.

"In the spring of 1980," he told the black-tie audience of 500 at the Capitol Hilton, "I received a call asking if I had any interest in going to the Office of Civil Rights in the Department of Education. Until then, for the good of my career, I had assiduously avoided any work that was related to civil rights, and frankly I had no interest in such a position. Then a dear friend of mine, Jay Parker, spoke to me about it, insisting that these issues were of great importance to me, and that I had a point of view that should be part of the policy process and the continuing debate. I had to admit that what happened in this area did mean a lot to me. But I didn't want to be the one arguing publicly for policies that would raise the ire of the civil rights establishment."

The Justice then went back to one of the points he'd made 14 years earlier (and at other times since his confirmation) in his interview with *Reason* magazine. "I had just gotten a taste of the penalties for candor and honesty as a result of the *Washington Post* op-ed, and I had no interest in a repeat performance. There is, of course, such a thing as self-preservation. Also, I was insulted that I was being offered the job for no reason other than my race. I hesitated, unsure of how to proceed. But Jay Parker's final words of advice to me were compelling: 'Put up or shut up.' What a choice!

"But he was right. Even with all the complications, in the end the choice is just that stark. One might shut up when it doesn't matter, but when it really counts, we are required to put up."

In mid-December of 1979, on his own nickel, Clarence Thomas flew to San Francisco to attend a conference of black conservatives that was held at the Fairmont Hotel (which caused it to be called, ever after, the Fairmont Conference). Ronald Reagan, who was to be inaugurated the next month, had been elected with little or no help from black America, and some of his advisors saw this meeting as an opportunity to win one for the Gipper. No less an administrative heavy than Edwin Meese was one of the speakers at the conference, which was sponsored by the San Francisco-based Institute for Contemporary Studies.

The day after the conference, *The Washington Post* ran two front-page stories about it. The first, a feature or "color"-type piece, began with an anecdote: "There were so many black men checking into the elegant old Fairmont Hotel on Nob Hill that one of the red-liveried bellhops wanted to know if there was some special musical event going on that he had not heard about."

It went on, "The men and a few black women retold the story as a joke, laughed about it and shrugged it off with an air of prosperous self-assurance. There were no musicians among their ranks, but there were Ivy League professors, lawyers, physicians, dentists and commentators—men in their 30s, 40s, and early 50s, dressed in dark blue pin-striped suits as befits the members of an emerging black professional class.

"Some had for years been that anomaly of American

politics, a black Republican. Many others were lifelong Democrats, disillusioned at the perceived failure of President Carter to champion legislation that aided blacks. They were not only turning away from the Democrats but from the traditional black civil rights organizations as well, in the belief that liberal philosophies of government intervention in behalf of blacks and creation of social programs for the poor had not worked."

In his speech, Edwin Meese promised the assembly that the Reagan administration was looking for people "at the highest level of decision-making—executive positions, management positions and other types of high positions— as he did in California." According to the *Post*, Meese said that the President-elect was committed to putting blacks in "non-traditional roles," adding, "'There is no black Cabinet "spot" as far as he's concerned. There will undoubtedly be blacks in the Cabinet but not in just the same department over and over again,' he said to cheers from the conference participants."

It's highly likely that Clarence Thomas was among those cheering, for what the top presidential aide was saying dovetailed perfectly with the young Hill aide's own career plans, especially the idea of "non-traditional roles." Meese made two other statements that night that had to have gone down well with Thomas, the newly-minted Republican. The first was: "I think there's going to be black people in the White House staff but they're not going to be the ambassadors to the black people. They're going to be there because they have a substantive role to fulfill. You're not going to have one person that all blacks have to funnel through. I think that's demeaning." The other statement referred to a meeting Ronald Reagan had just had with civil rights leaders that left them somewhat nervous as to his real intentions. "The difference between that meeting and this conference here is they were talking about the last 10 years and the ideas of the last

10 years. You're talking about the ideas of the next 10 years."

The article closed with this paragraph: "Meese promised the conference that the Reagan administration would 'adhere to the problems of this country and we hope that how we act will benefit black Americans.' He said Reagan would live up to a campaign promise to provide financial support for black colleges and would act to curb any 'zealous demons' at the Department of Education."

Sitting in the audience, waiting his chance to speak, Clarence Thomas had no way of knowing, but before too long he would be one of the Reagan appointees chosen specifically to counteract the zealous demons in the Department of Education. Through a series of steps, almost all of them fortuitous (in the sense of being accidental) he would find himself front and center when the time came to choose black appointees.

The first step involved the presence at the conference of a young editorial writer for the *Washington Post*, Juan Williams. On Tuesday, December 16, 1980, under the bold headline, "Black Conservatives, Center Stage," there was a picture—five inches high by five inches wide—of a non-smiling Clarence Thomas very much center stage on the op-ed page of the *Washington Post*. This was the story Thomas would refer to, again and again over the years, as the beginning of his "troubles."

Williams's story, which he'd filed from San Francisco, began, "You've heard about Clarence Thomas, but not by name. He is one of the black people now on center stage in American politics: he is a Republican, a long-time supporter of Ronald Reagan, opposed to the minimum wage law, rent control, busing and affirmative action. How a black man can say no to those policies is a mystery to most black people.

"But Clarence Thomas, 32, who paid his own way to fly here from his home in Bethesda for a weekend meeting of top black Republican policymakers, is convinced that the real mystery is how 90 percent of black Americans could support those policies and vote for Jimmy Carter." That was the first mention, in the media, of the mystery that continues to exist, in the minds of all sorts of people, to this very day, as far as Clarence Thomas is concerned.

Williams continued, quoting Thomas, "'I marched. I protested. I asked the government to help black people,' says Thomas. 'I did all those things. But it hasn't worked. It isn't working. And someone needs to say that.'"

So Clarence Thomas said that. And more.

"To talk with Thomas is to realize that his conservatism is born of the same personal anger at racism that fired the militants of the 1960s," wrote Williams. "The worst experience of his life, says Thomas, a lawyer who is an assistant to Sen. John Danforth (R.-MO), was attending college and law school with whites who believed he was there only because of racial quotas for the admission of blacks.

"'You had to prove yourself every day because the presumption was that you were dumb and didn't deserve to be there on merit,' Thomas says. 'Every time you walked into a law class at Yale it was like having a monkey jump down your back from the Gothic arches.... The professors and the students resented your very presence.'"

That statement, along with several others quoted by Williams in his op-ed piece, would follow Clarence Thomas for decades.

The article continued: "The same racism, the assumption that he got his job because he is black, trails Thomas to this day. He refuses to work on any issue directly related to black people because, he says, his colleagues would assume that he has the job only because he is black. Thomas works only on energy, environment and public works policy for Sen. Danforth, staying away from black issues until last weekend."

There were two quotes in particular in the remainder of

Williams's article that would bring significant attention to Clarence Thomas, both in the immediate future and for a long way down the road, attention that would come from whites as well as blacks.

The first quote, viewed in hindsight, seems downright prophetic. Thomas told the reporter, "If I ever went to work for the EEOC, or did anything directly connected with blacks, my career would be irreparably ruined. The monkey would be on my back again to prove that I didn't have the job because I'm black. People meeting me for the first time would automatically dismiss my thinking as second-rate."

The second quote, which would follow him all the way to his Supreme Court nomination hearings in 1991, had to do with his sister, Emma Mae. Williams led into it by writing, "Thomas is also a man who has a sister on welfare back in his home state of Georgia, but he feels that he must be opposed to welfare because of the dependency it can breed in a person. 'She [his sister] gets mad when the mailman is late with her welfare check,' he says. 'That is how dependent she is. What is worse is that now her kids feel entitled to the check too. They have no motivation for doing better or getting out of that situation.'"

Thomas even went so far as to "dis" Rev. Jesse Jackson, the liberal icon. As quoted by Williams, he said, "'I'm tired of blacks being thought of only as poor people, people on welfare, people who are unemployed,' says Thomas. 'That's the only way the Jesse Jacksons and the other black leaders talk about black people. To them, we're all a monolith. Well, they are not talking for the 80 to 90 percent of black people in this country who have never been on welfare or in jail."

In addition to mentioning, as did the news reporter in his front-page story, that Edwin Meese, the top presidential counselor who just happened to be heading up Ronald Reagan's transition team and therefore on the lookout for "talent," had promised open access to the new administra-

tion and a good shot at jobs that were not "directly connected with blacks," to use Thomas's phrase. Williams also
mentioned Thomas's hero Sowell. "As a follower of Thomas
Sowell, the black economist who was the star attraction at
the weekend conference.... Clarence Thomas also questions
black support for the minimum wage and government jobs
programs. 'The proof they do not work is in the high black
teenage unemployment rate,' says Thomas."

The *Washington Post* article, with its prominent place-
ment and its arresting picture of a shirt-sleeved Thomas staring up at the camera minus even the hint of a smile as it
entered the consciousness of hundreds of thousands of readers in the Washington area on Monday morning, ended with
this paragraph:

> Thomas' attitude and thinking, long the distant
> cousins of popular black thought, now come to the
> forefront because of Ronald Reagan's election. But
> blacks did not elect Ronald Reagan, and they did not
> ask for prominence to be given to a black silent
> majority.
>
> While the black conservatives like Clarence
> Thomas point out that not all blacks are poor or in
> jail, their challenge will be to remember that a dis-
> proportionate number of blacks are poor and are in
> jail. This country is not yet so sophisticated that
> blacks, even black Republicans can say it makes no
> difference what color an American is. But thanks to
> Clarence Thomas and other black Americans like
> him, new approaches to significant problems are
> being discussed for the first time since Martin Luther
> King, Jr.

Williams's December 1980 column about Thomas caused
several important reactions. One was from the left, another
from the right, and a third was from home. Liberal colum-

nists and commentators decried his statements, calling him both insensitive and opportunistic. As he would say many times in the years to come, he wasn't as bothered by the substance of what they said as he was by the virulence with which they said it. But while he may have been surprised by the degree to which African-American spokespeople reacted to the reports of what he had said, he probably should not have been, given the volatility of his comments. Seven years later, the same *Washington Post* reporter would write, this time in the *Atlantic Monthly*, in describing Thomas's coming-out speech at the Fairmont Conference, "Thomas was the most interesting of a very self-important crowd, because he was so brutally candid," citing as a prime example Thomas's comments about his sister. But it was that same year Clarence Thomas told *Reason* magazine, "...you have to remember, I was thrown on this scene."

The reaction from the right took a much more pragmatic form—job offers. As it happened, Jay Parker, who was, along with Thomas Sowell, Clarence Thomas's co-equal idol, was helping Edwin Meese with the transfer of power at the Equal Opportunity Employment Commission, the federal agency of greatest potential importance to black Americans, and, according to several Thomas biographers, had actually talked to Thomas as early as 1980 about the top job there. But that would have been way too much way too soon, and Thomas said he was not interested. Nonetheless, the fact that the new administration was even talking about such a lofty post to a 32-year-old Senate staffer who had barely been in Washington for a year is indicative of how hard they were looking for conservatives of color.

The reaction from home was his sister Emma Mae's displeasure at his speaking publicly about their ongoing argument over her being on welfare. There is disagreement as to what actually happened. According to Mayer and Abramson in *Strange Justice*, "Thomas told a personal aide that he had been so upset when his comments appeared in print, he had driven nonstop from Washington to Georgia to apologize to his sister (an event she says she has no memory of)." The co-authors relate her recollection that he called her on the phone, though not necessarily to apologize; rather, they continued their usual debate about the topic of welfare. Mayer and Abramson also mention, in a footnote, that in his 1992 book *Resurrection*, Thomas's boss at the time, Senator Danforth, wrote that Thomas *flew* to Georgia to apologize. (Interestingly, on one page Danforth lists 10 questions the media raised about Thomas at the time of the hearings, and on the next page denies or refutes them, one after the other. But he does so with only the first eight charges. The two he does not address are: "While in law school, had Clarence watched pornographic movies?", and, "While a youth, had Clarence tried marijuana?")

In May of 1981, in direct contradiction of what he had said publicly about accepting a "black slot" (and after turning down a mid-to-low level White House job working on energy and environment issues), Clarence Thomas became head of the civil rights office at the Department of Education.

Deciding to take the offer was not, in light of a number of his public comments but especially the one in the *Washington Post* about not wanting to accept a "black" job, the easiest of decisions. On the one hand, he'd just come right out and said he didn't want that kind of job, that it would ruin his career; but on the other, it was a presidential appointment in the brand-new administration of Ronald Reagan, the conservatives' savior. As a fellow aide in Danforth's office told him bluntly, "You'd have to be nuts not to take it." He took it.

Brief as it turned out to be—from May of 1981 to May of 1982—Thomas's tenure at the Department of Education was not the smoothest. Not only was he on record as having said he didn't want that exact kind of job, but he was also unfamiliar, as a lawyer, with its nature and substance. And if those two reasons weren't enough, there was the additional fact that his personal life was at a very low point.

Along with that of his friend Jay Parker, Clarence Thomas sought the advice of several other people about whether or not to take the civil rights post at Education. One of them was Allen Moore, with whom he worked in Senator Danforth's office. Basically, Moore said the same things as had Parker. "You are thirty-two years old, a legislative assistant, and you have been handed an opportunity to run an office in a federal agency with a large staff. Forget about being a stereotype. This is visibility, responsibility, a presidential appointment."

Judith Winston, a Carter appointee who stayed on as an assistant general counsel, told Mayer and Abramson, "As one of the few black conservatives, he ended up being treated by his own party in a way he said he opposed. I always felt he resented the position of having to defend these civil rights cases at all." Still others told the authors of *Strange Justice* that they found him harsh and abrupt, which they attributed not to his basic personality, but to the political and philosophical bind in which he found himself, and for which he could blame no one else.

The co-authors go so far as to report that *many* of Thomas's associates in the civil rights division at Education found him "chilly, sarcastic, and short-tempered" at this time. They quote Tony Califa, a classmate at Yale Law School and a Democrat: "You couldn't argue with him. Instead, I'd find myself having to back down, saying things like, 'Oh, I didn't know that,' to which he'd reply, 'I could fill a book with what you don't know.'"

Judy Winston had a different take on why he acted this way. She told Mayer and Abramson his attitude was a cover-up for a basic insecurity regarding the work. Winston said he "…intimidated a lot of white appointees because they didn't know how to read him. He had a way of sitting quietly and glowering, and giving very short yes and no answers to complicated questions. But I think it was a front. The fact was that he didn't know a lot about how the civil rights laws worked, and he didn't let on in meetings that he was less than knowledgeable."

Nonetheless, Winston gave him good marks for trying to walk a reasonable path between the hard line Reaganites on the right and the traditional civil rights establishment on the other side. There were many "stormy meetings," she said, as a result of which Thomas found himself "in no man's land. He was caught between blacks, who saw him as being used, and the whites in the administration, some of whom I remember him angrily describing as bigots who really thought blacks were inferior."

It didn't help Clarence Thomas's state of mind, or the mid-ground position he was trying to stake out, when the Reagan Justice Department came out in favor of tax-exempt status for the far-right, anti-black Christian school in South Carolina, Bob Jones University. His intra-administration protests fell on deaf ears, but there is no doubt he protested the decision.

Winston's read on Thomas during this period was that he was very confused. Mayer and Abramson quote her as saying, "The confusion, from my standpoint, stemmed from the fact that he was permitting himself to be used, and he knew it. He was a willing instrument, very pragmatic; he saw the opportunities for someone who would go along. But he resented some of the things that the Republican political appointees were trying to talk him into."

Thomas had an answer for Winston and others who suggested (or implied) that he should do the honorable thing and quit the post that had put him between a rock and a hard place. He said it was preferable to deal with "out-and-

out racists," rather than the behind-your-back variety, because then, "…at least you know where you stand."

Just how active Clarence Thomas was behind the scenes
of the new administration at this point is not generally
known, but there's little doubt he had a good idea of how
well-positioned he was for advancement. Compared not just
to other blacks in positions of power, but also to young
lawyers of any racial or ethnic background, he was, as they
would say in his native Georgia, "walking in tall cotton."
Only 32, he was a presidential appointee with a staff of 50
people under him. He had gone from being an obscure congressional aide to the civil rights chief of an important
Cabinet agency—even if it was one the Reagan administration had said, during the campaign, that it would like to
eliminate. For him to have given up this advantage, to have
taken himself off the fast track, *would* have been, as he'd told
Juan Williams, career suicide. It may also have been, by this
point in his development, out of character.

Clearly, during his time at the Department of Education, he was not as ideologically conservative as he would be
once he'd been at the EEOC for several years. In one of the
many speeches he gave during his 12 months at Education,
he was forthright in laying out for the student audience at
Clark College in Atlanta his belief that he and the traditional civil rights leaders did not see eye to eye on all the problems that beset black Americans.

"Today," he said, "we must recognize that, while discrimination continues as a pervasive barrier, many problems
of blacks are socio-economic." He cited some definitely
depressing statistics: functional illiteracy among young
blacks as high as 40 percent; percentage of black unwed
mothers, 48 percent; and blacks on welfare at some point in
their youth, over 40 percent. He praised the traditional civil
rights leaders, but accused them of sleeping at the switch.
He said, "These problems cannot be solved by the law, even

civil rights laws, but they can be solved by new ideas…we must also look to ourselves admitting that there are problems which anti-discrimination laws will not cure."

He told his audience that they could not continue, "…saying the same things, adhering to the same party, believing in the same solutions. We fought too long and too hard to stop others from saying we all looked alike. We cannot now accept people saying we all think alike. This is far more dangerous." As for help from the government in the past, he said, "Massive federal involvement still left us at the bottom rung of the economic ladder. Clearly then, the answer does not lie in more government intervention."

There was a fundamental irony operating here. If what Clarence Thomas was saying, both privately and in his speeches and writings at the time, sounded heretical to certain segments of the civil rights leadership, it would begin to sound less and less so as the years marched on, even though he would not receive much credit for that in the mainstream media. But that is not the ironic part. The irony is that not very many members of the Reagan administration agreed with him, certainly not in principle. To them, his idea of keeping traditional black colleges black by resisting forced integration (because of Thomas's oft-stated belief that blacks did not have to sit next to whites in class in order to get a good education) was just fine—but for the reason that they opposed forced integration of *any* school, meaning any white school.

In another speech Thomas gave a few years after his Clark College address, he elaborated on what he meant when he said that all too often in the present day it seems, "we look at our distant past as an indictment:"

Somehow we have permitted ourselves to be trapped in a rhetorical discussion of our race that is shamelessly negative, a discussion that ultimately leads to

102

the conclusion that we have no control over our fate—
the others, bigots, friends, enemies and politicians
have more to say about us than we do. For example,
we control the values that our kids have. I am raising
a young teenager so I know how difficult and critical
that is. When I was a kid…it was bad to say that
blacks are dumb but then it became all right to say we
could not perform as well as whites because of something beyond our control. What's the difference?

While he may have stayed on message, there were other
changes going on. In *Capitol Games*, Phelps and Winternitz,
state that as Clarence Thomas became more and more of a
Republican, he even began to look more like one. "At his
office within the education department," they write,
"Thomas began shaping his image. He started dressing like
a conservative in dark, expensive suits. And, predictably, he
got into political fights with members of his staff who
thought he was not enforcing civil rights laws in the nation's
schools. But Thomas stayed only a year at the civil rights
office and mostly kept himself out of the public eye. He did,
however, begin his fight with the civil rights community.…
On the face of it, though, nothing astounding happened
during Thomas's brief term in the civil rights office.

"…In the meantime, over at the White House, the
Republicans were having trouble finding blacks to fill other
posts. Many qualified blacks were just not interested in joining the Reagan administration's dismantling of social policies
that the civil rights movement had toiled years to establish."

There was another reason for Clarence Thomas to
"shape his image." By 1981, he and Kathy Ambush had
come to the conclusion that their marriage was doomed.
There had been separations and then reconciliations, at one
time or another they'd each had sole custody of their son
Jamal, then about eight years old, and attempts at counseling, but they now agreed on the futility of any further

attempts. Their differences were simply too great. Some friends of the couple have suggested that Clarence's growing political conservatism was a major impediment, while others have attributed it to differences in "ambition." Whatever the case, by the time he took the job at the Department of Education, he was no longer a happily married man. According to several interviews with friends who knew him at the time, Thomas was (understandably) unhappy, on edge, and snappish during this period. The final split came in August of 1981, with the official decree granted three years later, at which time he received sole custody of Jamal.

When it came time for him to leave the house they were renting in the Maryland suburb of Bethesda, Thomas moved in with his friend from both college and law school, Gil Hardy. Hardy, who was also getting divorced, had a two-bedroom apartment in Adams Morgan, a section of Northwest D.C. just a few miles from the Department of Education. A girl who was dating Hardy at the time later told Mayer and Abramson that each morning Clarence Thomas used to wake himself—and anyone else in the apartment—by blasting out Whitney Houston's version of "The Greatest Love of All," a paean to self-love.

"As the song suggested," the co-authors write, "Thomas seemed suspicious of romance and intent on embracing his new, independent status. It was, after all, something of a novelty. He had gone from the chaste life of the seminary directly to college, where he had married his first serious girlfriend only months after they had met. Thus the summer of 1981 was the first time in Thomas's adult life that he was truly free and on his own."

Gil Hardy, who was known for helping people, just as he had done for his friend Clarence, did another favor that summer. There was a young lawyer at his firm who'd had trouble fitting in, despite an excellent school record and a law degree from Thomas's alma mater, Yale. Also like

Thomas, she was an African-American from a poor family who had pulled herself up by her academic bootstraps. She was thinking of moving from the private sector into the government. Thomas said to send her over, he would check her out, and if she was as good as Hardy said, he'd give her a job. Hardy did so, Thomas was duly impressed, and she was hired. Her name was Anita Hill.

Chapter Six

Washington II, EEOC

*I thought I was heading for trouble when I came over
here, but no one could have prepared me for this
agency. It was like biting into a bad apple. The more
you bite, the more wrong you find.*

— Clarence Thomas
April, 1984

Established in 1965 under the umbrella of Title VII of
the Civil Rights Act of 1964, the EEOC is the government's chief enforcer of the country's laws against discrimination in employment. At the time Clarence Thomas
was named as its head, the principal federal statutes enforced by EEOC were Title VII (which covers cases involving race, color, religion, sex, or national origin), the Age
Discrimination in Employment Act of 1967 (which prohibits discrimination against people age 40 and above), and
the Equal Pay Act of 1963 (which prohibits discrimination
on the basis of gender in compensation for "substantially
similar work under similar conditions"). In later years, its
mandate would be broadened by the passage of the
Americans with Disabilities Act (1990) and the Civil Rights
Act of 1991.

In addition to its headquarters in Washington, the EEOC has 50 field offices throughout the United States. People who believe they've been discriminated against in employment start the process by filing administrative charges, and individual EEOC commissioners (there are five) may also initiate charges. After it investigates the charges, if the EEOC determines there is reasonable cause to believe discrimination has occurred, under the law, it must then try to reach a voluntary resolution between "the charging party and the respondent." If conciliation is not successful, the EEOC can bring suit in federal court. Whenever the EEOC concludes its processing of a case—or, prior to that time, upon request of a charging party—it issues a "notice of right to sue" which enables the charging party to sue in court.

While Clarence Thomas was getting his feet wet as a brand-new member of the brand-new Reagan administration, the administration was getting egg all over its EEOC face. Although Edwin Meese had promised the Fairmont Conference audience that blacks would not be offered "black jobs," it certainly looked that way at the Equal Employment Opportunity Commission. And the potential nominees caught on right away. When a reported dozen blacks said no to the post, that was bad, but when the administration found someone to accept, things got even worse.

The first to say yes to a post for which he could not get confirmed was a black businessman from Detroit named William Bell. Mr. Bell was telling the truth when he said he ran his own job-placement firm, but the administration was embarrassed when he turned out to be its sole employee. And, the firm had placed only two people a year, on average. What's more, Bell was not a lawyer, as all the other EEOC chairs had been.

Down the street at the U.S. Civil Rights Commission things were no better. Sam B. Hart, a black minister from Philadelphia whose religious radio program had a large following, had been nominated as a commissioner. But before he could gain approval he called a press conference at which he denounced affirmative action, school busing, civil rights for gays and lesbians, and the Equal Rights Amendment (ERA). There was an immediate firestorm of criticism from such groups as NOW, the Gay Task Force, and the NAACP's Legal Defense Fund, Inc. When it was learned, in the midst of this uproar, that Reverend Hart had a problem with back taxes and with the rent for his radio station, it wasn't long before he was no longer a contender.

Liberal Senator Thomas Eagleton told the media, "There is deep despair in the black community for many reasons, and the nominations of those two individuals really sent a message to the black community that we don't care. They were such glaring examples of poor appointments that it is almost shocking." And Vernon Jordan, who'd been the national executive director of the Urban League, said that in its selection of black nominees, the Reagan administration had been stressing "incompetence and ideology. In the process, they have ignored the extraordinarily competent middle-of-the-road blacks, many of whom campaigned for Reagan. They have ignored a fantastic political opportunity with blacks."

Reverend Walter Fauntroy, then the D.C. delegate to the House of Representatives and head of the Congressional Black Caucus, said the president's appointments were more insulting to black Americans than those of any president in memory. He said the nomination of Bell was "an insult to blacks, while the appointment of Hart added insult to injury."

Onto that stage, in May of 1982, walked Clarence Thomas of Pin Point, Georgia. There is no denying that things weren't exactly shipshape at the commission when Thomas arrived. His immediate predecessor, Eleanor Holmes Norton (by coincidence another African-American graduate of Yale Law School) had also inherited a troubled agency. While she may have been more activist than administrator, Norton had tried to straighten out the agency, but the task was Sisyphean. For a number of reasons, including political affiliation, her time at EEOC would be in marked contrast to that of Clarence Thomas.

As it happened, on the same day Thomas took over, May 17, 1982, the General Accounting Office (GAO) released a report that was scathing in its criticism of EEOC. It said the agency was "beset by acrimony, improper employee conduct, poor performance and favoritism," and estimated that the total amount of uncollected employee travel allowances was one million dollars. Later, EEOC's director of audit said publicly, "The building itself was a disaster. People didn't want to come to work. There was mold growing in the halls. Carbon monoxide was coming in from the garage. Thomas cleaned it up."

Thomas's approach to the agency's mission represented a fundamental shift in priorities that did not sit well with the civil rights establishment. According to David Brock in *The Real Anita Hill*, "Thomas focused on attaining real relief, like back pay and damages, for those who had been discriminated against instead of stretching the concept of discrimination." The author quotes Clint Bolick, who had been a legal advisor to EEOC, as saying that Clarence Thomas's attitude was that it would be far better to "'...nail the discriminator and make it hurt,' because quotas don't hurt. The EEOC changed from an advocacy group into an effective law enforcement agency."

Among the very pragmatic problems Thomas encountered when he got to the EEOC were a stack of outstanding travel vouchers that totaled more than *a million dollars*, suppliers of such items as copy paper refusing to provide any more until bills were paid, and a threat from one phone company to discontinue service because of the agency's chronic "slow pay" status.

In August, at which point he'd been on the job for three months, Thomas showed up in St. Louis at a rally in support of John Danforth's bid for re-election. The rally was billed as an attempt to gain the votes of blacks and Democrats. Danforth was praised by the rally's organizer, Alphonso Jackson, the deputy executive director of the St. Louis Housing Authority, who also had positive words for Thomas: "There are a number of people in the Reagan administration who are not sensitive to civil rights. But if you look at people like Thomas who are in the administration, these are independent-minded black persons whose voices are going to be heard. I don't think they would stay in their positions unless they were."

Thomas was heard from less than a week later in an interview he gave to a reporter for *The St. Louis Post-Dispatch*. "Personalities are not part of my management technique," he said, in reference to reports of disagreements between him and his general counsel, Michael Connolly, a Reagan appointee who'd sparked considerable criticism over *his* management style and aggressively pro-business attitude. "Rather," the account continued, "Thomas said, he would put reorganization at the top of his agenda because he wanted to make institutional improvements that would 'fine-tune the organization's systems for the next decade.'

"The EEOC was widely regarded as inept for many years and underwent an earlier overhaul under former Chairwoman Eleanor Holmes Norton.... Thomas appointed a task force to draw up the reorganization shortly after he joined the commission...one of the highest-ranking black appointees in the administration, [Thomas] is generally regarded as a sharp administrator who takes his responsibility to enforce the laws seriously. But he is also considered a conservative and has questioned some traditional civil rights approaches."

While shoring up the EEOC internally, Thomas was also shoring up his conservative Republican credentials on the outside. In late August, after he'd been at the commission but 90 days, he gave a speech attacking African-American criticism of Ronald Reagan. At a lunch in his honor hosted by the

Black Women and Business Dynamics, Inc., a St. Louis organization, he told a reporter, with what was becoming his trademark candor, "Everybody is now comfortable with the statement that the Reagan administration is cutting back on civil rights. I ran two shops [the civil rights office at the Department of Education and EEOC]. What are they talking about? Anybody who has ever worked for me will never substantiate a charge like that. That's nonsensical."

Thomas mentioned help for minority businesses and traditional black colleges and universities as areas in which blacks misperceived Reagan's actual record. "I just got forms across my desk asking, 'What are you doing for black colleges? What are you doing for minority businesses?' These are internal documents for department heads. I don't think people have really given [Reagan] the credit that he deserves for being committed to civil rights, to what is right, to what is fair and just. He has just gotten an awful, awful image. We all make mistakes."

As for his own image problems, Thomas was not about to give any ground, saying, "I am a Republican. I will continue to be a Republican, and I'll be damned well what I want to be. That's what I was in college [sic] and that's what I'll continue to be. This is a country in which we fought as hard as anybody to feel and believe in what we want to. One of the things Tom Sowell says that I agree with is that when they start characterizing me as a conservative or whatever, I say, 'Well, that's better than being called a transvestite.'"

Even though he'd only been at the Equal Employment Opportunity Commission for a few short months, Clarence Thomas had already established his main approach: that in going after employers who discriminate, EEOC would no longer stress the large class action suits and numerical goals, but would concentrate on individual cases with clear evidence of harm and loss. He said, "Affirmative action is not civil rights. It is an approach that was used to remedy some of the past effects of discrimination. There is so much more beyond that. Even with all of that, I think we can agree that minorities are still in trouble—very, very serious trouble—in the employment arena, in the education arena, in the housing arena. We shouldn't be just clutching one solution, one part of a solution to a tremendous problem. I accept the image problem as part of the price I have to pay to do what I believe in."

The following year, Thomas silenced some of his critics, at least temporarily, when the EEOC announced a $42.5 million settlement of a sex and race discrimination charge against General Motors Corporation (GM), the largest settlement in the commission's almost 20-year history. Although the case had been filed a decade earlier, August 1973 (also during a Republican administration), it came to fruition on Thomas's watch. Under the terms of the settlement, GM management and its unions agreed to a five-year pact that set out hiring and promotion goals for women and minorities, plus a $15-million education program for GM employees and their families, and a variety of training and career-development programs.

By the spring of 1984, approximately two years after Thomas took over, more substantive reviews of his, and the administration's, performance began to appear. On April 11, 1984, *The St. Louis-Post Dispatch* reported that while the EEOC was definitely more efficient that did not mean it was necessarily more effective.

Margaret W. Freivogel of the *Post-Dispatch's* Washington bureau, who covered EEOC (and other government agencies) during Thomas's years there, wrote an article which began, "When Clarence Thomas became chairman of the Equal Employment Opportunity Commission two years ago, he found a backlog of thousands of cases and a financial structure so shaky that the commission could not pay its bills on time. Today, the backlog is gone and suppliers no longer are threatening to cut off deliveries. But greater efficiency has not necessarily meant greater effectiveness in carrying out the agency's primary mission. Civil rights leaders and congressional critics say the EEOC continues to do a poor job of protecting workers' civil rights on the job. On the other hand, they think it is doing a better job than the rest of President Ronald Reagan's administration.

"Policy and operational disputes still surround the commission.... Nonetheless, the civil rights groups see improvements since the early months of Reagan's term, when the EEOC was adrift in controversy.... Thomas has overhauled the agency's organization and demonstrated what all sides consider a strong personal commitment to equal opportunity. Even Thomas concedes, however, that the EEOC is not operating as efficiently as it could. And critics continue to doubt whether Thomas' good intentions are actually bringing results in enforcing civil rights laws."

Freivogel presented a "composite view of the EEOC's performance under Reagan," which included the statement that, "The EEOC has been more outspoken than most executive agencies in support of civil rights laws. But in some key cases, the Justice Department has prevented the commission from seeking court rulings strengthening those laws."

It was an open secret within the administration that Thomas and Attorney General William French Smith's Justice Department did not always see eye to eye. Barry Goldstein of the NAACP's Legal Defense and Education Fund, Inc. (commonly called "the Inc. Fund," for short), while faulting the commission for "not fulfilling its mission—It's not only supposed to settle cases, but to litigate," nonetheless had some words of praise for Clarence Thomas's EEOC. He said, "One good thing you can say is that the commission fought the Justice Department over goals and timetables. But they lost. And they have continued to lose repeatedly." Reporter Freivogel wrote that "Goldstein and others say Thomas has been faithful to established civil rights principles, even if he disagrees with them. By contrast, they say, the Justice Department has tried to backtrack on precedents that the administration does not support."

In regard to the case backlog, Freivogel wrote that in order to reduce it, Thomas had continued "a rapid processing system that already had made headway under Carter's administration. He went one controversial step further by closely tying numerical production goals for the staff to their performance ratings. Despite the improvement, staff divisions persist along racial, ethnic and gender lines, Thomas said. When he promotes a member of one group, he often is inundated with complaints from the others. Thomas said he had attempted to choose the best employees for each job, regardless of race or sex. But he concedes that the agency remains less efficient than he would like. 'Before we can ask for a bigger staff, I must see that we are functioning as efficiently as we can,' Thomas said."

In March of 1984, Thomas went back to his undergraduate alma mater, Holy Cross, and participated in Black Awareness Month. In an interview for an article in an alumni publication, Thomas provided information that touched on his differences with the civil rights establishment. The author of the article, William Sprout, wrote, "In his present position [Thomas's] goal is to have a positive impact in the area of civil rights. Yet he is opposed to the use of numerical goals, timetables and quotas as a means of establishing equal opportunities for minorities, because he believes that if you force a company to hire a minority employee who is not capable of doing that job, you have done both the hiring company and the minority employee a disservice. Instead, he believes that one must understand that, for blacks in particular, the problems go much deeper: the disaffection of males 16 and older with the society as a whole; the economic and emotional hardships for the children of the many households headed by single black women, many of whom are in their teens or early twenties; and the decline in quality of life in the U.S. since WWII. 'In other words,' said

Thomas, 'the black is not only unemployed, he's often unemployable. And the solution may take a long time to occur, because it has been a long time in coming, though anyone who wanted to could have seen this train coming down the track.'"

The article ended with an anecdote:

On March 16, a few days before he came back to Holy Cross to participate in Black Week, Thomas was walking down 17th Street in Washington when a black man stopped him and asked for a handout. "I asked him about himself. He said, 'I've been out here for seven years, and there ain't nothin' left for me. Just lost my job in a car wash. Don't know where I'm gonna go next.' I gave him a $1 and my card and asked him to call me so I could help him get a job. He called once the next day, I couldn't talk, and he never called back. That's the kind of person I'm talking about when I say that the solution to equal opportunities for employment has deep social and academic implications that will not be easily solved."

Thomas's habit of speaking his mind brought him national headlines in the fall of 1984 when he took civil rights leaders to task, publicly, for what he termed excessive complaining. He told a *Washington Post* reporter that African-Americans were being "essentially disenfranchised" by their leaders who were refusing to work with "a popular president" like Ronald Reagan. Thus, he said, these leaders are "watching the destruction of our race." Instead of working with the administration on the problems that plagued so many blacks and their families, they would go to the media and "bitch, bitch, bitch, moan and moan, whine and whine."

He went on to say that even though he had been at EEOC for three and a half years, no fellow black had come to him for help in influencing the Reagan administration. Once again singling out Rev. Jesse Jackson, he said that he and other black leaders had "alienated blacks so badly from Reagan and the Republican Party—made him into some evil person—that there is no chance at this point for blacks to discuss the Republicans as an alternative to the Democratic Party. It's a basic law of politics that you should always have access to people in power. You don't alienate them, at any cost. You don't call the judge reviewing your case a jackass; you don't call the banker reviewing your loan application a fool. But that's exactly what black leaders have done with this administration."

The following summer Thomas stirred more feathers when he told the annual convention of the National Black Nurses' Association that while it was true that "Our main priority should be to find out what is happening to the black family," it would be futile for them to go to lawmakers and the government for programs to help blacks. Rather, he said, "The future of blacks relies on the commitment that you're going to educate yourselves to the realities of the world, that you will teach it at home, and it must come from within.... Nobody can tell me a government program prevented me from fathering a child out of wedlock. It was my grandfather who told me, 'You're not going to do that.'"

* * * *

I was practicing telecommunications law with Dow, Lohnes and Albertson, and in the course of that work I met Gil Hardy who was with Wald, Harkrader and Ross. Gil was a good guy, and I'd see him on the street, and from time to time we'd go to lunch. Clarence Thomas was at EEOC then, and I'd see op-ed pieces about him or something he'd written, and one day right after I'd read one of these, I was having lunch with Gil, and I said, "What is wrong with this guy? He's talking about his sister being on welfare, being real critical of her, and I just don't understand how he can be like that. The guy's really nuts!"

Gil laughed, and said, "You're talking about my

classmate. I went to undergrad and law school with him. I know he's writing all this stuff, but he really isn't a bad guy. The three of us ought to have lunch some time. I'll call him and set it up."

The speaker is Fred Cooke—full name Frederick Douglass Cooke, Jr.—a native Washingtonian, and a graduate of Howard University and its law school. Formerly the Corporation Counsel for the District of Columbia, and one of the most respected lawyers in Washington, he is a name partner in the firm of Rubin, Winston, Diercks, Harris and Cooke. About the same age as Justice Thomas, Fred Cooke also works hard and also likes a good discussion and hearty laughter. But that's about as far their commonalities go. He has always been very curious about Clarence Thomas, curious about "what makes him tick." In an interview conducted for this book in 2001, Cooke recalled his first impressions of the future Supreme Court justice.

"Gil did set it up, and sometime later Gil and Clarence and I had a lunch, and we just talked about *stuff*. It wasn't confrontational—I didn't say, 'You asshole, how the hell could you write…?' or anything like that. It was just kind of like, 'Hey Fred, this is my friend Clarence, he's working for the government as a lawyer, and you're a lawyer, and maybe you can just meet and talk.' And we did. We talked about a lot of fairly typical guy stuff, especially sports, because Gil was very interested in sports, as was I, and it turned out Mr. Thomas was too. He was very interested in football, and as far back as then was a Dallas Cowboys fan.

"We just talked about stuff, and to my surprise he was a pretty amiable, likable guy, in terms of somebody to sit down and have lunch and a conversation with, or have a beer with, whatever. We did not talk politics in any sense. My recollection is that it was not anything in which I got agitated or involved in a political argument. It was just guys talking, having lunch, and me just trying to get a better sense of who this guy was. And I left the lunch thinking, you know, he's not such a bad guy. He may have some ideas I don't agree with, but he's not a horned devil."

Cooke says he met with Hardy and Thomas several more times after that, and each time the conversations were, for the most part, general and social rather than issue-oriented. But, Cooke recalls saying to Thomas on several occasions that "…this position or that position he had taken that might have been in the news, or that someone had told me about, was sort of cockeyed, or something I disagreed with. But, again, it was not unpleasant conversation, just dispassionate discussion of the relative merits of, say, affirmative action."

Fred Cooke says he did finally confront Thomas to a certain extent by expressing his own belief that, "because of the position he was in, a guy like Clarence had an obligation to speak to certain issues. Whether he wanted to be or not, he was in large part a group representative, at least indirectly, and with that came certain responsibilities. His answer to that was, 'Nah, it's not like that. I represent *Clarence*. For good or bad, I don't represent anybody else. That's not my deal, I don't do that. I'm here to do what I can do. If you or the next guy or lady wants something, then you have to get up off your butt and get it, and not expect to get it vicariously through anything I've done, or would do, for you. I'm willing to try to help people who help themselves, but I'm not going to be involved in this Big Brotherism type of taking care of people.' And he was real clear about that. He wasn't hostile. It was just, 'That's not something I believe in.'"

With one notable exception to be mentioned later, Fred Cooke has had little or no direct contact with Clarence Thomas since those days, but he has followed his career with great interest. One of the reasons he lost touch was the death of their mutual friend Gil Hardy (who died in a diving accident on vacation in Hawaii in 1989). The other is Cooke's belief that Thomas has gone so far to the right in his politics that were they to meet today they could no longer have even a social dialogue.

"I think that he has for whatever reason embraced that political philosophy with great gusto and a real, almost religious fervor. He's a man of very deep beliefs. When he believes something he really believes it. It's not *surface* with him, which is why I call it religious because with him it's an article of faith. He doesn't require any more physical demonstration of it. He *accepts* it as an article of faith. He believes. It's just as simple as that. He is not looking for a sign from God; he is *there*. And that's why those conservative guys who really identify with Clarence feel so comfortable with him, because, as Barbara Jordan said in a very different context, 'His faith in his philosophy is whole. It is complete. It wraps and comforts him.'"

Despite not having talked with Thomas in years, Cooke continues to believe that anyone—even any political liberal—who went to lunch or dinner with the justice today would, as long as the conversation did not touch on religion or civil rights, find him to be excellent company. "Clarence is not an unlikable guy one on one or in a small setting. But I think that when he has his official persona on, he becomes a much less likable person. But I think if you are sitting down and having lunch or dinner with him and just talking about nonpolitical or nonreligious things that might tend to get people excited, you will have a pleasant time with him. Because he is not nearly as uncommunicative or monosyllabic as he appears to be when he sits up there on that bench."

It is not inaccurate to say that Clarence Thomas continues to make the kind of statements he made when he first appeared on the national scene. Nor is it inaccurate to say that when he does so, they continue to rankle Fred Cooke.

"I think that Mr. Thomas has a point of view that he is absolutely, positively entitled to hold," Cooke said in a 2001 interview, "but I don't think his point of view is particularly helpful, in either the short or the long term, to the minority community in this country, whether it's black or Hispanic or Asian. And I think it's important that people don't get confused about this. The reason that Clarence Thomas, or people who are black and hold the same or similar views, are not in any significant number in the black community is because black people pretty quickly understand that that's not to their advantage. Some conservatives will go off on crusades and tirades against the NAACP and Jesse Jackson and Al Sharpton as if these people have all black people hypnotized and that we can't think for ourselves. The reason there are so few black conservatives is that there's been so little offered from the conservative agenda that is, in the view of most black people, constructive for them. And that is *not* the result of overwhelming ignorance or blind loyalty to the causes of the left.

"The reality of it is that there is no way that an objective reader can say that arguing to have my rights as a citizen under the Constitution honored is a liberal notion. That is a conservative notion. That is being true to the words and concepts of the Constitution. That is not a liberal notion. The reality of it is that aside from the civil rights issues that have been put into a liberal category by popular opinion, black people in this country tend to be, overwhelmingly, conservative in their overall philosophy of how the world ought to work. So it's not that black people are afraid of conservatism *qua* conservatism, it's that they're afraid of the conservatism offered by these people which is fundamentally racist. *That's* the problem—and it doesn't take a brain surgeon to figure that out. Black people are not averse to conservatism; they're averse to racism."

* * * *

It is 1986, and Clarence has been nominated by President Reagan for a second term as EEOC chairman. We are walking across the parking area immediately in front of the Senate steps of the Capitol.

Clarence is expecting a grueling confirmation process.... I ask Clarence why he allowed himself to be renominated for a job he never wanted in the first place and which had become a battleground of controversy. He replies, "Because I have so much to do."

– Senator John C. Danforth
Resurrection, 1994

By the time Clarence Thomas came up for reappointment as chairman of EEOC for another four-year term, he was determined to stay with the job, to stick it out because of his principles. He believed his track record was one of which he could be proud—particularly when contrasted with the chaotic condition of the agency under his immediate predecessor—and his conservative philosophy was stronger than ever. If he woke in the night worrying that he might be a pawn of the kind of conservatives described by Fred Cooke as "fundamentally racist," he gave little or no sign of it.

At the confirmation hearings before the Senate Labor and Human Resources Committee, Thomas had the strong support of its chairman, Republican Orrin Hatch of Utah, who called him an excellent manager and said he had taken "a very troubled agency and put it on a solid foundation." But two committee Democrats, Paul Simon of Illinois and Howard Metzenbaum of Ohio, voted against the renomination. While Simon agreed with Hatch that Thomas was a good manager (he wouldn't go so far as to say "excellent"), he faulted him for not being a strong leader, stating, "The agency should be leading the charge, not dragging its feet." Metzenbaum said Thomas had "failed to show that kind of leadership which the civil rights community is entitled to." The vote was 14-2 in favor of Thomas.

One of the reasons there weren't more anti-Thomas votes was that the EEOC had suddenly performed a flip-flop on affirmative action. Earlier in 1986, Thomas, as instructed, had quietly done away with the practice of using "goals and

122

timetables" as part of settlement negotiations to ensure compliance with EEOC laws, justifying the change by saying goals and timetables amounted to "quotas." But after the same committee that would hear Thomas's renomination rejected Jeffrey Zuckerman as EEOC's general counsel – *The St. Louis Post-Dispatch* editorialized, "In rejecting Mr. Zuckerman, the Senate panel has sent the administration a message that it will oppose civil rights nominees whose words and deeds are at variance with federal law and congressional intent."—the administration quickly got the point. In late July, less than two weeks before the hearings on Thomas's renomination, the EEOC announced it would resume using goals and timetables.

"Whatever reservations I have are purely personal," Thomas told the committee that would soon decide if he'd get a second four-year term. "The Supreme Court has ruled, and that's that." Then he added, "Whether I like it or not."

As for Thomas's social life, that too was beginning to pick up. His first years at the commission had coincided with the final dissolution of his marriage, and he'd found it hard to adjust from married to single to single parent. But from all accounts he'd done a fine job with his son, Jamal, and there was a certain rough parallel between his time with his grandfather years ago, and the life he and his young son led when they were under the same roof (whereas his father had been away from home in the seminary, young Jamal Thomas was away from home at a military academy).

Clarence Thomas had been seeing one young woman for a while, but the relationship did not become serious. He would give the occasional ride home to women on his staff, such as Anita Hill, who'd followed him over from the Department of Education, or do them some small domestic favor (such as the time he hooked up Hill's new stereo equipment) but these were not "dates." And then, in 1986, he met Virginia Lamp.

Lamp, a fellow conservative and a fellow attorney, was

not also a fellow black. But the difference in races made no difference to either of them, as they found acres of common ground, starting with their strict moral upbringings. When they met, she was a lawyer-lobbyist for the Chamber of Commerce, but later she would go to work as a lawyer for the Department of Labor, and still later for the Heritage Foundation. Thomas's critics, a group that was increasing in number in direct proportion to his increasing "celebrity," gloated over the fact that the EEOC director was on record as "frowning upon" black-to-white marriages. But that did not bother Clarence Thomas, who put the situation well, and very succinctly, to a friend: "I know what it's like to be unhappy; this is someone I'm happy with."

* * * *

I have always found a way to get in my two cents.
—Clarence Thomas, 1987

As Thomas's social and home life improved, he recovered his normal smiling, laughing demeanor. And not only did he speak more often, but he also spoke more boldly.

In a June 1987 speech at the conservative Heritage Foundation entitled "Why Black Americans Should Look to Conservative Policies," he again lauded his mentors (and friends) Thomas Sowell and Jay Parker: "Much has been said about blacks and conservatism. Those on the Left smugly assume blacks are monolithic and will by force of circumstances always huddle to the left of the political spectrum. The political Right watches this herd mentality in action, concedes that blacks are monolithic, picks up a few dissidents, and wistfully shrugs at the seemingly unbreakable hold of the liberal Left on black Americans.

But even in the face of this, a few dissidents like Tom Sowell and Jay Parker stand steadfast, refusing to give in to the cult mentality and childish obedience that hypnotize black Americans into a mindless, political trance. I admire them and only wish I could have a fraction of their courage and strength."

He went on to give the hardscrabble particulars of his upbringing, the story that would have so much appeal when President Bush was casting about for qualified blacks to appoint to the federal judiciary.

He told the audience, "I may be somewhat of an oddity. I grew up under state-enforced segregation, which is as close to totalitarianism as I would like to get. My household, notwithstanding the myth fabricated by experts, was strong, stable, and conservative. In fact, it was far more conservative than many who fashion themselves conservatives today. God was central. School, discipline, hard work, and knowing right from wrong were of the highest priority. Crime, welfare, slothfulness, and alcohol were enemies. But these were not issues to be debated by keen intellectuals, bellowed about by rousing orators, or dissected by pollsters and researchers. They were a way of life; they marked the path of survival and the escape route from squalor. Unlike today, we debated no one about our way of life—we lived it. I must add that my grandparents enforced the no-debate rule. There were a number of concerns I wanted to express. In fact I did on a number of occasions at a great price. But then, I have always found a way to get in my two cents...."

In 1987, Clarence Thomas once again spoke, on-the-record and for attribution, with Juan Williams, the *Washington Post* reporter who'd written the op-ed page article that appeared earlier that Thomas always claimed had caused him so much trouble. This time Williams's work appeared in the pages of *The Atlantic Monthly*.

Williams offered up as significant a story Thomas told him that dated back to the lawyer's youth. It entailed a group of boys playing cards for pennies on a back porch. One boy keeps winning until it's discovered that he's been cheating. A fight breaks out, during which everyone attempts to grab his coins back out of the pile, and of course only the bigger and faster boys are able to do so. But, because they would all rather play cards than fight, rough justice is meted out in the form of warnings and admonitions, and the game resumes with a new deck and everyone's promise not to cheat.

Williams wrote, "The story, Thomas said, is a lot like the story of race relations in America. Whites had an unfair advantage. But in 1964, with the passage of the Civil Rights Act, the government stopped the cheating. The question now is, should the government return the ill-gotten gains to the losers—the blacks, the Hispanics, and the women who were cheated by racism and sexism? Does fairness mean reaching back into the nation's past to undo the damage?... Should American businesses have to compensate for the legacy of slavery?... How would society, especially the society of government and business, make amends, even if making amends were its fervent goal?

"Thomas believes that government simply cannot make amends, and therefore should not try. The best it can do is to deal a clean deck and let the game resume, enforcing the rules as they have now come to be understood. 'There is no government solution,' Thomas said, 'It hasn't been used on any group. And I will ask those who proffer a governmental solution to show me which group in this country was pulled up and put into the mainstream of the economy with governmental programs. The Irish weren't. The Jews weren't.'"

Returning to his analogy of the boys on the back porch, Thomas told the reporter, "'I would be lying to you if I said that I didn't want sometimes to be able to cheat in favor of those of us who were cheated. But you have to ask yourself whether, in doing that, you do violence to the safe harbor, and that is the Constitution, which says you are to protect an individual's rights no matter what. Once you say that we can violate somebody else's rights in order to make up for what happened to blacks or other races or other groups in history, then are you setting a precedent for having certain circumstances in which you can overlook another person's rights?'"

"Clarence Thomas," wrote Williams, "has resolved to play by the rules. Once again one sees that boy on the porch, the respect for method and procedure. Thomas is consistent. Because the courts in the past have mandated goals, time-tables, and quotas, and because these are therefore the law of the land, Thomas's EEOC continues to enforce (though it may occasionally challenge) such decisions. This stance has sometimes left Thomas isolated within the Reagan adminis-tration. But when it comes to new business before the com-mission, there is little in Thomas's record with which a right-wing administration could find fault."

There were, however, instances in the conduct of the right-wing Reagan administration with which Thomas could find fault. As a prime example, there was the ceremony cel-ebrating his swearing in for his second term as EEOC head. Among the most notable right-wingers were Senator Strom Thurmond of South Carolina (once an arch segregationist), Attorney General Edwin Meese, and William Bradford Reynolds, Assistant Attorney General for Civil Rights. Just before he left, Reynolds raised his glass and proposed a toast, saying, "It's a proud moment for me to stand here because Clarence Thomas is the epitome of the right kind of affir-mative action working the right way."

Clarence Thomas, the Reagan administration's highest-profile foe of affirmative action, visibly flinched.

Section III
From Judge To Justice
1988-2001

Chapter Seven

From Bureaucracy to the Bench

The picture of the Clarence Thomas I know comes to me in flashbacks.... It is the spring of 1990, and Clarence Thomas has just taken his place on the U.S. Court of Appeals for the District of Columbia. I am standing outside my office door, looking down the long corridor at a silhouetted figure pushing a cart that is used to deliver government papers to Senate offices. It is Robert Foster, the black employee of the Senate Commerce Committee responsible for office deliveries. Walking slowly beside Robert as he pushes his cart, engaged in animated and obviously friendly conversation, is the newest member of the second highest court of the land, making personal delivery to me of a photograph of his swearing-in ceremony.

–John C. Danforth
Resurrection

By the late 1980s, Clarence Thomas was ensconced in his post as the chairman of the Equal Employment Opportunity Commission. On the friend vs. foe scale, while his critics were no less numerous, they were somewhat less vocal, whereas his friends were growing in number—and power.

True to form, Thomas had made believers of most of his close associates, both the people for whom he worked and those who worked for him. One person who came to know and admire him in the later years of his chairmanship was Janine Kemp, widow of the late Evan Kemp, the former EEOC commissioner who succeeded Thomas as chairman.

In a 2001 interview solely for this book, she spoke candidly of Clarence Thomas, whom she had met in about 1987 when her husband-to-be was an EEOC commissioner. "I'm not sure if Evan knew Clarence Thomas before he went to the commission in 1987, but soon after that they became close professional associates. I think it's both fair and accurate to say that they liked *and* respected one another. Evan came to the commission from the Disability Rights Council, the oldest nonprofit 'cross-disability' group in the country. He'd been its director. Before that he'd been, as a lawyer, at the Securities Exchange Commission and the IRS. As for me, I probably met Clarence at about that same time, and my first impression was that he was strong and funny and bright."

Janine Kemp is of the firm opinion that "Justice Thomas has not been fairly portrayed in the books I've seen that have come out about the issue," the Anita Hill controversy, "so it's very frustrating for me to read them, because the whole thing, particularly around the Thomas-Hill hearings, really had nothing to do with sexual harassment." What it in fact had to do with, she says, "...was that the traditional civil rights community did not want a conservative African-American justice on the Supreme Court bench, and would have done anything to fight it. If the tables were turned," she adds, "the Republicans would have done the same thing, because this was the pinnacle of what has become a very bitter and nasty Washington, D.C., game, which is the result of politics having completely lost touch with issues that involve serving the people. That's the context within which I remember the hearings, and that's why, had I not been asked to, I would not have gone back and read these accounts.

"In fact, the whole confirmation and hearing process was such a painful time for Evan and me—and we were by no means the closest people to it—that we got so depressed we almost split up. When we looked back on it, we saw it was the stress and pressure of that whole time. Perhaps everyone is jaded by now, given all that politicians and public servants have put us through in recent years, but people in the outlying areas think that our representatives in Washington should be serving the people, so it's very disconcerting."

Kemp says one of the things that so impressed her about Clarence Thomas was that "He really viewed people according to what kind of work they did, who they were, and what they were capable of. Many times I heard him talking about people in terms of advancing their career. So the allegations of sexual harassment just didn't fit with the man that I knew at that time. But then we all have flaws—I'm a former urban guerrilla!"

Clarence Thomas, says Janine Kemp, deserves high praise for rescuing the EEOC. "It was an administrative disaster, but in his seven years there he turned it around totally. When he got there, they had to mail case files to Kansas, I think it was, and back before anything could really be decided. Things were being lost. It had been *horribly* managed before. He could not get an increase in funding to computerize the agency, so he introduced the policy of offering a ten percent discount to vendors who would pay their bills within 30 days, and when that money came in he put it aside and used it to computerize the entire agency. You hear about uncaring bureaucrats and people working for the government not doing their jobs, but people at EEOC, both at national headquarters and around the country—and I got to know quite a few of them because Evan and I would travel around to all these different offices—were on the whole an incredible group of people committed to fighting discrimination in the workplace. And the loyalty to Clarence Thomas, overall, at that agency was amazing."

* * * *

Of course not everyone felt that way. In late October of

1992, just minutes before it was to go to trial, Shoney's restaurant chain settled an employment discrimination case brought as a class action by 21,000 former employees for the record-breaking sum of $132.5 million. Also unprecedented was the fact that the company's long-time CEO, who had fought the case bitterly, had to pay $67 million out of his own pocket. While the settlement came after Thomas had left the commission, the case had roots that actually predated his tenure.

In *The Black O*, a 1997 book about the case by Steve Watkins, a journalist and English professor at Mary Washington College, the lawyers for the ultimately successful plaintiffs have harsh words for the EEOC and the two men who headed it during this time period, Clarence Thomas and Evan Kemp.

Tommy Warren (he and Barry Goldstein were the chief lawyers for the plaintiffs) said the EEOC's interest in the case, which took the form of an offer to join the litigation in 1991, was "too little too late." He told Watkins, "The ideal situation in the Shoney's case would have been for the EEOC to have done its job. To track complaints against the company over the years and measure them against the EEO-1 reports. They should have a system for monitoring charges that raise issues of systemic, overt racism. They should do what congress created them to do, which is to look at these things from a mountaintop perspective. That's the EEOC's job. If they're not going to do their job, then why have it?"

"The EEOC chairmen under the last two Republican administrations, Clarence Thomas and Evan Kemp, were 'ostriches,'" Warren said; they were men who for years chose to ignore the evidence laid out in front of them about racism in society, he charged, including the evidence in *Haynes v. Shoney's*. "Their approach has been to say, 'Look, there's a little fire, let's take a fire extinguisher and put it out,' but never mind the huge fire over there blazing," Warren said. "There was an incredible amount of backsliding on civil rights under the Reagan Administration. The message was, 'Hey, it's okay to discriminate. We're not going to do anything about it.'"

Watkins quotes an unnamed "highly placed source" within EEOC as agreeing that there were problems in-house under Thomas and Kemp: "In that particular time frame, from private counsel's point of view, there may have been some reservation about the EEOC getting involved for political reasons. There were lots of suspicions about the nature and quality of our work during that period, given the national administration."

According to author Watkins, Tommy Warren was frustrated because he'd been contacting the EEOC since 1988, trying to get the commission interested in the case, believing "the agency had sat on its hands when it was needed the most." In the summer of 1989, still trying to get the EEOC involved, the plaintiffs' lawyers, who had by this time filed suit, sent copies of the 68-count complaint to the EEOC, and kept sending them relevant documented information and further complaints. In May of 1991 (two years after Thomas had left), the EEOC did file a friend of the court brief in support of the plaintiffs' charges against the Shoney's chain, but it was, as Warren described it, too little too late. All the heavy lifting had already been done.

Writing in 1997, Watkins concluded: "The lack of involvement by the EEOC in the Shoney's case came as little surprise to many observers of the commission during the 12 years from 1980 to 1992, most of that time under the direction of Clarence Thomas, now a U.S. Supreme Court justice. For one thing, Thomas…made it EEOC policy to de-emphasize class cases, stating publicly on numerous occasions that discrimination was an individual act and each allegation should thus be treated on an individual basis. Congressional investigators reported that at one point during the mid-

1980s, 75 workers who had been fired en masse from the same plant in Birmingham, Alabama, marched together into an EEOC district office to file discrimination charges, only to have every single worker's charge taken as an individual complaint and those complaints divided up among several different investigators."

As to how many class actions were handled by the EEOC before—or during—Thomas's tenure, the author reports a former EEOC general counsel as saying there's no reliable way to determine such a number because before 1991 the agency had no definition of what constituted a class action case.

"Whatever the actual class numbers," Watkins wrote, "settlement figures show that individual charges of discrimination received significantly different treatment under Thomas than they had under previous administrations. At the same time resources for systemic investigation and litigation units were being cut. In 1980, the EEOC was settling 32.1 percent of the cases it closed, meaning the complaining party agreed to the resolution of his or her case, whether it involved money, a job, a promotion, or simply an agreement by the employer to end a discriminatory practice. Six years later, that rate had dropped to 13.6 percent. One outside study found that in 1980, 15,328 victims of discrimination received monetary benefits through charges filed with the agency, but in the first half of 1985, only 2,964 received such benefits. Meanwhile, 'no cause' findings during that same period doubled from 28.5 percent of all charges brought before the commission."

As for Clarence Thomas's decision to end the use of goals and timetables because that would be the same as establishing quotas, Watkins says one EEOC official in the Northeast called that "like sending soldiers into battle without guns or bullets."

These specific charges mirrored the more general complaints of the traditional civil rights organizations. However, by this point, the late 1980s, such complaints were rolling off the chairman's back. Happier in his home life than he had been in years, and sure of the support of his superiors, he continued to speak out. And also to write.

In August of 1988, Thomas gave the keynote address celebrating the formation of the civil rights task force of the Pacific Research Institute, a San Francisco-based conservative organization. This speech is of interest for several reasons, one being his careful elucidation of his ongoing strong belief in natural rights (a subject that would be raised at the time of his Supreme Court confirmation hearings), and another being his use of the term "enemies" to describe people who disagreed with him philosophically and politically, a habit that would grow stronger as he rose in the national consciousness.

After thanking his hosts for asking him to be the keynote speaker, Thomas said, "For my comments, let me focus on the proper attitude we must have in approaching our subject. Keeping in mind two simple imperatives will prove absolutely necessary for a conservative libertarian group such as ours. First, we must be principled. Second, we must be positive.

"By being principled, I mean standing for the fundamental principles on which this nation is predicated. When arguing for the protection of individual rights, we must connect them directly to our democratic institutions and practices. That is, we cannot discuss 'civil rights' apart from a general discussion of individual rights, and how they fit into the American concept of democratic self-government. We need, in other words, to make sure that our civil rights arguments are derived from and strengthen sound morality and justice.

"Such a concept of civil rights necessarily involves higher law and natural rights principles. That is, this view calls forth the strongest elements of the American political tradition—what Martin Luther King did in his best moments.

"Second, and this is something I have underscored in my years in the administration, have a positive agenda. We must not merely be critical of the many blunders and follies that have occurred in the practice and theory of civil rights. We must show how our reliance on American principles produces better results than those of our enemies. Later, I will discuss briefly how I have attempted to have such a positive agenda at the EEOC. But first I need to explain what 'being principled' involves. Being principled does not mean being aloof from the practical consequences of those principles. Quite the contrary. The best practice takes place when our actions are informed by an overarching principle. Moreover, our principles must be ones that take us beyond conservative versus libertarian or individualist, and certainly beyond Republican versus Democrat. I am trying to articulate what I take to be the fundamental *American* principles, principles of freedom and responsibility...."

Citing Abraham Lincoln as a prime authority for these principles, he wrote, "Thus, when Lincoln spoke of Equality as 'the standard maxim' by which our institutions and practices should be guided, he meant *the equal and natural right of each individual to enjoy the fruits of his or her labor. Lincoln spoke of this as a natural right* [emphasis added]. Today, we call this equality of opportunity.

"But Lincoln also noted that such equality necessarily means democratic self-government, and all the institutions it requires, especially the separation of powers. Legitimate majority rule and the protection of individual rights go hand in hand." The idea that natural rights might in certain instances transcend the law of the land, the law that judges on the nation's highest courts are sworn to uphold, raised a question of some import when Clarence Thomas was called to the bench.

Continuing, he said, "Unfortunately, conservative

heroes such as the chief justice [Rehnquist] failed not only conservatives but all Americans in the most important court case since *Brown v. the Board of Education*. I refer of course to the independent counsel case, *Morrison v. Olson*. As we have seen in recent months, we can no longer rely on conservative *figures* to advance our cause. Our hearts and minds must support conservative *principles* and *ideas*. As Judge Lawrence Silberman concluded...his D.C. Circuit Court of Appeals opinion: 'This is no abstract dispute concerning the doctrine of the separation of powers. The rights of individuals are at stake.'"

Thomas then went on to praise a liberal hero and chide a couple liberal "enemies:" "Justice Antonin Scalia's remarkable dissent in the Supreme Court case points the way toward these principles and ideas. He indicates how again we might relate natural rights to democratic self-government and thus protect a regime of individuals rights." Of the two so-called enemies, he wrote that the governor of Massachusetts, "...undoubtedly takes a government of laws to mean government by ACLU lawyers," and of Delaware Senator Joseph Biden (who would play a major role in Thomas's own life just a few short years later) he said, "The conservative failure to appreciate the importance of natural rights and higher law arguments culminated in the spectacle of Senator Biden, following the defeat of the Bork nomination, crowing about his belief that his rights were inalienable and came from God, not from a piece of paper. We cannot expect our views of civil rights to triumph, by conceding the moral high ground to those who confuse rights with willfulness."

It was speeches like these, and articles in which he made the same and similar points, that brought Clarence Thomas onto the radar screens of not just those who disagreed with him, but also onto those of people highly placed, and highly powerful, within the administration of

President George H.W. Bush.

As he grew older and even more Republican, Clarence Thomas would increasingly downplay the fact that he had been trained at one of the Ivy League's premier law schools. But in 1989, shortly before his time as EEOC's chairman came to an end, he saw fit to contribute an article to the Journal of Law and Public Policy at Harvard. Entitled, "Civil Rights as a Principle Versus Civil Rights as an Interest," it began with an explanation.

"My comments on civil rights," he wrote, "will take a broad perspective, which reflects my experience in seven years in the Reagan administration.

"In 1980 I was confident great strides could be made on behalf of individual liberty. Now, I take comfort in having made several relatively modest but significant reforms. Although we are able to take credit for much good, I believe that the administration's efforts did go awry, in both rhetoric and substance. Perhaps its faults can best be examined if I focus on one particular theme: our failures to enunciate a principled understanding of what we were about and to articulate the meaning of individual rights and how we might best defend them."

Continuing (and with a bit more "attitude" than one usually sees in legal journals), he took a mild swipe at *The New York Review of Books*, calling it "that august journal of learning," and then focused on NYU law professor Ronald Dworkin ("who rivals the sainted John Rawls in some circles") for what he called his "trashing" of Robert Bork in a review in that publication.

In answer to Dworkin's comment that the ideal of constitutional integrity would not have been safe in the hands of Robert Bork, Thomas wrote, "Let me dissent. It reflected disgracefully on the whole nomination process that Judge Bork is not now Justice Bork."

Thomas continued: "But the issue of Judge Bork aside,

Dworkin does go to the core of the civil rights debate today [by correctly noting] the primacy of the principle of freedom and dignity, but I think he misunderstands the substance of that principle. He reveals his error by applying that principle to groups, rather than to individuals. For it is above all the protection of *individual* rights that America, in its best moments, has in its heart and mind.

"To develop and implement a just civil rights policy, the Reagan administration had first to make clear its principled understanding of this issue. Simply put, we failed to do so— not because we lacked commitment to equal justice under law, but because we did not present our case for civil rights on the highest possible plane. In that way, we complemented the failure of the Supreme Court to deal adequately with race-related issues. It is nowhere clearer than in the field of jurisprudence how distant the Court and the political branches remain from an understanding of the principles of equality and liberty that make us one nation. Thus has civil rights become entrenched as an interest-group issue rather than an issue of principle and universal significance for all individuals."

He went on, in a fascinating trifecta of interests, to comment on: affirmative action, Oliver North's congressional testimony in the Iran-Contra hearings, and Barry Goldwater's famous speech to the Republican convention in 1964.

"Having been critical of the overemphasis on 'affirmative action,'" he wrote, "I am hesitant to say more about it at this time. Let me say for now that what is known as affirmative action arose precisely because of the congressional and bureaucratic attitudes I have sketched above. And they have been aided and abetted by lazy businesses, especially large corporations. I am confident it can be shown, and some of my staff are now working on this question, that blacks at any level, especially white collar employees, have simply not benefited from affirmative action policies as they have developed. Therefore it is wrong for politicians to focus implicitly on blacks when attacking 'affirmative action.' Such an attack, however justified on the principle of colorblindness, places the blame primarily on blacks, who have not been helped. No one in this country should be made the fall guy for some other person's easy way of solving problems. And this resentment is what hiring-by-the-numbers policies have produced. A positive civil rights policy would aim at reducing barriers to employment, instead of trying to get 'good numbers.' Those who have been in the government know the artificial barriers to hiring someone you want. That is the sort of practice we should be seeking to eliminate. That is the sort of affirmative action I practice at my agency."

As for Oliver North and Senator Goldwater, the soon-to-be-moving-on bureaucrat had this to say: crediting North with defending "the always arduous task of preserving freedom," he wrote, "Partly disarmed by his attorney's insistence on avoiding closed sessions, the committee beat an ignominious retreat before North's direct attack on it and, by extension, all of Congress. This shows that the people, when not presented with distorted reporting by the media, do retain and act on their common sense and good judgment, and that members of Congress can listen if their attention is grabbed. Self-government need not be an illusion!"

As for Senator Goldwater's bell ringer of a perfomance some three-and-a-half decades ago, Thomas wrote, "If one reads Barry Goldwater's 1964 speech accepting the Republican nomination for the presidency, one sees how little the political world has changed, even after two terms of Ronald Reagan. The threats to freedom remain as strong as ever, both at home and abroad. The power of the central government has grown dramatically since 1964, as has the Soviet menace. But the speech's most famous words implied to many listeners—it certainly did to me then, a high school student—an endorsement of extremist groups, such as the Ku Klux Klan and the John Birch Society, which were so hotly disputed during the convention. But one must reread the whole speech to see such a conclusion is wrong."

Instead, he wrote, people should have paid attention to what he called the "stirring passages" in which the senator extolled the positive things for which his party stood. Thomas then provided examples, ending with this one, "'And beyond that we [Republicans] see and cherish diversity of ways, diversity of thoughts, of motives, and accomplishments. We don't seek to live anyone's life for him. We only seek to secure his rights, guarantee him opportunity to strive with government performing only those needed and constitutionally sanctioned tasks which cannot otherwise be performed.'" Those last two sentences probably come as close as any others to capsulizing Clarence Thomas's philosophy of government."

He closed the article with a reprise of his main theme: "A civil rights policy based on principle, replacing the one based on interest-group advantages, would be a blessing not only for black Americans but for all Americans. That is what I have been working for as chairman of the EEOC. Partisans of freedom should be alert to seizing the opportunities as well as warning of obstacles awaiting them."

At about this same time, Thomas gave another speech in which he covered many of these same points. Liberal critics of Thomas would find this a good-news-bad-news appearance. The good news was that he again spoke at Harvard; the bad news was that he spoke to the Federalist Society (a then-new group of lawyers and law students pledged to very conservative principles).

In this speech, he again elaborated on one of his favorite themes, the importance of natural rights as a basis for our legal system: "So we must constantly keep in mind the higher-law, natural rights principles for which the Civil War was fought. Other than the speeches of Lincoln, the best source for understanding the application of these ideals to American politics is Justice John Marshall Harlan's dissent in *Plessy v. Ferguson*. Unfortunately, his noble phrase 'color-blind constitution' became a prominent part of the solely anti-affirmative action rhetoric that appeared to be the sum and total of [the] Reagan Administration civil rights policy." Later in the same speech, he wrapped up this line of reasoning by stating, "The higher law background of the American Constitution, *whether explicitly appealed to or not* [emphasis in original], provides the only firm basis for a just, wise, and constitutional decision. The Supreme Court may not always have the latitude of an American Abraham Lincoln in appealing directly to natural rights and 'the laws of nature and of nature's God.'"

In what was becoming standard in his speeches, Thomas got in plugs for Robert Bork and Oliver North. In regard to Bork, he told his audience,

> Given our historical experience, it is second nature that black Americans' politics is one of distrust; and Administration rhetoric (much more than politics) concerning civil rights enforcement has raised this distrust of Republicans to new heights. Unfortunately, the civil rights establishment has played on this distrust to the detriment of the true needs of blacks. It is preposterous to think that by spending so much energy in opposing as decent and sensible a man as Bob Bork that this establishment was actually protesting the rights and interests of black Americans. Or that the interests of black Americans are really being served by minimum wage increases, Davis-Bacon laws, and any number of measures that pose as beneficial to low-income Americans but actually harm them. On the brighter side, it is encouraging to know that increasing numbers of younger blacks no longer iden-

tify themselves as Democrats. This reflects a healthy skepticism about the old approaches.

As for Colonel North, the EEOC chairman used him to support his criticism of Congress, which in the late 1980s was still controlled by the Democrats: "...over the past several years, Congress has cleverly assumed a neutral ombudsman's role, and thrust the tough choices on the bureaucracy, which it dominates through its oversight functions and the courts. *As Ollie North made perfectly clear last summer, it is Congress that is out of control* [emphasis in original]."

He finished by saying, "...let me emphasize the importance of upholding our ideals. What else could have kept me defiant in the face of some petty despots in Congress or in the various different interest groups which have plagued EEOC in the past! As we conservatives make our pro-freedom arguments, let us keep in mind that we not preach only to the fellow committed conservatives. The conservatism I know has an appeal, because it reflects a belief in the good sense and decency of the American people, and hence in freedom as the main source of all that is good politically. And what could be more conservative than the revolutionary proposition that America was founded on: 'All men are created equal.'"

The frequency—and increasingly combative tone—of these writings and speeches was not lost on the powers-that-be within the Reagan administration. Clarence Thomas was no longer a voice crying in the bureaucratic wilderness; he was a high-profile black conservative who happened to be a lawyer at a time when his party was finally shaking off the aftereffects of its bitter defeat in the case of Judge Bork, and beginning to look around for fresh candidates who might soften the party's image as overly harsh and unbending ideologues—but without giving in on any of their main philosophical points.

"I wasn't interested in becoming a judge," Thomas told

his biographer Norman Macht in 1991. "I wanted to get out of public life and out of Washington. I didn't see it as a job for a guy 40 years old. I had never had any interest in it, which is the irony of ironies." Macht continues: "Ricky Silberman, Thomas's second-in-command at the EEOC, urged her boss to take the judgeship. 'I thought it would be the perfect place for Thomas, who is at heart an intellectual who loves thinking through ideas and getting to the heart of the matter,' she said. 'But he was reluctant.'" The author also quotes Silberman as saying that while it was the administration's plan, as early as 1989, to elevate Thomas to the U.S. Supreme Court just as soon as there was a vacancy, "It was not Clarence Thomas's."

Macht made another point that in retrospect sounds like, to quote Thomas, "the irony of ironies." He wrote, "There was one consolation: being a judge would take him out of the politics of turmoil."

The idea that Clarence Thomas did not have his eye on the federal bench, or that if he did it was only with reluctance, would be greeted with hoots of laughter by the coterie of liberal special-interest groups (*and* certain of their conservative counterparts) around Washington. Why else, they would reason, had Thomas been speaking and writing at such a suddenly accelerated pace? And why had he picked, as prime targets, some of the high court decisions most fervently disliked by conservatives? Or why had he lavished such praise on what liberals considered an *un*holy trinity—Antonin Scalia, Robert Bork, and Oliver North?

Professional court watchers, both in the media and academia, did not notice any reluctance on Thomas's part to go on the bench. In *Turning Right*, his book on the Rehnquist court, David Savage, who has covered the U.S. Supreme Court for *The Los Angeles Times* for 15 years, wrote, "Thomas also seemed to have his eye on much more than the EEOC. He churned out newspaper opinion pieces, sounded off in interviews, and gave dozens of speeches across the country. He denounced 'quotas' and racial preferences, advocated black self-help, and complained that the nation's established civil rights leaders did little but 'bitch, bitch, bitch, moan and whine.'"

His speeches as EEOC chair were also sprinkled with comments that appealed to the top attorneys of the Reagan-Bush administration. He praised Justice Antonin Scalia's dissent in the 1987 case of *Paul Johnson v. Santa Clara County*, which called for outlawing affirmative action in the workplace. In a speech at the Heritage Foundation in Washington, Thomas praised as "splendid" an article by conservative philanthropist Lewis Lehrman that called abortion a "holocaust" and maintained that the constitution gave fetuses an absolute "right to life." By this interpretation, not only was the *Roe v. Wade* decision wrong, but also abortion at any stage of a pregnancy and in every state of the union was murder. Thomas also called the 1988 case of *Morrison v. Olson*, involving the independent counsels "the most important court case since *Brown v. Board of Education*" ending segregation. Once again, he praised Scalia's dissent, which had called for striking down the law. Not many Americans would even recognize the case of *Morrison v. Olson*, and fewer yet would consider it of vast significance. Still, the top attorneys at the Justice Department and at the White House certainly shared Thomas's view. Because of this law, Ed Meese, Michael Deaver, Oliver North, and John Poindexter, among others, had come under criminal investigation.

Continuing, Savage wrote, of a liberal activist special-interest group, "To [Nan] Aron and the [Alliance for Justice] staffers, the blizzard of Thomas speeches meant only one thing: he was running for higher office. Certainly, he had made a name for himself at the top levels of the administration. As vice president, George Bush got to know the outgoing and personable EEOC chair...."

In *Capitol Games* (also written in 1992) Timothy Phelps and Helen Winternitz had this to say about Thomas's path to the judiciary: "Clarence Thomas kept moving to the political right, until he was outstripping the average Republican. Within three short years he was transformed from a moderate to a conservative to a member of the radical right. By 1987, he was ranting and raving about liberals in Congress, in the Supreme Court, in the media. He was delivering key speeches to very conservative audiences to whom he extolled the virtues of right-wing heroes like Ayn Rand, Oliver North, and Robert Bork. They were fiery words, like those of a man on the stump. As Thomas grew more conservative, he became more strident and more impatient with the moderate positions he himself had espoused just a couple of years before."

The authors, while suggesting that Thomas was "born again in a political sense," point out that his chief speechwriters at the time were "proteges of Harry Jaffa, a California guru of esoteric new right jurisprudence. In his earlier years, Jaffa had written for Barry Goldwater the famous 'Extremism in defense of liberty is no vice,' speech."

Phelps and Winternitz see Thomas as a blend of opportunism and anger. Indulging in a bit of psycho-history, they write: "It is not easy to explain Thomas's transformation. Signs had appeared before of his deep conservatism. It had perhaps been repressed during his moderate phase by a desire, typical enough of any rising political bureaucrat, to get along and be accepted. But he found little encouragement for his moderation from the civil rights community. At the same time, it was clear to this very ambitious young man that political survival meant the adoption of the hardline Republicanism that ruled Washington."

Continuing:

In addition, Thomas was an impressionable per-son, a man who imbibed new ideas and spouted them out again with great fervor before moving on to something else. In his later years at the EEOC, he was surrounded by conservatives who showed him the way to greater power and prestige. Thomas's new far-right speechwriters were clever enough to find the right words to match the rage that had built up inside him over the years.

They gave expression to his anger at the injustice of a racist society, white and black, which had rejected him because of the darkness of his skin and the curli-ness of his hair. Thomas undoubtedly carried a more personal anger from his boyhood, when his parents had essentially abandoned him, and his grandfather had taught him not to expect compassion. In the con-servative atmosphere of Washington, Thomas's indig-nation blended easily with his ambition.

* * * *

In the spring of 1989, Clarence Thomas took the penul-timate step toward his seat on the Supreme Court of the United States when President George W. Bush nominated him for the U.S. Court of Appeals in Washington, D.C. He had reached this lofty perch by virtue of an impressive net-work of conservative friends and acquaintances, most of whom were lawyers. Of these, the most powerful was C. Boyden Gray, White House Counsel to President Bush.

One of the few men active on the upper rungs of national party politics who could be (and was) legitimately referred to as a "scion," Gray was an heir to R.J. Reynolds Tobacco Company wealth. Generally labeled not just conser-vative but arch-conservative, Gray had very definite ideas about politics and politicians (his most fervent wish was to find the reincarnation of Barry Goldwater). When he learned—in part through Thomas's avid cooperation with the Federalist Society—that Clarence Thomas thought as he did on the matters closest to his heart, he became his new best friend. Whether Gray or Senator John Danforth was Thomas's biggest booster is debatable, but not particularly important: Boyden Gray was President Bush's close personal friend as well as his in-house lawyer, which meant he was in the White House, not down the street in the U.S. Senate. Thus Thomas could hardly have found a better guide through the thickets of highest-level judicial appointments.

According to Mayer and Abramson in *Strange Justice*, Thomas's way to the Court of Appeals was paved by several people, including Patrick McGuigan, at that time a top lawyer with the Free Congress Foundation, an important (and powerful) conservative group founded and run by Paul Weyrich and Lee Liberman, another White House counsel with impeccable conservative credentials. Further help was provided by two of Thomas's best friends at EEOC, his successor Evan Kemp and vice-chair Ricky Silberman (the wife of Laurence Silberman, a judge on the same court to which Thomas was soon to be named).

Also present at the creation of Judge Clarence Thomas was Clint Bolick, another lawyer who'd worked for Thomas at EEOC. Mayer and Abramson state that President Bush, who was carrying on Ronald Reagan's efforts to turn the high court to the right, had decided—in the aftermath of the Willie Horton affair—to put a "kinder and gentler" face on his efforts by seeking out not just women and minorities but qualified blacks.

"This shift in emphasis," they write, "at last presented Thomas with the opportunity he'd been waiting for. As he had long reckoned, the list of well-connected, conservative African-American officials with law degrees was very short, and his name belonged at or near the top. The White House just needed to be reminded of this.

"His friend and former EEOC employee Clint Bolick was the eager messenger. Bolick described Thomas's many attractive qualities to Lee Liberman, underscoring Thomas's devotion to the philosophy of Ayn Rand. Good to his word, McGuigan helped Thomas's cause by calling in a favor. Earlier, when Richard Thornburgh had been nominated for attorney general, McGuigan had denounced him as too moderate. Asked by the White House to keep quiet, however, he had agreed to hold his fire. As soon as Thornburgh was confirmed, he invited McGuigan to have breakfast—and McGuigan's first order of business was to lobby for Thomas's appointment to the appeals court....

"The campaign to make Thomas judicial timber was successful. Soon he occupied a solid position on the short list of candidates. And one year after the campaign was launched, his name rose to the top: with Gray's and Liberman's final blessings, President Bush nominated Thomas to the D.C. Circuit on July 11, 1989."

* * * *

Some African-Americans, mostly conservative ones, were very pleased with the appointment. Others, such as Washington, D.C., attorney Fred Cooke, were, to put it mildly, skeptical.

"I think," says Cooke, "there are a lot of black people like Clarence who on the one hand are looking for a way to distinguish themselves to show that they can be significant, so they step out of the mainstream as a way to distinguish themselves. They become Republicans or conservatives because it gives them a better opportunity."

Laughing, Cooke continues, "You can get to be a prominent black Republican a lot quicker than you can get to be a prominent black Democrat 'cause the line's a lot shorter."

But doesn't Clarence Thomas have a right to be a conservative black Republican if he wants to be?

"Absolutely," says Cooke without any hesitation. "I

don't quibble with that. In the history of the dynamic of intellectual discussions within the black community there's always been that kind of yin and yang, with the classic example being W.E.B. DuBois and Booker T. Washington. And it's probably a good thing to have the ability to balance these two views and to force some sort of synthesis. The left can't be right all the time, just like the right can't be *wrong* all the time. They got to be right about something at some point— even though I don't know what the hell it is!"

Chapter Eight

Court of Appeals

C ompared to what would happen 15 months later when he was nominated for the Supreme Court, Clarence Thomas's nomination to the second highest court in the land was met with a whimper, not a bang.

The National Association for the Advancement of Colored People (NAACP) had considered opposing the nomination, but decided to remain neutral instead, thus heading off a possibly lengthy battle. As *Jet* magazine reported, "A secret 2 and 1/2 hour meeting with NAACP Washington Bureau Director Althea Simmons broke a threatened Liberal-Democratic campaign against EEOC Chairman Clarence Thomas' nomination to the U.S. Court of Appeals in Washington."

President Bush nominated the Yale Law School graduate and former Missouri assistant attorney general to serve on the 12-member panel described as the second most powerful court next to the U.S. Supreme Court. Conservatives hail the ranking Black Reagan-Bush judicial appointee as the possible replacement to Justice Thurgood Marshall.

Faced with a dilemma of opposing the scholarly, respected conservative lawyer on the basis of "personal views and his EEOC record of carrying out court dictates," Ms. Simmons decided on an eyeball-to-eyeball confrontation with Thomas on the eve of the Senate confirmation hearings.

Confirming that Mr. Thomas "understands" the role of Blacks, the roles of courts, and the duties of a federal judge, Ms. Simmons recommended that the nation's leading civil rights organization neither oppose the Thomas nomination nor endorse it. The neutral position, however, canceled what was expected to be a prolonged hearing on Capitol Hill.

Speaking to a packed Judiciary Committee hearing, Thomas promised he would not apply his personal views on the law in reaching judicial decisions. "My personal view, when there is a precedent, when there is case law, is irrelevant," he testified. "In the policy arena, one has options. In the judicial arena, the rule of law applies."

In fact, the meeting was far more dramatic than the account in *Jet* would suggest. The meeting with Althea Simmons took place in a hospital room—hers. The NAACP official (who would die a short time later) apparently found Thomas more simpatico than she had expected, and persuaded her organization not to oppose him. She told the same magazine, "He has not forgotten his roots or black folk. I gained a new meaning of Clarence Thomas and felt he will help us. He's a very dedicated man."

One of the liberal groups that had actively opposed Robert Bork only two years prior but remained neutral this time was the Leadership Conference on Civil Rights. Nan Aron's Alliance for Justice came out against Thomas, citing his "disdain for the rule of law," and the fact that he had, in its opinion, "shown hostility to Congress," and made "insensitive comments" about his sister (when he criticized what he said was her dependence on welfare). On the plus side, Thomas was helped by an endorsement letter from a prominent and well-respected black Republican, William T. Coleman, Jr., then the chairman of the NAACP Legal Defense and Education Fund.

There was concern for quite some time among Thomas supporters that the powerful American Association of Retired Persons (AARP) would come out in opposition to Thomas. As *National Review* columnist "Cato" wrote in early December 1989, "Others close to the process tell us that the key to the Thomas nomination will be the position taken by the thirty million member American Association of Retired People. Although the group has never before taken a position on a nominee for a judgeship, AARP has been critical of Mr. Thomas's tenure at the Equal Employment Opportunity Commission, where he refused to sanction group rights for the elderly. AARP lobbyist Michelle Pollack says her organization 'hasn't yet decided' whether it will break with precedent and get involved in the Thomas nomination process." After due consideration, the organization decided to stay out of this fight, but began to keep tabs on Thomas for future reference.

As for the judicial rating panel of the American Bar Association (ABA), which has four listings—not-qualified, qualified, well-qualified, and exceptionally well-qualified— it declared Clarence Thomas to be "qualified." As endorsements go, that was rather lukewarm. Nonetheless, it was better than the "not-qualified" rating they had given Judge Bork two years earlier.

On March 19, "Cato" weighed in with a follow up to his pre-confirmation column. He began this one by asking, "Oh Biden, where is thy sting?"—a stinging reference to Delaware Democrat Joe Biden, chairman of the Senate committee that had passed, favorably, on Clarence Thomas. Continuing, he wrote, "After remarkably civil treatment by the Senate Judiciary Committee, Clarence Thomas sailed through his confirmation hearings for the U.S. Circuit Court of Appeals here in Washington...tak[ing] the seat vacated by Robert Bork and thus moved closer to a Supreme Court nomination that will doubtless come when Justice Marshall's body goes the way of his mind."

Still in a sarcastic, if somewhat less mean, mode, "Cato" went on: "Of course, that a man of Mr. Thomas's caliber has to vindicate himself before a jury including Senators Biden and Kennedy says something about the curious state of our nominating process." Contrasting the efforts of the Thomas backers with the administration's recent unsuccessful effort to get William Lucas approved as head of the Justice Department's civil rights office, the columnist wrote:

> The difference this time was that the Right got out front and stayed out front, setting the terms of the debate. The Landmark Legal Foundation Center for Civil Rights came out with a 14-page paper on Mr. Thomas's record, leaving no doubt of his qualifications. The American Conservative Union kept the pressure on; National Right to Work and National Right to Life helped rally the troops. The Free Congress Foundation and the Coalitions for America did yeoman's work starting in August when the issue first came up. In particular, the former's personal profile of Mr. Thomas in *The Family, Law, and Democracy Report* made it impossible to depict the nominee as some kind of civil-rights ogre.

Other factors contributed. The campaign for Mr. Thomas picked up two key Democratic supporters in Senators Sam Nunn (Ga.) and Chuck Robb (Va.). *The Wall Street Journal's* publication of the absurdly detailed request for information from Mr. Thomas helped foil any plans for a Biden Inquisition, and the White House waged what one activist called a successful "low-intensity conflict," with John Mackey at Justice and Lee Liberman in C. Boyden Gray's office, providing critical help. Whether this would have been enough had the Democrats decided to make it Bork II is another matter altogether.

While Silberman and Thomas himself (through his biographer Macht) are on record as saying he was not interested in becoming a judge in 1989, the media and (eventually) Thomas's other biographers treated it as a given. In *Strange Justice*, Mayer and Abramson report that he was given a "full-time consultant" to help him survive the bipartisan-shark-infested waters of the Senate confirmation process.

"Perhaps sensing the shaky nature of the appointment," they write, "the White House treated the Thomas nomination with particular care. Eddie Mahe, a GOP consultant with strong ties to the new administration, called Murray Dickman, the attorney general's top lieutenant, and convinced him that Justice needed to hire a full-time consultant to help Thomas prepare for his confirmation hearings—an unusual precaution for an appointment other than to the Supreme Court. 'He wasn't getting the right help,' Mahe explained. 'The Bush administration was sloppy in its confirmation prep.'"

The job, report the authors, went to Phyllis Berry, an African-American whose background included stints at both the Republican National Committee and Thomas's EEOC—

where she'd either resigned or been fired, depending on who was telling the tale. Nonetheless, she was said to have good political skills and contacts. She became, as Mayer and Abramson put it, "Thomas's de facto campaign manager." They quote her as saying, "I ran this like a campaign. We needed a strategy. I made a plan. I looked at the opposition, who had spoken against him at EEOC reconfirmation. I had Clarence make courtesy visits to civil rights leaders. I thought about disgruntled EEOC workers, feminists—anywhere opposition was likely to come from."

One person Berry didn't think of in 1989 and 1990 was the one person who would be center stage in 1991, Anita Hill.

Mayer and Abramson also mention the help given Thomas by William T. Coleman, Jr., the well-respected black Republican who was a close and trusted friend of Thurgood Marshall's, and whose daughter Lavidia had been Thomas's classmate at Yale Law School. In a letter to President Bush on Clarence Thomas's behalf late in 1989, he wrote, "I think this is a fine appointment.... Mr. Thomas will add further luster and judicial ability to the Court. His starts and advantages in life at the beginning were in no way equal to that of my children's."

By the time the hearings began in February of 1990, Thomas, with the help of Berry and various others, had sanded down most of the rough spots on the slide. Getting the support of his old boss, Senator Danforth, or Missouri's senior senator, Thomas Eagleton, was no problem. Getting help from the other side of the aisle was a bit more difficult, but not, as things turned out, all *that* hard. Eventually, he was able to enlist the respected moderate Democrat Sam Nunn of Georgia, Thomas's home state. That connection was made with the help of an old friend from his days in the legal department of Monsanto Chemical, fellow attorney (and African-American) Larry Thompson, who just happened to be with the prestigious Atlanta-based law firm of

King & Spalding, whose chief rainmaker was former Attorney General Griffin Bell.

A former U.S. District Court Judge, Bell was a Democrat, but he warmed to Thomas's plight, especially after he'd been supplied—by Clarence Thomas himself—with the details of the prospective judge's rise from humble beginnings.

In an interview in 2001, Judge Bell still had a vivid recollection of that event. "Thomas was brought to my law office by Larry Thompson, one of my law partners. He and Clarence had been friends in St. Louis at Monsanto. Larry later came to Atlanta to work on a case for Monsanto that our firm was handling, and he decided he liked Atlanta, so we just got him to come on and join up with us. The years went by, and then one day he told me Clarence had a problem that he wanted to discuss with me, and asked me if I would discuss it with him. I asked what it was, and Larry said, 'He's from Georgia, was reared in Georgia, and he's going to be nominated for the Court of Appeals, but he doesn't have a senator from Georgia that has agreed to sponsor him. He's got both senators from Missouri, but he feels badly that he hasn't got a Georgia sponsor.' So I said I'd be glad to talk with him, and Larry brought him to my office, and we had a nice talk.

"I was impressed with him, and I thought it was a shame that he was getting such a high post and that Georgia senators were not supporting him. So I got in touch with the Georgia senators, and Senator Nunn did then support him."

Judge Bell not only recalls how impressed he was with Clarence Thomas, he also recalls how impressed former President George Bush was with Thomas.

"I was representing President Bush in the Iran-Contra matter, and we got in a conversation about Clarence Thomas. He told me he was so impressed with his life story, and I said anyone would be. It was a remarkable story. Only in this country could something like that happen." Bell says that amazing life story was what made him decide to help Thomas—"That and the fact that I'm very big on Georgia. If someone from Georgia is up for an important post like that, the two senators from Georgia ought to stand up for him, even though they might not even agree with him. They ought to stand up for him on a character basis."

With Sam Nunn and Danforth and Eagleton backing him, as well as both Virginia's senators, the Democrat Chuck Robb and Republican John Warner, Clarence Thomas had little to fear from Joe Biden, Ted Kennedy, et al., by the time the hearings began. This is not to say there was no opposition. Illinois Senator Paul Simon was one who had reservations.

In *Advice and Consent*, his book about the Bork and the Thomas nomination fights, he wrote (referring to 1991), "No stranger to the Senate Judiciary Committee, Thomas had twice been approved for the chairmanship of the Equal Employment Opportunity Commission (EEOC), once for Assistant Secretary of Education, and once for the U.S. Appellate Court. After Reagan's reelection, when the President reappointed him as chair of the EEOC, I joined several of my colleagues on the committee in voting against his confirmation, though he carried the majority in the committee. He had a good relationship with the employees at EEOC, and he had the ability to do the work, but he found himself caught in a squeeze between a law that required him to act against those who blatantly discriminated and the Reagan administration, which had no interest in enforcing the law. How much zeal Thomas himself had never has been clear."

Simon was clearly bothered by what he saw as a contradiction in regard to Thomas's attitude toward age discrimination cases. He wrote, "Age discrimination cases were massively neglected. Thomas said he did not have adequate staff to carry out all these responsibilities, yet he wrote for the Cato Institute: 'I am confident it can be shown, and some of my staff are now working on this question, that blacks at any level, have simply not benefited from affirmative action policies.' What is key in that sentence: he had staff working on undermining the basic mission of the EEOC but he said he did not have adequate staff to carry out the assignment given him by law. Overall, his record was not impressive." Nonetheless, Senator Simon told the White House he would vote for Thomas at this level, but not if and when he were nominated for the Supreme Court.

The vote turned out to be 12 in favor and one against. The lone dissenter was Senator Howard Metzenbaum of Ohio.

In voting against the nominee, Metzenbaum, one of the Senate's most liberal members, said his main concern was that under Thomas's aegis, the EEOC had cared less and less about age discrimination cases. This was also the concern of both the AARP and of Arkansas Senator David Pryor. The association sent Chairman Biden a long angry letter denouncing Thomas, suggesting that he had not told the truth about age cases, a suggestion seconded by Pryor, but in the end the powerful older citizens' lobbying group decided to wait and fight another day. There was a feeling among a number of like-minded groups that if they came at Thomas with all their guns blazing at this point, and *missed*, then they would have a much harder time should he (as they were all but certain would happen) be put up for the highest court in the land.

Women's advocates, who also frowned on Thomas, also declined to go all out at this stage. One spokesperson who did testify against Thomas at his confirmation hearings was Nancy Kreiter, the research director of Women Employed, a Chicago-based group. Mincing few words, she said, "We think the bottom line performance profile was dreadful. There was a steady decline in settlements, a building backlog of cases. When he left we were hard pressed to tell anybody that they should take their case there."

One woman who felt quite differently was Janine Kemp, wife of the man who would succeed Clarence Thomas as the head of EEOC, Evan Kemp. In her interview for this book in 2001, she said, "I think Clarence Thomas, like Evan, was concerned about the Balkanization of our society and also the victim mentality in society and how damaging that was to individuals. During the time I knew him he had really taken the reins of that agency and changed it, and people really responded well. He would walk through that agency and he had a good word for people no matter what their station as long as they were doing their job. Evan used to say that he would 'more readily be fooled by the first 50 names in the Boston phone book than the Harvard faculty.' That was an indication of his populist mentality and trust in people, which I believe was shared by Justice Thomas who always related well to rank and file workers."

Washington lawyer Frederick Douglass Cooke Jr., who is on the opposite side of the political fence as Janine Kemp, nonetheless agrees that at this point in his career Clarence Thomas was no villain. "He's a fascinating guy because he doesn't really hide. He goes out and he talks to school groups, for example.

"I think people are usually pleasantly surprised by the dichotomy between the public, media persona and what they see when they actually see him. He's not an ogre. He's not a stiff, stern kind of guy. You talk to him and he says the right things. You can't argue with self-sufficiency or about making the most of your opportunities, taking advantage of the chances you get wherever they are. How can you say that's a bad thing to promote? He says that and he believes that. And most people I know believe that.

"But what gets people—black people I know, that is—off the track with him is his refusal to acknowledge the impact that the history of racism has had in this country. And how do you get at resolving it.

"It's well and good to wake up one day and pronounce, that racism in the United States is over and we're not going to discriminate any more. But there is, arguably, 400 years of racism that's in place, that happened. So how do you then make both the victims and the perpetrators of the racism move ahead in a relatively equal way? How do you do that? How do you level the playing field? And Clarence *just doesn't get that*.

"This is what black people want to say to Clarence: 'Look, you were born and raised a poor black kid in Pin Point, Georgia. You got the opportunity to go to a Catholic grade school, and to Holy Cross and to Yale. Do you think any of that happened just because you were the most brilliant person these people had met? They were reaching out to you as a member of a class of people who had been discriminated against to give you an opportunity to shine. And you *did*, to your credit. You did the work. But don't be confused and think that somehow you got here on merit, that you got here just because you're the most wonderful person on the planet. They *reached out*. They didn't know you. They said here's a black guy among a number of black guys who might have something to offer the world, and we're going to give him a chance. Otherwise you wouldn't have been at Holy Cross. You wouldn't be at Holy Cross just because you're smart, you wouldn't be at Yale because you're smart.'"

"And then for Clarence to say, 'Well, I think that's bullshit. I'm not going to advocate any legal philosophy or any Supreme Court doctrine that would perpetuate that because I think that's a bad thing!' Well, that's what drives people I know completely crazy. Because Clarence Thomas is a direct beneficiary of that whole concept called affirmative action, but he somehow wants to turn his back on that and say to people behind him, 'you got to get there on merit.' And because he is black and he says that, he does such harm to the legitimate argument for affirmative action, which is *not* reverse racism, which simply says, in some way, make sure that what you do includes a methodology to include people who would not otherwise be included."

Summing up, Fred Cooke says, "Clarence thinks that if the government requires an employer to cast as broad a net as possible in order to have as diverse a pool as possible, then that is discriminatory, and the government can't require that. Well, that's just *nuts*. Because that's really what affirmative action is. Affirmative action is about making sure employers take affirmative steps to bring about a diverse workforce. It doesn't mean giving a job to a guy just because he's black and he shows up. That's not what affirmative action is. It's about trying to diversify the pool to the greatest extent possible. And for a guy who did that, who's been a beneficiary of that, both at Holy Cross and at Yale, to say that's bad, I just find that really difficult to fathom. But then, to say again, and somewhat in his defense, I think he really believes it. I think he's *wrong*, but I think he really believes it."

* * * *

The United States District Court of Appeals for the District of Columbia Circuit, the court on which Clarence Thomas would sit for 15 months before getting the call to become one of the nine "Supremes," the court on which he would, so to speak, cut his judicial teeth, has a proud and distinguished history. Generally considered the second-most important court in the country, it was referred to for a long time as "the Bazelon court," for its chief judge, the venerated liberal David L. Bazelon.... Another leading liberal member of the court for years was J. Skelly Wright. By the time Clarence Thomas was named to the court, however, its liberal heyday was over, despite the continuing presence of such Democratic appointees as Patricia Wald, Abner Mikva (former U.S. Representative from Illinois and later a presidential counselor in the Clinton White House), and Ruth Bader Ginsburg, the second woman named to the U.S. Supreme Court.

As Mayer and Abramson write, "But by the end of the Reagan years, Bazelon and Wright had both died and the court became ideologically divided. Mikva...Ginsburg... and Wald remained energetic Democratic holdovers.

"Equally influential, however, were two conservative former law professors, Antonin Scalia and Robert Bork, who in the 1980s radically shifted the panel's direction toward judicial restraint. Joined later by another forceful conservative, Kenneth Starr, the Reagan appointees moved to limit the scope and source of suits against the government as well as the panel's power of judicial review, which had been used during the Bazelon era to override Congress and the executive branch. By the time Clarence Thomas arrived, Scalia and Bork were gone—Scalia to the Supreme Court, Bork to private practice."

Another member not long for the court was Kenneth Starr. In 1990, he was appointed Solicitor General of the United States, making him the government's top appellate lawyer. The SG and his office (as of 2001 there's not been a female Solicitor General) decide which cases the government will seek to ask the Supreme Court to review, which losses in lower federal courts should be appealed, and in which cases the government will file a friend of the court (*amicus curiae*) brief or enter the case as an "intervenor." All of these matters are handled by lawyers from the Solicitor General's office, and in most cases before the highest court the SG himself makes the oral argument. (Not only was Thurgood Marshall the Solicitor General, so was Robert Bork. Indeed, that was the position he held when he was ordered by President Richard Nixon to fire Special Prosecutor Archibald Cox in what would become known as the Saturday Night Massacre.)

On June 1, 1998, Solicitor General Seth Waxman began an address to the Supreme Court Historical Society with these words:

Some 60 years ago, a letter found its way into the United States mail addressed simply "The Celestial General, Washington, D.C." The Postmaster apparently had no trouble discerning to whom it should be delivered. It went to Robert H. Jackson, then Solicitor General of the United States.

Now neither Justice Jackson nor any of my other predecessors, I am sure, had pretensions of other-worldliness. But they—we—have all been fortunate indeed to have been able to serve in what Thurgood Marshall called "the best job I've ever had." For the office of Solicitor General of the United States is a wonderful and unique creation.

The Solicitor General is the only officer of the United States required by statute to be "learned in the law." He is one of only two people (the other being the Vice President) with formal offices in two branches of government. And perhaps more than any other position in government, the Solicitor General has important traditions of deference to all three branches.

As important and interesting as the position is, it is quite different from that of a sitting judge, and thus it was with some ambivalence that Bush appointee Kenneth Starr, later to become famous (some would say notorious) as the Special Prosecutor in charge of the Clinton Whitewater scandal accepted the post. In 1992, in an article in *The Washington Lawyer*, the magazine of the District of Columbia Bar Association, Starr discussed some of his feelings about the famous court that he was leaving and Clarence Thomas would soon be joining.

"My principal concern," on becoming a federal judge at age 37 (in 1983), "was, frankly, whether I would be able to carry on well and effectively on a very distinguished court with a very distinguished tradition...."

(By contrast with Clarence Thomas, who was 41 at the time he was named to the court, and had been a federal bureaucrat for most of his legal career, by 1983 Starr had been, in reverse order, counselor to the Attorney General and chief of staff at the U.S. Department of Justice, a litigation lawyer for Gibson, Dunn & Crutcher, one of the top firms in the country, and had spent three years as a law clerk, one year on the Court of Appeals and two as law clerk to U.S. Supreme Chief Justice Warren Burger.)

"...And my second concern had to do with my sense that it was a *moral* commitment for life, that federal judges enjoyed life tenure for a reason, namely to assure their independence and their isolation from the political branches."

Starr told the magazine that he'd wanted to become a judge ever since his first clerkship, that it would be "a marvelous way to spend one's professional life, a very noble kind of professional life. I'd very much enjoyed being in a judge's chambers, working with a judge and advising a judge." As early role models on the appellate level, he mentioned Second Circuit judges Henry Friendly and Learned Hand. "Everyone has idols on the Supreme Court, and my particular idol was Holmes. Then, as I grew somewhat professionally, the number of idols expanded to include—I'm talking about other than persons who are still alive—Justices Jackson and Harlan." As for the work of the court, Ken Starr admitted it was even harder than he'd thought it would be— "And I had expected it to be difficult. I always felt intellectually stretched and challenged."

At the end of the article, Starr answered a question as to how he felt about leaving the D.C. Court of Appeals to become the U.S. Solicitor General.

I had loved the court and I'd loved my work, and I was not only content, I very much wanted to remain where I was. Regrets? Yes and no. I very much love this position and feel very privileged to be here, but I also regret having left the bench.

That was the court Clarence Thomas joined on March 12, 1990.

* * * *

For once, there was a period in Thomas's life that was not marked by controversy, at least not any of great substance. By all accounts he too enjoyed life as one of the 12 judges on the U.S. Court of Appeals for the District of Columbia Circuit. Like Ken Starr, he was surprised by the amount, and in some cases, the difficulty of the work, but hard work had never been a problem for Clarence Thomas.

Fellow judges who knew him at the time, such as Stanley Sporkin, previously of SEC and FBI fame, but at that time a federal district court judge in the same building if not the same court, remember him fondly. "Great guy," said Sporkin in 2001, with characteristic exuberance. "A very nice fellow, always pleasant, fun to be around."

Another judge, who asked not to be named, said that to his surprise Thomas was "more progressive and liberal" while on the Court of Appeals. "I remember one search and seizure case in which he got outraged over the facts. But he had to be told by me and [another judge] that there was very little we could do about it because of the way the Supreme Court had narrowed the issue that was before us. It took ten minutes for us to talk him down." This same judge remembers the Clarence Thomas of that year as being quite open and friendly and mixing with the other judges and their families "easily and well. He was always quite personable. You could hear that booming laugh all over the building."

Of Thomas's work on the Court of Appeals, not much stands out, in the sense of being either memorable or indicative of what was in the wind for him. Mayer and Abramson claim to have seen evidence of puppeteering—with Clarence Thomas the puppet, not the puppet master:

> Unlike his speeches and writings at the EEOC, Thomas's D.C. Circuit opinions read as if they have been stripped of controversy.
>
> As an appeals judge, Thomas would not leave a problematical paper trail when, and if, he was nominated to the Supreme Court. He also rarely expounded opinions from the bench. During the twenty [sic] months that Thomas served on the court, he was generally quiet during oral arguments, according to most clerks there. And in a departure from the normal practice, the administration took an active role in helping Thomas pick his clerks. Most were carefully culled from the best law schools, and many of them were Federalist Society alumni; their draft opinions needed little embellishment. According to clerks from other chambers, Thomas leaned especially heavily on them.

Thomas supporters would disagree with a number of statements in that paragraph, the last being not the least among them.

Continuing, they wrote:

> During his time on the D.C. Circuit, Thomas heard more than a hundred and fifty cases and wrote twenty-five opinions. Several clerks remember that he was a very slow writer. His votes show him to be generally tough on criminal defendants, and in affirming a number of convictions, he rejected defenses of entrapment, inadmissible evidence, and inadequate legal representation.
>
> In keeping with his philosophy of judicial conservatism, Thomas was inclined to defer to the decisions of administrative agencies....

One might wonder, using hindsight, if Supreme Court Justice Clarence Thomas ever looks back on his brief period as a federal appeals court judge and wishes he'd never stepped up. While difficult, the work was, as Kenneth Starr said, both worth doing and intellectually challenging. Having "got the job," Thomas could put his political dog and pony show in the stable for as long as he wished, maybe forever. Few people were calling for his scalp.

As a married man for three or four years, he no longer had the emotional uncertainty of his days as a born-again bachelor. He had a lovely wife, a nice home, and when he wanted to see his son, all he and Virginia had to do was get in the car, his beloved black Corvette, and drive the 100 miles to Fork Union, where his son Jamal attended (and played sports for) Fork Union Academy. He had a good job and a good life.

All in all, Clarence Thomas's time on the appellate bench was a period of calm, which was just as well, considering the firestorm that lay ahead.

Chapter Nine

A Supreme Promotion

*I didn't start out saying I'm going to have a black
to replace Thurgood, or Mr. Marshall to me. But it
worked out very well, and he went through tough
times. But I don't know what his position is going to
be on any issue. I like the background, the grass roots
feel of his character, and I like what I was told was
his record on the bench.*

–President George Bush
"Talking with David Frost"
December 23, 1991

All hell did not break loose on the day George Bush
nominated Clarence Thomas for the Supreme Court
of the United States, at least not immediately. But on
that day the crack appeared and the fissures began to
spread. And as bad and contentious as the battle between
the pro- and anti-Thomas forces would become, on that July
day, three days before the Fourth, no one anticipated it was
going to be *that* bad. It was just that, as happens in
Washington from time to time, things got out of hand.

It did not help either side that President Bush tripped
over his text and declared that Clarence Thomas was "the
best qualified person for the job." But once uttered, the
superlative hung out there, reverberating, until it settled,
and looked to both sides like a line drawn in the sand.

* * * *

Although Justice Marshall's resignation had been expected, given his age and poor health ("I'm old and I'm coming apart," he told reporters), its sudden arrival was still something of a surprise. And an omen. As David Savage wrote near the end of *Turning Right: The Making of the Rehnquist Supreme Court*, "[Marshall's] resignation added an exclamation point to the term's end. The last of the Warren court liberals was gone. Rehnquist and the conservatives had control, and now even the voice of liberalism had vanished." The element of surprise was also present when the White House announced the nomination of Clarence Thomas. "If credit accrues to him for coming up through a tough life as a minority in this country, so much the better," said the President. "The fact that he is black and a minority has nothing to do with this sense that he is the best qualified at this time. I kept my word to the American people and to the Senate by picking the best man for the job on the merits. And the fact that he's a minority, so much the better."

"Only in America could this have been possible," said Clarence Thomas, on the lawn at Kennebunkport, Maine, where President Bush had invited him so he could make him an offer he couldn't refuse. "As a child I could not dare dream that I would ever see the Supreme Court, not to mention be nominated to it." It was July 1, 1991, a Monday, and Thomas was being presented to the nation in a media-heavy coming out party on the grounds of the Bush family's sprawling seaside home, known in the curious nomenclature of the rich as a cottage.

Several hours later, and a thousand miles away, on 32nd Street in Savannah, the phone rang as Leola Williams walked in the door from work.

"Turn on Channel 6," said a woman's voice. "Your son's on it!" She did so, and, "There was Clarence standing behind the President and a message flashing on the screen saying he was the nominee to the Supreme Court.

"Well, I screamed so loud I dropped the phone."

If Thomas had been nervous, and he clearly had been, so was the President. At least he was nervous enough, or George Bush enough, to mix up his words. According to his written text, he was to refer to Judge Thomas as "the best man" for the job, but instead it came out as the "best qualified," raising the ears of even Thomas's backers—and the hackles of his detractors.

When a reporter asked the nominee what he'd say to critics who'd say he was only chosen because he was black, Thomas replied, "I think a lot worse things have been said. I disagree with that, but I'll have to live with it."

Arlen Specter, the sometime maverick of a Republican senator, wrote in *Passion for Truth*, his political memoir that came out in 2000, "Bush announced that Thomas was the 'best qualified' nominee he could find for the high court, and that 'the fact that he is black and a minority has nothing to do with this.' Immediately I said publicly that Thomas certainly was *not* the best-qualified nominee available and that race *was* a factor—and properly so."

He goes on, perhaps damning with faint praise, to say, "I did not object to Thomas's nomination, because I thought he was entitled to a hearing and because of his record, with his degrees from Holy Cross and Yale Law School plus his tenure on the Court of Appeals, he appeared at least marginally qualified."

Other senators did object. Senator Paul Simon of Illinois, who'd warned the Bush administration when he voted for Thomas's nomination to the Court of Appeals that they could not count on his vote if and when they tried to elevate him to the highest court, kept his word. Only two years later, in *his* book—books on Thomas, Hill, and Thomas and Hill, became an instant cottage industry in the years immediately following the famous hearings—he quoted a trio of anti-(Clarence)Thomists. The first was the venerable liberal columnist James Reston: "One mystery of this avoidable scandal is why President Bush ever nominated Clarence Thomas in the first place. He said he never even considered Judge Thomas's race but sent his name to the Senate because he regarded Judge Thomas as the best qualified person for the job, and nobody even laughed." Next he quoted the *Economist* magazine: "The system has been abused. Prime among the abusers is George Bush. The President said he nominated Mr. Thomas because he was the best man for the job. That is simply not true.... His sterling qualities were not his ability or his experience but the color of his skin combined with his right wing views." Finally, he quoted from a letter sent to the Senate Judiciary Committee from the chairs of a dozen U.S. House committees and subcommittees who'd dealt with Clarence Thomas as head of EEOC. They said that when they wrote to President Bush two years earlier and urged him not to name Thomas to the Court of Appeals, they did so after concluding that Thomas had "...demonstrated an overall disdain for the rule of law." Now, they said, "More recent, detailed reports reaffirm that conclusion.... His confirmation would be harmful to [the U.S. Supreme Court] and to the nation."

Once Thomas was the nominee, Simon had his staff compile an 800-page dossier on him and his record, and on a return trip from Africa (Simon was chair of the Senate subcommittee on that continent) he read the whole thing. "The picture that came across," he later wrote, "was of an extremely conservative person." And then Simon asked the sixty-four-thousand-dollar question that has intrigued (and bothered) Thomas-watchers for as long as he has been in the public eye: "But how much of that extreme conservatism did Thomas simply design to please his bosses in the Reagan administration? What did Clarence Thomas really believe?"

Two Republican Senators with reservations about Thomas were the aforementioned Arlen Specter and Warren

Rudman, of Pennsylvania and New Hampshire, respectively. This is what they had to say (in *their* books) about the President nominating Clarence Thomas to fill the seat of Thurgood Marshall:

Specter: "I did not like a number of Thomas's views, but I thought there should be considerable latitude for the president's appointment. I disagreed with Thomas about affirmative action, but there was some basis for what he was saying. I had fought hard for pro-choice candidates on the ground that there should not be a litmus test, so how could I act differently toward a nominee on the other side of the issue? Thomas, forty-three, had been on the bench less than a year when Bush nominated him for the Supreme Court. He had never argued a case before a jury and had not practiced law in a decade. But he had a compelling personal story, an impressive resume, and the political outlook the White House was looking for. Thomas would come before the Senate a year before the 1992 elections, and getting a conservative like Thomas on the Court would make important inroads."

Rudman: "One of my achievements during my final months in the Senate was winning the nomination and confirmation of three outstanding candidates for federal judgeships, and my success was due in part to my vote, the previous year, to confirm Clarence Thomas's appointment to the Supreme Court. It isn't a vote I'm proud of, but it's a textbook example of how our system works....

"A lot of federal judges are appointed after senators cast votes they'd rather not cast. That was the case with my support for Clarence

173

Thomas in the fall of 1991. I don't know what inspired George Bush to nominate Thomas. Perhaps his staff convinced him it would be clever to challenge liberals to vote against a black conservative. Bush had the audacity to call Thomas the best-qualified candidate for the job, but he wasn't even close to being that...."

* * * *

Early in the morning of June 28th, John Danforth received a call from Vice President Dan Quayle, who was on his way into a meeting regarding Thurgood Marshall's replacement. Quayle wanted to know how far Danforth would go in support of Clarence Thomas. Danforth's reply: "At least as far as Senator Warren Rudman went in supporting David Souter."

As a result, Thomas had all the senators he needed in that one man, John Danforth. Former employer, mentor, friend, Danforth put Clarence Thomas on his back, almost literally, and carried him around the halls of the Senate making nice until he had all the votes he needed.

In *Advice & Consent*, Paul Simon relates the careful work done by Thomas's champion. "Before the actual hearings began, Senator Danforth came to my office with Judge Thomas, and we discussed some of my concerns. I told him I wanted a Supreme Court Justice who would defend civil liberties and civil rights and be willing to do what may be temporarily unpopular." The senator from Illinois told the nominee that in his experience, people who had overcome tough odds to become successful fell into two camps. In one, that person would remember his own difficult past and try to help those on the bottom make it as far up the ladder as they could; or, that person would ignore those below, and adopt an if-I-made-it-on-my-own-so-can-they attitude. He said Clarence Thomas assured him he would be in the first camp.

"I told him," Simon later wrote, "the general nature of

the questions I would be asking: on privacy, on civil liberties, on separation of church and state, on his sensitivity to the powerless in our society. As they started to leave my office, Danforth leaned over to me and said, 'You'll never get a better nominee from this administration.'" Simon added that some days later, when he encountered Danforth and Thomas in a Senate office building and asked, "Still at it?" that Danforth replied, "We've just visited our fifty-ninth senator."

John Danforth, a man of his word, was merely living up to it—"in for a penny, in for a pound," as the old saying has it. Total commitment. As he told the tale in his book, *Resurrection*, he was merely following the lead of the distinguished gentleman from New Hampshire: "Rudman, a good friend and a highly regarded senator...had set the standard for all-out support for a nominee the year before.... Rudman not only lent his stature to the Souter nomination, he personally escorted Souter on visits to the offices of individual senators. To make a similar effort on behalf of Clarence Thomas would require a major commitment of time and of whatever standing I had in the Senate, for this was certain to be a controversial nomination.... I did not hesitate a second. That I would give this everything I had was the promise I made to the vice president." As Paul Simon indicated, Senator Danforth gave it everything he had.

* * * *

While all of this schmoozing was going on, the Forces of Evil (as seen by Clarence Thomas's backers) were gathering strength. Perhaps the best prepared was Nan Aron's Alliance for Justice, a coalition formed early in the Reagan administration by such groups as the NAACP, the National Wildlife Federation, the National Organization for Women (NOW), and the Consumers Union. For several years, they'd been saving string—in the form of speeches, memos, legal opinions, briefs, articles in legal journals as well as the popular print media, all of which would go toward providing the kind of paper trail that had proved so successful in derailing the nomination of Judge Robert Bork. (In fact, so successful was that effort that it gave us a new word—"borking," for bringing someone down under a barrage of well-documented literature, the great majority of which having come from the nominee's own head and hand.) As David Savage wrote, "When the nomination finally went to the Senate for confirmation, reporters, civil rights advocates, and even Senate staffers could count on the alliance to have the thickest file of information on the candidate."

However, as Savage points out, the Alliance's track record was not the greatest. "Despite the efforts of the alliance, the president's nominees were rarely defeated. During Reagan's eight years in office, he filled 378 judgeships in the three-tiered federal court system. Only three of his nominees were rejected by the Senate: Jefferson B. Sessions of Alabama...Bernard Siegan, a San Diego law professor and friend of Attorney General Meese...and Judge Robert Bork.... By the fall of 1991, Reagan and Bush together had filled 439 of the 837 seats in the federal judiciary. Undaunted by the statistics, the alliance lawyers kept gathering information. They made sure that none of the president's nominees got a free ride." Savage wrote that the alliance was "especially ready" for one nominee in particular: "It had two full file drawers marked 'Clarence Thomas.'"

At the beginning, the main opposition came from the women's groups, all of whom were deeply concerned that Thomas would soon be yet another Reagan-Bush hit man for *Roe v. Wade*. One of the men, however, did get off a good line. Arthur Kropp, head of People for the American Way, said, "Clarence Thomas is closer to Ed Meese than to Thurgood Marshall." But then, to the man who picked him (and the men who helped the man to pick him) that was the idea.

Caught somewhat by surprise—and, for many, also between a rock and a hard place—were the nation's African-

Americans. Pleased to see a black man get the nod for Thurgood Marshall's seat, they were not of one mind as to whether this was the right black man, and that he had been chosen for the right reasons. While 54 percent of the black Americans polled by USA Today said they approved of the nomination of Clarence Thomas (with 17 percent disapproving and 29 percent saying they didn't know), 52 percent, an almost equal number, said they did not believe Thomas reflected the views of most blacks (24 percent said he did, and 19 percent responded "don't know"). That same newspaper reported that the nomination of Thomas brought "unprecedented attention to the nation's black conservative movement, and emboldens its leaders as they seek to become a major political force. After years of enduring scorn from better-known black liberals, black conservatives are barely restraining their joy at President Bush's selection of one of their own...a USA Today poll of black Americans finds substantial agreement with Thomas and other black conservatives on some key issues. While more than half believe Thomas does not represent the views of most blacks, the poll nonetheless finds 47 percent agreeing with Thomas that black self-help is better than hiring quotas. Four out of 10 blacks say blacks should embrace more conservative views. And only a third think Thomas is not a good role model for blacks.

"Whatever the fate of the black conservative movement, most think blacks will be hard-pressed to oppose Thomas' nomination. 'This is it....' says David Bositis [senior research associate for the Joint Center for Political and Economic Studies, a black think tank], 'If there's going to be a black member of the court, it's going to be Clarence Thomas.' Adds [U.S. Representative from Georgia and civil rights pioneer John] Lewis: 'It will be difficult for some blacks to oppose his nomination—because of the fact that he's black. He's a brother.'"

The Congressional Black Caucus—of which John Lewis

was a member—did not have any particular difficulty opposing Thomas. Even though its vote would have no official impact, being a House not a Senate body, it moved to go on record as opposing the nomination while the NAACP and other traditional black-led civil rights organizations stalled for the moment. The chairman of the caucus said that the group felt that Thomas "was not the person to carry on the legacy of Thurgood Marshall."

The nomination was still a very hot topic two weeks later when the NAACP met in Houston for its annual convention. Jesse Jackson said, "Judge Thomas has not asked for our support, indeed he has shown disrespect for our leadership heritage. Without some expression of contrition and change, and the will to be fair and just, it would be a betrayal of the heritage of our struggle to support anyone who threatens to undermine it." While no one exactly leapt to Thomas's defense, there were a number of others who took more moderate positions. But it was clear that the group, as a group, found the situation unsettling, to say the least. NAACP executive director Benjamin Hooks was quoted as saying, "When we get through looking at his record we may oppose him, support him, or take no position." But he admitted that despite the major differences in their respective positions on issues of paramount important to African-Americans, Thomas's statements about his impoverished upbringing had given him "the feeling he has not forgotten he is black. Who knows how much that bruised his heart and gives him a feeling of looking at cases from a human consideration. That is what the Supreme Court lacks."

Those who opposed Thomas were in the difficult position of needing to attack his positions without seeming to attack the man himself. As Sara Fritz reported in *The Los Angeles Times* less than a week after the nomination: "Ever since he ran for president in 1988, George Bush has been engaged in an emotional debate with liberal Democrats over civil rights issues—a battle that appears to have escalated with his choice of Clarence Thomas for the Supreme Court. For the president, Thomas, 43, a conservative black man who overcame poverty to become a prominent federal jurist, serves as a potent symbol of self-made success, challenging the strongly-held belief of many liberals that without some special preference, minorities cannot succeed. As such, the nomination is being viewed by Democrats as well as Republicans as a deft political stroke on Bush's part. 'It's brilliant, if not a bit cynical,' said William Schneider, political scientist at the American Enterprise Institute, a think tank for many conservative figures.... Thomas's nomination puts liberal Democrats and black leaders in a difficult position in which they must attack a black man in order to defend their own view of civil rights."

"If civil rights groups soft-pedal their opposition," wrote black columnist DeWayne Wickham, "there will be an inclination on the part of Senate Democrats to support him because he's black. Everyone is going to be uncomfortable voting against Clarence Thomas unless there is a tidal wave of opposition."

On September 5, 1991, less than a week before Clarence Thomas would take the witness chair before the Senate Judiciary committee, its chairman, Joseph Biden, received a letter signed by nine professors of constitutional law at the following six law schools: Harvard, Cornell, NYU, Stanford, UCLA, and UC Berkeley. It began:

> As teachers and scholars of constitutional law committed to the protection of constitutional liberty, we submit this report to convey our grave concerns regarding the nomination of Judge Clarence Thomas to be an Associate Justice of the United States Supreme Court. Careful examination of Judge Thomas' writings and speeches strongly suggests that his views of the Constitution, and in particular his use of nat-

ural law to constrict individual liberty, depart from the mainstream of American constitutional thought and endanger Americans' most fundamental constitutional rights, including the right to privacy.

Among the most alarming aspects of his record, and the primary focus of this report, are the numerous instances in which Judge Thomas has indicated that he would deny the fundamental right to privacy, including the right of all Americans, married or single, to use contraception and the right of a woman to choose to have an abortion. Judge Thomas has criticized the Supreme Court's decisions in the landmark privacy cases protecting the fundamental right to use contraception. He has endorsed an approach to overruling *Roe v. Wade* that is so extreme that it would create a constitutional requirement that abortion be outlawed in all states throughout the nation, regardless of the will of the people and their elected representatives. Recent Supreme Court decisions in *Webster v. Reproductive Health Services* and *Rust v. Sullivan* have seriously diminished protection for the right to choose. Replacing Justice Thurgood Marshall with Judge Clarence Thomas would likely result in far more devastating encroachments of women's rights, perhaps providing the fifth vote to uphold statutes criminalizing virtually all abortions....

We submit this report prior to Judge Thomas' testimony before the Judiciary Committee in the hope that it will assist the committee, and the Nation, in formulating questions to discern Judge Thomas' views on fundamental rights to individual privacy and liberty. We urge the committee to question Judge Thomas on these matters and to decline to confirm his nomination unless he clearly refutes the strong evidence that he is a nominee whose special concept of the Constitution "calls for the reversal of decisions dealing with human rights and individual liberties." [the quote is from the Executive Report of the Senate Judiciary Committee on the Bork nomination].

The White House response to this, and similar statements, was simple. President George Bush said, "There's a fight on. I am confident we are going to win it."

* * * *

The producers of "West Wing" could not have staged it better. Held in the wonderfully historic main caucus room of what used to be called the Old Senate Office Building, then later the Russell Building after the Hart Building made the "New Senate Office Building" no longer the newest kid on the block, it was a room replete with echoes of grand drama. This was the same room in which two venerable senior citizens, both looking as if they'd been sent over by Central Casting, left their mark not just on the history of the Senate, but of the country as well. The first was Joseph Welch, the Boston lawyer, he of the bow ties and the righteous indignation who, frustrated with the sleazy machinations of the junior senator from Wisconsin, asked Joe McCarthy that blistering question, "Have you, sir, no sense of decency?" The other was Senator Sam Ervin of North Carolina, whose plain-spoken questions and gentlemanly Southern decorum wore down one Watergate witness after another, as the nation watched mesmerized. Both of these men, and countless others, had played out their hours on the national stage in this very same ornate chamber, thus carving their names into the national memory for decades to come.

On September 10, 1991, that same stage was definitely set, even if no one expected this particular drama to have two acts, or for the second to be so shocking and riveting that to this day people remember, almost to the extent they remember the assassination of President Kennedy, where they were and what they were doing as it unfolded in front of them on national television.

"Good morning, Judge. Welcome to the blinding lights. It's a pleasure to have you here and let me begin by indicating that the morning is going to be painless, or maybe the most painful part of the whole process because you're going to hear from all of the committee who have an opening statement and then half a dozen senators who are going to introduce you. And so you'll hear from about 20 senators before you get to speak. It could be the most painful part of the process."

As predictions go, that one by Delaware Democrat and Senate Judiciary Chairman Joseph Biden was pretty much on the money. Clarence Thomas had entered the huge ceremonial room on the arm of South Carolina Republican Senator Strom Thurmond, a man who'd known a controversy or two in his time, one of them being the Dixiecrat Revolt, when he, then a Democrat, led his supporters out of the national convention in protest against the inclusion of a civil rights plank in the presidential platform.

The staging was a bit heavy-handed. Thomas sat alone at a long witness table. Directly behind him were his wife, mother, sister, and son. Biden, continuing on a more serious note, laid some interesting recent historical groundwork. "This committee begins its sixth set of Supreme Court confirmation hearings held in the last five years—a rate of change that is unequaled in recent years. If you're confirmed, Judge Thomas, you will come to the Supreme Court in the midst of this vast change. In four years, Justices Powell, Brennan, and Marshall will have been replaced by Justices Kennedy, Souter, and Thomas. Because of these changes, many of the most basic principles of constitutional interpretation of the meaning that the Supreme Court applies to the words of the Constitution are being debated in this country in a way they haven't for a long time—in a manner unlike anything seen since the New Deal. In this time of change, fundamental constitutional rights which have been protected by the Supreme Court for decades are being called into question."

Then Biden got to his main point, "Judge Thomas, you come before this committee in this time of change with a philosophy different from that which we have seen in any Supreme Court nominee in the 19 years since I have been in the Senate. For as has been widely discussed and debated in the press, you are an adherent to the view that natural law philosophy should inform the Constitution. Finding out what you mean when you say that you would apply the natural law philosophy to the Constitution is, in my view, the single most important task of this committee, and, in my view, your most significant obligation to this committee."

A touch of humor crept in as Biden was closing his remarks. Commenting on Judge Thomas's age, he stopped for a moment, and then said, "I never thought I'd be sitting here talking about the youth of a nominee to the Supreme Court, but I am. Heck, you're six, seven years younger than—I'm 48. How old are you, Judge, 42, 43?

Thomas, never one to pass up an opportunity to lighten the proceedings, said, to general laughter, "Well, I've aged over the last 10 weeks, but, 43."

"Forty-three years old," Biden repeated, and then commented, "Because of your youth, Judge, you will be the first Supreme Court justice the Senate will ever have confirmed, if it does, that will most likely write more of his opinions in the 21st century than he will write in the 20th century. To acknowledge that fact alone, Judge, is to recognize the unique significance of your nomination and the care with which this committee must look at it."

* * * *

Among the many advisors who were helping Clarence Thomas prepare for the hearings, there was a certain amount of difference of opinion as to how he should conduct himself. One camp, chiefly made up of administration people, and led by political consultant Ken Duberstein and Fred McClure of the White House, felt he should emphasize his roots, thereby hoping to forestall serious negative questioning on the implied grounds that the nominee had come so far and overcome so much that it would be unseemly, and perhaps even unfair, to subject him to the kind of issue-oriented interrogation that had undone Judge Bork four years earlier. The other camp, made up mainly of friends and colleagues of Thomas's, felt they should to borrow a phrase from the previous occupant of the White House, "let Thomas be Thomas." The reasoning of this latter group was that Clarence Thomas—who loved to argue, even if it meant taking a position he did not necessarily favor—would be more than able to stand up under tough questioning. Indeed, they felt he could and would give at least as good as he got. In the end, however, the administration forces won out, and it was agreed that he would take the Horatio Alger route. It was a decision some of them would come to regret.

In *The Real Anita Hill*, David Brock asserts that it was Thomas himself who called the shots as to what stance he'd take before the committee. "Contrary to the widespread notion, even among some of his supporters, that Thomas was a creature of his White House handlers, the nominee himself directed all aspects of the confirmation strategy. He had agreed that emphasizing his background over his beliefs would provide the most effective introduction to the committee and the public. He had personally courted black leaders over the summer, hoping to gain their support and split the opposition. And he instantly provided the information needed to rebut each new charge aired by the critics."

Thomas, dressed in what over the next decade would become the male Republican uniform of the day—dark suit, white shirt, red tie—began by telling his story. "My earliest memories are those of Pin Point, Georgia, a life far removed in space and time from this room, this day, this moment. As kids, we caught minnows in the creeks, fiddler crabs in the marshes, we played with plovers, and skipped shells across the water. It was a world so vastly different from all this. In 1955, my brother and I went to live with mother in Savannah. We lived in one room in a tenement, and we had a common bathroom in the backyard which was unworkable and unusable. It was hard but it was all we had and all there was. Our mother only earned $20 every two weeks as a maid, not enough to take care of us, so she arranged for us to live with our grandparents later in 1955. Imagine, if you will, two little boys with all their belongings in two grocery bags...."

After detailing the major highlights of his life story, Clarence Thomas paid further tribute to his grandparents, and then addressed the issue at hand: "It is my hope that when these hearings are completed, that this committee will conclude that I am an honest, decent, fair person. I believe that the obligations and responsibilities of a judge in essence involve just such basic values. A judge must be fair and impartial. A judge must not bring to his job, to the Court, the baggage of preconceived notions of ideology, and certainly not an agenda. And a judge must get the decision right because when all is said and done, the little guy, the average person, the people of Pin Point, the real people of America will be affected not only by what we as judges do, but by the way we do our jobs.

"If confirmed by the Senate, I pledge that I will preserve and protect our Constitution and carry with me the values of my heritage, fairness, integrity, open-mindedness, honesty and hard work. Thank you, Mr. Chairman."

* * * *

With the exception of some prodding from Senator Biden regarding what he and others whose work he admired (such as the conservative scholar Lewis Lehrman) had written about natural law, as the chairman had predicted, Clarence Thomas got through the first day without any major chinks in his armor. He did so by saying, when pressed to explain something he'd written, said, or praised that too much time had passed, or that in his review he'd only had time to skim the material in question, not to read it carefully.

On the second day, however, things got hairier. Ohio Democrat Howard Metzenbaum, no fan of Thomas's, came back to those same points and pressed much harder, at one point charging bluntly that, "Instead of explaining your views, though, you actually ran from them and disowned them."

Lest there be any doubt, Metzenbaum got specific:

Now, in a 1989 article in the Harvard Journal of Law and Public Policy, you wrote, "The higher law background of the American Constitution, whether explicitly referred to or not, provides the only firm basis for just, wise, and *constitutional* decisions."

Judge, you emphasized the word "constitutional" by placing it in italics. By that emphasis, you made it very clear you were talking about the use of higher law in constitutional decisions. But yesterday you said, "I don't see a role for the use of natural law in constitutional adjudication. My interest was purely in the context of political theory."

Then in 1987, in a speech to the ABA, you said, "Economic rights are as protected as any other rights in the Constitution." But yesterday you said, "The Supreme Court cases that decided that economic rights have lesser protection were correctly decided."

In 1987, in a speech at the Heritage Foundation, you said, "Lewis Lehrman's diatribe against the right to choose was a splendid example of applying natural law." But yesterday you said, "I disagree with the article, and I did not endorse it before."

In 1987, you sign on to a White House working group report that criticized as "fatally flawed" a whole line of cases concerned with the right to privacy. But yesterday you said you never read the controversial and highly publicized report, and that you believe the Constitution protects the very right the report criticizes.

In all of your 150-plus speeches and dozens of articles, your only reference to a right to privacy was to criticize a constitutional argument in support of that right. Yesterday you said there is a right to privacy.

Now, Judge Thomas.... Our only way to judge you is by looking at your past statements and your record. And, I will be frank; your complete repudiation of your past record makes our job very difficult.

We don't know if the Judge Thomas who has been speaking and writing throughout his adult life is the same man up for confirmation before us today. And I must tell you, it gives me a great deal of concern.

Clarence Thomas, who had been very well coached, was wise enough not to interrupt or to attempt to answer until his questioner had finished. He sat there, silently awaiting his turn to respond. If any of Senator Metzenbaum's charges were getting to him, you couldn't tell it by looking at him.

Metzenbaum continued:

For example, yesterday, in response to a question from Senator Biden, you said that you support a right to privacy. Frankly, I was surprised to hear you say that. I have not been able to find anything in your many speeches or articles to suggest that you support a right to privacy.

Unfortunately, the committee has learned the hard

way that a Supreme Court nominee's support for the right to privacy doesn't automatically mean that he or she supports that fundamental right when it involves a woman's right to abortion. At his confirmation hearing, Judge Kennedy told us he supported the right to privacy. Since he joined the Court, Justice Kennedy has twice voted with Chief Justice Rehnquist in cases that have restricted the right to abortion.

Likewise, Judge Souter told us that he supported the right to privacy, and then when he joined the Court, Justice Souter voted with the majority in *Rust v. Sullivan.*

My concern is this—and I know I have been rather lengthy in this first question—your statement yesterday in support of the right to privacy does not tell us anything about whether you believe the Constitution protects a woman's right to choose to terminate her pregnancy. I fear that you, like other nominees before the committee, could assure us that you support a fundamental right to privacy, but could also decline to find a woman's right to choose is protected by the Constitution. If that happens soon, there could be nowhere for many women to go for a safe and legal abortion.

I must ask you to tell us here and now whether you believe that the Constitution protects a woman's right to choose to terminate her pregnancy, and I am not asking you as to how you would vote in connection with any case before the Court.

Clarence Thomas was not about to walk that particular plank. Not right then, and, as far as these hearings were concerned, not ever.

Senator, I would like to respond to your opening question first and, if you think it is appropriate, to consider each of your questions seriatim.

Yesterday as I spoke about the Framers and our Constitution and the higher law background—and it is background—is that our Framers had a view of the world. They subscribed to the notion of natural law—certainly the Framers of the Thirteenth and Fourteenth Amendments.

My point has been that the Framers then reduced to positive law in the Constitution aspects of life principles that they believed in; for example, liberty. But when it is in the Constitution, it is not a natural right; it is a constitutional right. And that is the important point.

But to understand what the Framers meant and what they were trying to do, it is important to go back and attempt to understand what they believed, just as we do when we attempt to interpret a statute that is drafted by this body, to get your understanding. But in constitutional analysis and methodology, as I indicated in my confirmation to the Court of Appeals, there isn't any direct reference to natural law. The reference to the Constitution and to using the methods of constitutional adjudication that have been traditionally used. You don't refer to natural law or any other law beyond that document.

What I have attempted to do with respect to my answers yesterday is to be as fair and as open and as candid as I possibly can. I have not spoken on issues such as natural law since my tenure as chairman of EEOC. At that time it was important to me—it was very important—to find some way to have a common ground underlying our regime and our country on the issue of civil rights. I thought it was a legitimate ground. I wondered. I looked back at Lincoln, saw him here in Washington, D.C., surrounded by a pro-slave State yet pro-Union, and a confederate state.

And I asked myself what was it that sustained him in his view that slavery was wrong. And it was through that process that I came upon the central notion of our regime, that all men are created equal, as a basis or as one aspect or trying to fight a battle to bring something positive and aggressive to civil rights enforcement. And I thought it was a legitimate endeavor.

At no time did I feel nor do I feel now that natural law is anything more than the background to our Constitution. It is not a method of interpreting or a method of adjudicating in the constitutional law area.

With respect to your last question—and I assume for the moment that perhaps you don't want me to address each of the underlying questions or specific questions seriatim. I would say this about them, though: I have written and I have been interviewed quite a bit. I have been candid over my career. My wife said to me that to the extent that Justice Souter was a "stealth nominee," I am "Bigfoot." And I have tried to think through difficult issues without dodging them.

As a judge, though, on the issue of natural law, I have not spoken nor applied that. What I have tried to do is to look at cases, to understand the argument, and to apply the traditional methods of constitutional adjudication as well as statutory construction.

I am afraid, though, on your final question, Senator, that is is important for any of us who are judges, in areas that are very deeply contested, in areas where I think we all understand and are sensitive to both sides of a very difficult debate, that for a judge—and as I said yesterday, for us who are judges, we have to look ourselves in the mirror and say, are we impartial or will we be perceived to be impartial? I think that to take a position would undermine my ability to be impartial, and I have attempted to avoid that in all areas of my life after I became a judge. And I think that is important.

I can assure you—and I know, I understand your concern that people come here and they might tell you A and then do B. But I have no agenda. I have tried to wrestle with every difficult case that has come before me. I don't have an ideology to take to the court to do all sorts of things. I am there to take the cases that come before me and to do the fairest, most open-minded, decent job that I can do as a judge. And I am afraid that to begin to answer questions about what my specific position is in these contested areas would greatly—or leave the impression that I prejudged this issue.

Metzenbaum wasn't buying. "…I am not asking you to prejudge the case. I am just asking you whether you believe that the Constitution protects a woman's right to terminate her pregnancy."

Thomas ducked. Metzenbaum fired again, and Thomas ducked again, saying, "Senator, I think to do that would seriously compromise my ability to sit on a case of that importance and involving that important issue."

The Democratic Senator from Ohio then tried to go around the barn a different way.

> Let us proceed. Judge Thomas, in 1990, I chaired a committee hearing on the Freedom of Choice Act, where we heard from women who were maimed by back-alley abortionists. Prior to the Roe decision, only wealthy women could be sure of having access to safe abortions. Poor, middle-class women were forced to unsafe back alleys, if they needed an abortion. It was a very heart-rending hearing.
>
> Frankly, I am terrified that if we turn the clock

back on legal abortion services, women will once again be forced to resort to brutal and illegal abortions, the kinds of abortions where coat-hangers are substitutes for surgical instruments.

The consequences of Roe's demise are so horrifying to me and millions of American women and men, that I want to ask you once again…appealing to your sense of compassion, whether or not you believe the Constitution protects a woman's right to an abortion.

Clarence Thomas responded, for what may have been the first time, with some emotion. "Senator, the prospect— and I guess as a kid we heard the hushed whispers about illegal abortions and individuals performing them in less than safe environments, but they were whispers. It would, of course, if a woman is subjected to the agony of an environment like that, on a personal level, certainly, I am very, very pained by that. I would not want to see people subjected to torture of that nature. I think it is important to me, though, on this issue, the question that you asked me, as difficult as it is for me to anticipate or to want to see that kind of illegal activity, I think it would undermine my ability to sit in an impartial way on an important case like that."

As might have been expected, that answer did not satisfy Senator Metzenbaum. Indeed, he got a bit heated.

I have some difficulty with that, Judge Thomas, and I am frank to tell you, because yesterday you responded, when Senator Biden asked if you supported the right to privacy, validated in *Moore v. City of East Cleveland*, by agreeing that the Court's rulings supported the notion of family as one of the most private relationships we have in our country. That was one matter that might come before the Court.

You also responded, when Senator Thurmond asked you whether, following the Court's ruling in

Payne v. Tennessee, families victimized by violence should be allowed to participate in criminal cases. You went on to respond by indicating that the Court had recently considered that matter, and you expressed concern that such participation could undermine the validity of the process. [And you responded] to Senator Thurmond's questions about the validity of the death penalty cases, the fairness of the sentencing guidelines, which was another one of his questions, and the good-faith exception to the exclusionary rule, which was another one of his questions.

Finally, you responded, when Senator Hatch asked you whether you might reply on substantive due process arguments to strike down social programs such as OSHA, food safety laws, child care legislation, and the like, by telling him that "the Court determined correctly that it was the role of the Congress to make complex decisions about health and safety and work standards."

Now, all of those issues could come before the Court again, just as the *Roe v. Wade* matter might come before the Court again. So, my question about whether the Constitution protects the woman's right to choose is, frankly, not one bit different from the types of questions that you willingly answered yesterday from other members of this committee. (The senator did not mention that, with the exception of Senator Biden, all the senators whose questions Clarence Thomas had answered were Republicans.)

So, I have to ask you, how do you distinguish your refusal to answer about a woman's right to choose to terminate her pregnancy with the various other matters that have come before the Supreme Court, to which you have already responded to this committee?

At this point, Senator Thurmond, having heard his name mentioned several times, asked to interrupt for a question, but Senator Metzenbaum would not let him, and they bantered back and forth for a moment or two until the chairman, observing that the witness was about to answer, ruled against Thurmond. The interchange gave Judge Thomas additional time to think about how, and if, to answer the question.

His intitial response did not please the senator from Ohio and they sparred some more. At one point, Thomas summed up his position rather succinctly:

"I do not believe that a sitting judge, on very difficult and very important issues that could be coming before the Court, can comment on the outcome, whether he or she agrees with those outcomes as a sitting judge." Then he added, "I think those of us who have become judges understand that we have to begin to shed the personal opinions that we have. We tend not to express strong opinions, so that we are able to, without the burden or without being burdened by those opinions, rule impartially on cases."

Metzenbaum had other concerns, which he voiced, but it was clear when his time ran out that he was not satisfied with the nominee's answers, and he appeared reluctant to sign off. If Clarence Thomas was relieved, and he had to be, it did not show.

* * * *

Metzenbaum had kept at it too long and, in the opinion of many, too hard, and the questioners who followed him— especially Senator Leahy of Vermont, who elicited from Thomas the rather startling statement that even though it had been decided while he was in law school (and a young husband and father) he had never had a significant discussion about the epochal case of *Roe v. Wade*, and Erwin Griswold, former long-time dean of Harvard Law School and former U.S. Solicitor General—kept their inquiries shorter, and, perhaps as a result, seemed to score more points. By the time Thomas stepped down, for what everyone at the time thought was his final appearance, there was relief, and frustration, on both sides.

No one raved about the nominee's performance. "Even the White House team was aghast at Thomas's weak performance," wrote Jane Mayer and Jill Abramson in *Strange Justice*. "'I thought he was terrible, wooden,' one of the court coaches conceded later. But they publicly blamed Duberstein, not the nominee. 'He was so overcoached... that he didn't show he was a bright and interesting person. We overdid it.' The result was a disservice not only to Thomas but to the entire process. As an aide to Biden with extensive experience in previous confirmation battles put it later, 'At the end of Souter, you knew a little more about his philosophy than when it started. But with Thomas, at the end you knew less. It showed that the process had been reduced to a game.'"

"In trying to make himself sound harmless, even opinionless," wrote Phelps and Winternitz in *Capitol Games*, "Thomas had lost support from more than one quarter. The moderate members of the Judiciary Committee could not but doubt the nominee's sincerity, even his veracity. Also, Thomas was alienating right-wing groups that had helped organize the nomination for him in the first place.

"'By the second day, Clarence Thomas had begun to sound too much like David Souter to be Clarence Thomas,' said Tom Jipping [head of the judicial selection project at the conservative Free Congress Research Education Foundation]. Conservatives had had high expectations about this hearing. We knew what he believed in, we knew what his character was and we were looking at this as an opportunity to come back at the committee and champion what we all believed in. It wasn't that what he said was objectionable. It was what he didn't say that we were hoping he would. After the first day, we just thought he might be off to a shaky start.

After the second day, we were more confused by his [per-formance] and disappointment was increasing.'"

* * * *

One opinion of the Thomas nomination that was (quite properly) absent was that of Thurgood Marshall, the justice Clarence Thomas was slated to replace. Never the shy and retiring type, Marshall was not one to keep his opinion of important matters of the day to himself, but this was, as Justice Brennan had written about the death penalty, "differ-ent." Much as he may have wanted to speak out, he never did, at least not publicly. However, because he was known to friends and enemies alike as having strong views about the nominee, segments of the public who knew that found it frustrating not to be able to hear his singular voice on this issue. The tough question was whether Marshall's silence was harder on his admirers or on the justice himself.

Marshall friend and biographer Carl Rowan, also not a shrinking violet, discussed this point in *Dream Makers, Dream Breakers*, his biography of Thurgood Marshall that came out in 1993, less than two years after Thomas had been confirmed.

> Marshall was not preoccupied with reading his clippings on June 28 [1991]. He had no power or right to tell President Bush how to fill his seat. But he feared that under the cover of keeping a minority per-son on the Court, Bush would name a black conser-vative of the stripe of Scalia—someone who would move without conscience to undo everything Marshall had done. You didn't have to read much between the lines spoken by Marshall at the press conference on June 29, two days following his letter of retirement, to understand what was on the mind of the old civil rights warhorse:
>
> Q.: Do you think the president has any kind of obli-gation to name a minority justice in your place...?

A.: I don't think that should be a ploy, and I don't think it should be an excuse, one way or another.
Q.: An excuse for what?
A.: Doing wrong. I mean for picking the wrong Negro and saying I'm picking him because he's a Negro. I'm opposed to that.... My dad told me way back...that there's no difference between a white snake and a black snake. They'll both bite....

It was suddenly obvious to all but the densest reporters in the room that Marshall feared Bush was going to name a reactionary black, at worst, or a conservative Hispanic, at best, and assume that his or her skin color would provide such a shield that the Senate could not refuse to confirm....

Q.: What do you think about the idea of having Clarence Thomas as the person to succeed you?
A.: I think the president knows what he's doing and he's going to do it.

Marshall knew in his heart that Bush was going to nominate Thomas, but he let a reporter speak Thomas's name first. The retiring justice had delivered a not-so-subtle message to Bush, but he knew the President would ignore it.... No one could read [Marshall's] final dissent in *Payne* and other cases without sensing that Marshall was an angry man, bitterly hostile toward some of the most recent arrivals on the Court, frustrated by his knowledge that he couldn't change them, worried that his seat would probably be filled by a black man who would ally himself with the most socially myopic justices that Marshall had ever confronted in the Court's conference room....

Even in retirement, Marshall was still one of the brethren, whose bond forbade harsh public criticism of each other...he couldn't say publicly what he thought personally of Scalia or Kennedy. He absolutely could not personally attack Clarence Thomas, the black man who was taking his seat, no matter the depth of his ideological disagreements with Thomas, or of his personal contempt for him.

So Marshall would bridle in anger that newsmen would write that he was pointing to Thomas when he said that "a black snake will bite you as quick as a white one."

* * * *

Many people, both those who were for Thomas and those against him, as well as many members of the general public, found the first part of the hearings, to borrow Tom Jipping's description, "confusing and disappointing." But that was only a pale preview of what was about to happen. Waiting in the wings, though reportedly still ambivalent about what might transpire, was a young black law professor by the name of Anita Hill.

Chapter Ten

Speaking Truth (?) To Power

"She could testify behind a screen."

"That's ridiculous. You can't do that. This isn't the Soviet Union."

That snippet of conversation overheard by an aide to Senator Thurmond was, according to John Danforth, the first inkling Thomas's supporters had that they might have a problem. The first speaker was a Senate staffer, the second his boss, Judiciary Committee Chairman Joseph Biden. The brief exchange took place on September 16, several days before what Thomas and his backers fervently hoped would be the end of the hearings.

The "she" being spoken of was Anita Hill, and when the inkling became a full-fledged rumor, the pro-Thomas forces learned, to their great dismay, that it involved allegations of sexual harassment.

Ironically, on the day the Thurmond staffer overheard the cryptic conversation between Senator Biden and his aide, Thomas's prospects looked quite good. True, he'd embarrassed himself with some of his backing and filling as to previous beliefs and statements—especially the one about *never* having discussed *Roe v. Wade*—but none of this was considered to be fatal damage.

Fifty-three senators were on record as being ready and willing to vote yes, a total that included 13 Democrats. As for the members of the Judiciary Committee, at that point there were two Republican defectors, Pennsylvania's Specter and Hank Brown of Colorado. But when Democrats Heflin (Alabama), Kohl (Wisconsin) and Biden announced that they were going to vote against Thomas, Specter and Brown hurried home to their side of the aisle.

When the committee voted on whether or not to recommend that the full Senate confirm Clarence Thomas, it deadlocked seven to seven along party lines. Strom Thurmond then moved to send the nomination to the floor without a recommendation, and that motion passed by a margin of 13-1. (The lone holdout was Paul Simon who explained his no vote by citing his belief that "a committee should do its work," meaning that if it can't get a favorable majority, then a nomination, or bill, should remain in committee.)

Thus the nomination of Judge Clarence Thomas was on its way to the Senate floor for a vote, up or down, by the 100 members of that august body.

At least that's the way it looked when word of Anita Hill and her bombshell testimony was leaked to the media.

As the facts of the matter finally unfolded, it became known that Prof. Hill had spoken to Senator Biden *before* the first round of the hearings and given him the details of her information against Judge Thomas. But the chairman did not see fit to bring the charges to the attention of the full committee at that time. (That was but one of the factors that would eventually bring the Judiciary Committee into something less than high repute.)

The nation heard the news on Sunday night at six o'clock.

"Good evening, everybody," said Paula Zahn of CBS. "Clarence Thomas ran into trouble today in what had seemed to be a certain confirmation as a Supreme Court Justice. Reports accused him of sexually harassing a woman who worked for him at the Department of Education and the Equal Employment Opportunity Commission. Rita Braver has more on that story from Washington. Rita?"

RITA BRAVER: Paula, the Senate Judiciary Committee and the White House today confirmed that the FBI did indeed interview Anita Hill, a former subordinate of Thomas' who alleges that between 1981 and 1983 he repeatedly pressured her to go out with him, and when she refused, lured her into discussions where he talked about pornographic sexual materials. Thomas categorically denies the charges.

Hill, now a professor at the University of Oklahoma Law School, did not respond to calls today but did talk to National Public Radio earlier.

[clip from NPR broadcast]
ANITA HILL: He is using his position of power for personal gain, for one thing, and he did it in a very— just ugly and intimidating way.
[end of clip]

BRAVER: Thomas chief Senate advocate, Senator John Danforth, today blasted the charges as a desperate last-minute tactic by Thomas opponents.

SENATOR JOHN DANFORTH: But when the worst sleaze of political campaigns now gets involved in the matter of confirming a Supreme Court Justice, I think that this is something that's contrary to the values of most people.

201

BRAVER: One law professor who knows both Hill and Thomas well, says he was shocked at the allegations.

CHARLES KOTHE (former Dean, Oral Roberts U.): I just can't believe it. I think it's preposterous. In all my experience with her, and it's all been favorable, she never, ever made any comment that was adverse about Clarence Thomas.

BRAVER: But a current colleague of Hill's says she is totally credible.

DEBORAH CASE (U. of Oklahoma Law School): If she says it, I believe it.

BRAVER: Senator Paul Simon is calling for more investigation of the issue even though he admits the full Senate Judiciary Committee has known about the allegation for some time and done nothing.

SENATOR PAUL SIMON: Well, we knew the report but it is one thing to know a report; it is another thing to have someone be willing to go public on it....

That may well be true, but the fact that the Judiciary Committee had known about Hill's charges "for some time and done nothing" would infuriate most women (and quite a few men as well) around the country and the world in the weeks that followed, and would help to account for the hearings becoming a landmark event in the national consciousness.

While Rita Braver was reporting the story on CBS, over at WJLA, the ABC affiliate in Washington, local anchor Carole Simpson had led off by saying:

Trouble today for President Bush's already controversial Supreme Court nominee, Clarence Thomas, enough trouble that some senators are calling for a postponement of this week's confirmation vote. A woman who worked for Thomas in the early 1980s at the Department of Education and at the Equal Employment Opportunity Commission, claims that he sexually harassed her. Thomas insists that he never touched the woman. More from ABC's Jim Wooten.

JIM WOOTEN: Judge Thomas has said he did ask the woman out, but when she declined he says he did not pursue her further. Anita Hill insists he did, declaring his sexual interest in her in explicit terms and describing to her scenes from pornographic films. A law professor at the University of Oklahoma, she made her charges last month to the Senate Judiciary Committee, but until now was unwilling to speak publicly. She told National Public Radio....

[Clip from NPR interview]
ANITA HILL: Here's a person who is in charge of protecting right[s] of women and other groups in the workplace, and he is using his position of power for personal gain, for one thing, and he did it in a very— just ugly and intimidating way. [End of clip]

WOOTEN: And she says Judge Thomas told her that if she ever disclosed his behavior it would ruin his career. The White House said the President knew of Ms. Hill's allegations and after seeing an FBI report on them, dismissed [them]. So did I, said Republican Senator John Danforth, Thomas' chief defender on Capitol Hill, and so did the other members of the committee.

SENATOR JOHN DANFORTH: No member of the committee who was briefed suggested that the evidence was sufficient to warrant a delay or suggested the need for any further investigation....

WOOTEN: It could be difficult to delay the Senate vote on Thomas' confirmation since the Democratic leadership there is said to have known about Ms. Hill's charges before the vote was scheduled.

But that was before she made the charges public, and that could change a few Democrats' minds.

There was a very good reason why the networks were so generously crediting National Public Radio: Nina Totenberg, NPR's Supreme Court reporter, had scooped them. (As had *Newsday*'s Timothy Phelps, who, with colleague Helen Winternitz, would later write *Capitol Games*, their book on the Hill-Thomas story). Totenberg's evening report, which ran a half-hour earlier than the networks' six o'clock news, was a much fuller account.

This morning, NPR reported that Anita Hill, a tenured law professor at the University of Oklahoma, told the Senate Judiciary Committee, and later the FBI, that she'd been sexually harassed by Clarence Thomas when she worked as his personal assistant in the early 1980s. She said that when she worked for Thomas at the Education Department, and later the EEOC, he constantly pressured her to go out with him socially and that he would call her into his office to discuss work and turn the discussion to his, quote, "sexual interests." According to Hill's sworn affidavit, a copy of which was obtained by NPR, Thomas, quote, "spoke about acts that he'd seen in pornographic films involving such things as women having sex with animals and films involving group sex or rape scenes. He talked about pornographic materials depicting individuals with large penises and breasts," close quote. Hill said that despite her attempts to forestall this behavior, it continued. She said she told only one person about what was happening to her, a friend from law school. The friend, now a state judge in the West, corroborated Hill's story, in part, both in

204

an interview with the FBI and with NPR. She said that Hill had told her at the time of the alleged harassment in general, though not in detail.

Hill, in an interview with NPR, said she had initially intended to keep quiet about her experiences, fearing retaliation and not wanting to relive the experience. But in early September she changed her mind.

By the week of September 10th when Clarence Thomas was testifying at his confirmation hearing, Hill was talking with the staff of the Senate Judiciary Committee. But it was more than ten days before the committee sent an FBI agent to interview Hill, and it was not until the day before the vote that most committee members learned of her allegations. Indeed, her affidavit was given to Democratic senators an hour before the vote. As for Republicans, it is not clear how many knew about the allegations. Senator Charles Grassley said today he did not learn of the allegations until this morning. Last night the White House dismissed the allegations as unfounded. Republican Arlen Specter said he'd spoken to Thomas about the allegations shortly before the vote.

Totenberg then played a portion of her interview with Specter: "Judge Thomas forcefully denied to me that he had made any inappropriate statements to the lady, woman, who made the accusations. I questioned him in detail about the specific statements which she had complained about [to] the FBI and complained to the committee about. I noted the long time lapse, some ten years, since the statements had been made and the fact that they had come very late in this investigation and that there had not been any allegations of touching or any intimidation, and that the woman had, in fact, moved from one federal agency to the EEOC with Judge Thomas. And on those totality of circumstances, that put the matter to rest in my own mind."

The reporter then quoted Senator Strom Thurmond, who had put out a statement calling the allegations without merit, as saying he was "surprised anyone would pursue them further." She also quoted Democratic Senator Patrick Leahy of Vermont who said he was always worried about late-blooming charges, "because the more explosive the allegation, the more difficult it is for a person to rebut it. But these are allegations that actually came out weeks and weeks ago. And they have been available. The FBI report has been available to both the Republican and Democratic leadership of the committee, and I would hope to all senators to look at long before now."

NPR's Totenberg closed with another quote from Hill. "The committee...is nervous about raising any issues, because someone will say, oh, it's another political ploy. But I really resent that in this case. I think it trivializes and really takes away what was a very unfortunate personal experience. And I believe that if this was my experience, that it was probably an experience of other people, or that it can be the experience of other people, other women. And I think that's irresponsible to call this political."

* * * *

The event known as the Hill-Thomas hearings has been described variously as a watershed in American politics, a turning point in the awareness of sexual harassment, and a wake-up call for women. For me it was a bane which I have worked hard to transform into a blessing for myself and for others. And because it brought to bear for the average public issues of sexual harassment, issues of race, gender, and politics, the hearing and all of the events that surrounded it deserve honest assessment.

–Anita Hill
Speaking Truth To Power

In her introduction to a book containing the complete transcripts of the Hill-Thomas portions of the Clarence

206

Thomas confirmation hearings (Academy Chicago Publishers, 1994) Nina Totenberg described her own surprise at all the media attention she encountered on Friday, October 11th, the first day of the reconvened hearings. "The story at that moment was nothing more to me than Clarence Thomas, Round II of the confirmation process. To my astonishment, though, the building was not its usual quiet self. Workers were everywhere. Cables, lights, cameras were everywhere. Network anchors were munching catered food, going over scripts, talking on telephones. Crews were frantically taping down wires, hauling in more and more equipment...suddenly I realized that the Clarence Thomas/Anita Hill hearings would be broadcast live, not just by NPR and PBS (as the first round had been) but by every network that could buy, rent, or steal the equipment necessary to do it. The *world* was going to carry this hearing, in living color and lurid detail. My mouth literally fell open as I recognized, for the first time I think, that the story I had broken just a few days earlier had turned into a mega-story."

The initial phase of the Thomas confirmation hearings had played to a packed house, but, as Totenberg observed, the second was SRO—standing room only—and even people with clout were being turned away. United States Capitol Police Force Captain Charles T. Kindsvatter recalled (in an interview in 2001, several years after he'd retired) that it was tantamount to a mob scene.

By that point a 30-year veteran of Capitol Hill, Kindsvatter, a specialist in planning and research, had seen all the demonstrations of interest, from the public wake of President John F. Kennedy to the protests against the war in Vietnam, not to mention Dr. King's March on Washington for Jobs and Freedom.

"This one," he recalled, "was different. The interest was immense, and very widespread. We had to turn away people who, under any other circumstances, we'd have found

207

room for, somehow. I remember Judge Harry Alexander of D.C. Superior Court of Appeals, asking politely if there was any way we could find a seat for him, but it was just impossible. Ordinarily, we'd have been able to make *some* arrangement, but we simply couldn't. Judge Alexander was very nice about it, but there wasn't a seat to be had!"

Captain Kindsvatter also noted the proliferation of celebrities, both major and minor. "There was an attractive blond woman I kept seeing, nicely dressed, wearing a bright red blazer, and at one point we found ourselves in the same elevator and started to talk. She turned out to be Rita Jenrette," former wife of disgraced (and convicted) South Carolina congressman John Jenrette.

"She was covering the hearings for the *Playboy* channel, which is related to a magazine whose pages, if I'm not mistaken, she once graced."

At exactly one minute after ten on the morning of Friday, October 11th, Chairman Biden opened the hearings with a warning—and an apology.

"Let me inform the Capitol Police," he intoned most seriously, "that if there is not absolute order and decorum here, we will recess the hearing and those who engage in any outburst at all will be asked to leave the committee room."

After greeting Clarence Thomas—"Good morning, Judge"—who looked so stolid and silent as he sat at the witness table that he might as well have been across Constitution Avenue in Statuary Hall, Biden continued. "I want to speak very briefly about the circumstances that have caused us to convene these hearings. We are here today to hold open hearings on Professor Anita Hill's allegations concerning Judge Thomas. This committee's handling of her charges has been criticized. Professor Hill made two requests to this committee: First, she asked us to investigate her charges against Judge Thomas, and, second, she asked that these charges remain confidential, that they not be made public and not shared with anyone beyond this committee. I believe that we have honored both of her requests."

Given that the whole world now knew of those charges, that comment caused a few raised eyebrows in the hearing room.

"Some have asked how we could have the U.S. Senate vote on Judge Thomas's nomination and leave Senators in the dark about Professor Hill's charges. To this, I answer, how could we have forced Professor Hill against her will into the blinding light where you see her today. But I am deeply sorry that our actions in this respect have been seen by so many across this country as a sign that this committee does not take the charge of sexual harassment seriously."

Biden explained how the hearings would proceed, that only Senators Leahy, Helfin, and himself would handle the questioning for the Democrats, and just Hatch and Specter (with Thurmond as a possible third) for the Republicans. He said Judge Thomas, who, as the nominee, had the right to go first or second, had elected to go first, and then to rebut after Anita Hill had "testified." He also explained that normal courtroom rules of evidence would be relaxed somewhat in these proceedings. With that, he recognized the nominee, who came out swinging.

> Judge Thomas: Mr. Chairman, Senator Thurmond, members of the committee: as excruciatingly difficult as the last two weeks have been, I welcome the opportunity to clear my name today. No one other than my wife and Senator Danforth, to whom I have read this statement at 6:30 a.m., has seen or heard the statement, no handlers, no advisers.
>
> * * * *

It wasn't as if there weren't any handlers and advisers, or that they did not very much want to have input into the form and content of Thomas's reaction to Ms. Hill's charges.

As John Danforth explained, so candidly, in *Resurrection*, "Mike [Luttig, lawyer and close friend of Thomas's who was soon to be named to the 4th District U.S. Court of Appeals]...raised the possibility that Clarence might consider withdrawing. This was not meant as a recommendation but as an option for Clarence's consideration. He told Clarence that withdrawal would be relatively easy. All Clarence would have to say would be, 'There is nothing to these allegations at all, but I am not going to put myself and my family through the kind of charade that it would take to establish that.' Clarence would have none of it. He replied, 'Mike, this has all been made up. I don't know what she is talking about. And were I to leave at this point, I could never live with myself.... Mike recalls that during that meeting, he and Clarence disagreed about how confrontational Clarence should be with the committee. Clarence said that members of the committee and committee staff were in concert with interest groups in an effort to destroy him. Mike, thinking that it would be a mistake to attack the committee, said that he had no reason to believe that the committee was trying to get Clarence. Clarence summarily rejected Mike's point."

According to Danforth, the time before the hearings would resume and Thomas would have to respond to Hill's charges, was pure hell for Thomas, his wife, and all those close to him. By Thursday night, the night before both he and Anita Hill were to testify, the nominee still did not have a prepared statement. Preferring to write it himself, he had rejected the help offered by any number of friends and associates. But, just as he'd had trouble sleeping for several days, he also had trouble writing. Then, in the early hours of Friday morning, it came together. At 4:00 a.m., he woke his wife, who had volunteered to type the final product, and then tried to steal a couple hours' sleep.

A few short hours later, with but 15 minutes to go before the opening bell, Thomas and his wife were with

Danforth and his wife in Danforth's Senate office.

As Danforth tells it:

It was time for prayer. They asked me to get Sally, who was in the next room. The four of us sat on two adjacent couches. We held hands, and I said the prayer. I acknowledged that we were calling to God in weakness. I asked God to give Clarence strength, for he had none. I prayed that God would give Clarence the words to say and the power to speak from his heart. Clarence remembers that I asked that he be free of the burden of wanting to be on the Supreme Court and that God's will be done. I was to offer similar prayers that evening and the next day as Clarence returned to continue his testimony.

Clarence remembers that as we stood up, I said, "This is going to sound a little hokey." I asked them to follow me. Clarence, Ginny, Sally, and I crowded into the bathroom. There was barely room for the four of us to stand in a circle. I closed the door behind us and pressed the play button on the tape player. We reached out to each other and held hands as he listened:

Onward Christian soldiers
Marching as to war
With the cross of Jesus
Going on before.

I looked at Clarence. His eyes were closed, his head bowed; his foot beat time to the music.

The choir sang two verses of the old hymn. I pushed the stop button, put my hands on Clarence's shoulders, and spoke as a minister:

"Go forth in the name of Christ, trusting in the power of the Holy Spirit."

Clarence says by the morning of the hearing he felt "pure." He had asked God's forgiveness for past sins, and he "felt as though God had cleansed me." Now he was ready to give his testimony. As he left my office for the walk to the Senate Caucus Room, he said he "felt as though I was armed for battle then. I was still scared, but I felt that God was with us. That God was going to guide me. That God had given me these words. And that I was going to speak these words. And that if they ran me out of town, I had spoken what I thought God had put on my tongue....I know that mentally I did not have the capacity to speak those words. I didn't have the capacity to make a speech or to develop a speech, I had to sit there at one in the morning and open up when I was dead tired. So I felt that God had given me those words and that God had opened me up. I felt that God was with me. That I was doing God's will as I went upstairs."

* * * *

The first I learned of the allegations by Professor Anita Hill was on September 25, 1991, when the FBI came to my home to investigate her allegations. When informed by the FBI agent of the nature of the allegations and the person making them, I was shocked, surprised, hurt, and enormously saddened.

I have not been the same since that day. For almost a decade my responsibilities included enforcing the rights of victims of sexual harassment. As a boss, as a friend, and as a human being I was proud that I have never had such an allegation leveled against me, even as I sought to promote women, and minorities into non-traditional jobs.

In addition, several of my friends who are women, have confided in me about the horror of harassment on the job, or elsewhere. I thought I really understood the anguish, the fears, the doubts, the seriousness of the matter. But since September 25, I have suffered immensely as these very serious charges were leveled against me.

I have been wracking my brains and eating my insides out trying to think of what I could have said or done to Anita Hill to lead her to allege that I was interested in her in more than a professional way, and that I talked with her about pornographic or X-rated films.

Contrary to some press reports, I categorically deny all of the allegations and denied that I ever attempted to date Anita Hill, when first interviewed by the FBI. I strongly reaffirm that denial....

He then chronicled his relationship with Hill, beginning with his giving her a job at the Department of Education at the suggestion of Gil Hardy (with whom she'd worked at the law firm of Wald, Harkrader & Ross) taking her with him to EEOC, and her departure to accept a teaching position in Oklahoma. He included mention of the time or two he had seen her when he went to Oklahoma, and stressed that he'd had very few contacts with her since the mid-1980s.

"This is a person I have helped at every turn in the road, since we met," he said. "She seemed to appreciate the continued cordial relationship we had since Day One. She sought my advice and counsel, as did virtually all the members of my personal staff. During my tenure in the executive branch as a manager, as a policymaker, and as a person, I have adamantly condemned sex harassment. There is no member of this committee or this Senate who feels stronger about sex harassment than I do. As a manager, I made every effort to take swift and decisive action when sex harassment raised or reared its ugly head. The fact that I feel so strongly about sex harassment and spoke loudly about it at EEOC has made these allegations doubly hard on me. I cannot imagine anything I said or did to Anita Hill that could have been mistaken for sexual harassment."

The cavernous hearing room, which had been buzzing with a light undercurrent of whispered conversations, was now quite still, almost silent, as Thomas continued to speak. His distinctive deep bass tones gave some of his words and phrases an almost biblical cast.

> ...I have not said or done the things that Anita Hill has alleged. God has gotten me through the days since September 25 and He is my judge. Mr. Chairman, something has happened to me in the dark days that have followed since the FBI agents informed me about these allegations. And the days have grown darker, as this very serious, very explosive, and very sensitive allegation or these sensitive allegations were selectively leaked in a distorted way to the media over the past weekend.
>
> ...I have never in my life felt such hurt, such pain, such agony. My family and I have been done a grave and irreparable injustice. During the past two weeks, I lost the belief that if I did my best all would work out. I called upon the strength that helped me get here from Pin Point, and it was all sapped out of me. It was sapped out of me because Anita Hill was a person I considered a friend, whom I admired and thought I had treated fairly and with the utmost respect. Perhaps I could have better weathered this if it were from someone else, but here was someone I truly felt I had done my best with.
>
> Though I am by no means a perfect person, I have not done what she has alleged, and I still do not know what I could possibly have done to cause her to make these allegations.
>
> When I stood next to the President in Kennebunkport, being nominated to the Supreme Court of the United States, that was a high honor. But as I sit here, before you, 103 days later, that honor has been

crushed. From the very beginning charges have been leveled against me from the shadows—charges of drug abuse, anti-Semitism, wife-beating, drug use by family members, that I was a quota appointment, confirmation conversion and much, much more, and now, this.

Sternly, edging closer and closer to anger, Thomas went on.

I have complied with the rules. I responded to a document request that produced over 30,000 pages of documents. And I have testified for five full days, under oath. I have endured this ordeal for 103 days. Reporters sneaking into my garage to examine books I read. Reporters and interest groups swarming over divorce papers, looking for dirt. Unnamed people starting preposterous and damaging rumors. Calls all over the country specifically requesting dirt.

This is not American. This is Kafkaesque. It has got to stop. It must stop for the benefit of future nominees, and our country. Enough is enough.

And then he laid it on the line:

I am not going to allow myself to be further humiliated in order to be confirmed. I am here specifically to respond to allegations of sex harassment in the workplace. I am not here to be further humiliated by this committee, or anyone else, or to put my private life on display for a prurient interest or other reasons. I will not allow this committee or anyone else to probe into my private life. This is not what America is all about.

To ask me to do that would be to go beyond fundamental fairness. Yesterday, I called my mother. She was confined to her bed, unable to work and unable to stop crying. Enough is enough.

Mr. Chairman, in my forty-three years on this Earth, I have been able, with the help of others and

215

with the help of God, to defy poverty, avoid prison, overcome segregation, bigotry, racism, and obtain one of the finest educations available in this country. But I have not been able to overcome this process. This is worse than any obstacle or anything that I have ever faced.... I am proud of my life, proud of what I have done, and what I have accomplished, proud of my family, and this process, this process is trying to destroy it all. No job is worth what I have been through, no job. No horror in my life has been so debilitating. Confirm me if you want, don't confirm me if you are so led, but let this process end. Let me and my family regain our lives. I never asked to be nominated. It was an honor. Little did I know the price, but it is too high.... I want my life and my family's life back and I want them returned expeditiously.

...Instead of understanding and appreciating the great honor bestowed upon me, I find myself here today defending my name, my integrity...I am a victim of this process and my name has been harmed, my integrity has been harmed, my character has been harmed, my family has been harmed, my friends have been harmed. There is nothing this committee, this body or this country can do to give me my good name back, nothing.

Concluding his statement, Clarence Thomas used a word he would use again, later, before the same committee, when he was even more upset, even more angry: "I will not provide the rope for my own lynching or for further humiliation. I am not going to engage in discussions, nor will I submit to roving questions of what goes on in the most intimate parts of my private life or the sanctity of my bedroom. These are the most intimate parts of my privacy, and they will remain just that, private."

* * * *

If the Senate allowed drum rolls, there would have been one just a few minutes later, right after Chairman Biden made the following statement: "In further discussion...it has been determined that we will excuse temporarily Judge Thomas and we will call momentarily as the witness Anita Hill. Anita Hill will be sworn and will make her own statement in her own words. At that time, we will begin the questioning of Professor Hill, after which we will bring back Judge Thomas for questioning.

"Now, the committee will stand in recess until—and I imagine it is only momentarily, until Professor Hill arrives. We will stand in recess until she is able to take her seat, which should be a matter of a minute or so.

"I am told that security is clearing the hall. She is in the hall, so that she can come down.

"[Pause. Anita Hill enters the room.]"

* * * *

Mr. Chairman, Senator Thurmond, members of the committee, my name is Anita F. Hill, and I am a Professor of Law at the University of Oklahoma.

I was born on a farm in Okmulgee County, Oklahoma, in 1956. I am the youngest of thirteen children. I had my early education in Okmulgee County. My father, Albert Hill, is a farmer in that area. My mother's name is Erma Hill. She is also a farmer and a housewife.

My childhood was one of a lot of hard work and not much money, but it was one of solid affection as represented by my parents. I was reared in a religious atmosphere in the Baptist faith, and I have been a member of the Antioch Baptist Church in Tulsa, Oklahoma, since 1983. It is a very warm part of my life at the present time.

For my undergraduate work, I went to Oklahoma State University, and graduated from there in 1977....

I graduated from the university with academic honors and proceeded to the Yale Law School, where I received my J.D. degree in 1980. Upon graduation from law school, I became a practicing lawyer with the Washington, D.C. firm of Wald, Harkrader & Ross. In 1981, I was introduced to now-Judge Thomas by a mutual friend. Judge Thomas told me he was anticipating a political appointment and asked if I would be interested in working with him. He was, in fact, appointed as Assistant Secretary of Education for Civil Rights. After he had taken that post, he asked if I would become his assistant, and I accepted that position....

Having laid that groundwork, Professor Hill went on to explain, briefly, the projects she worked on for Thomas at Education, adding that she thought their working relationship was "positive," and that she thought he respected her work and trusted her judgment. Then, having covered the professional aspects, she turned to the social, mentioning that he had asked her out, and adding, "What happened next and telling the world about it are the two most difficult things, experiences of my life. It is only after a great deal of agonizing consideration and a number of sleepless nights that I am able to talk of these unpleasant matters to anyone but close friends."

Hill stated she had declined his request for a date, explaining that she didn't think it was a good idea to date coworkers, especially when one of them was the boss. She said she'd hoped that was the end of it, but several weeks later he asked again, and when she declined once more, the situation began to get uncomfortable for her.

My working relationship became even more strained when Judge Thomas began to use work situations to discuss sex. On these occasions he would call me into his office for reports on education issues and projects or he might suggest that because of the time pressures of his schedule, we go to lunch to a Government cafeteria. After a brief discussion of work, he would turn the conversation to a discussion of sexual matters. His conversations were very vivid.

Given Anita Hill's extremely polite and professional demeanor, the softness of her manner and appearance, the crude specificity of what she had to say created an almost surreal air.

He spoke about acts that he had seen in pornographic films involving such matters as women having sex with animals, and films showing group sex or rape scenes. He talked about pornographic materials depicting individuals with large penises, or large breasts engaged in various sex acts.

It had been quiet when Professor Hill began speaking. It was even quieter now. Could she *really* be saying these things in this room about this man?

On several occasions Thomas told me graphically of his own sexual prowess. Because I was extremely uncomfortable talking about sex with him at all, and particularly in such a graphic way, I told him I did not want to talk about these subjects. I would also try to change the subject to education matters or to non-sexual personal matters, such as his background or his beliefs. My efforts to change the subject were rarely successful.

Throughout the period of these conversations, he also from time to time asked me for social engagements. My reaction to these conversations was to avoid them by limiting opportunities for us to engage in extended conversations. This was difficult, because at the time I was his only assistant in the Office of Education or Office for Civil Rights.

Then, she stated, toward the end of her employment at the Department of Education, things got better, by which she meant Thomas cleaned up his act. ("I began both to believe and hope that our working relationship could be a proper, cordial, and professional one.") So, when Thomas was appointed EEOC head, and asked her to join him, she decided to go. "The work itself was interesting, and at that time, it appeared that the sexual overtones, which had so troubled me, had ended." Her decision was also, she said, a pragmatic one. "I also faced the realistic fact that I had no alternative job. While I might have gone back to private practice, perhaps in my old firm, or at another, I was dedicated to civil rights work and my first choice was to be in that field. Moreover, at that time the Department of Education, itself, was a dubious venture. President Reagan was seeking to abolish the entire department."

She went on to say that in the fall and winter of 1982, Thomas reverted to his earlier behavior and started commenting on her appearance, in sexual terms, and pressing her to go out with him or to explain why she would not. She said that all of these incidents took place "in his inner office at the EEOC."

And then she mentioned something that would top all the media reports the next day and become one of the specific charges best remembered by the public to this day, a decade later:

> One of the oddest episodes I remember was an occasion in which Thomas was drinking a Coke in his office. He got up to the table, at which we were working, went over to the desk to get the Coke, looked at the can and asked, "Who has put pubic hair on my coke?" (In her book, Anita Hill recalled the

incident: "...I was twenty-five years old...standing in the middle of Thomas's office. By that time I had had several jobs and worked with many different people, but never before had anyone ever uttered such an absurdly vulgar and juvenile comment to me. Disgusted and shocked, I could only shake my head and leave the office. I heard him laughing as I closed the door.")

The audience sat transfixed, wondering if there could possibly be more along these same lines. They were not disappointed.

On other occasions he referred to the size of his own penis as being larger than normal and he also spoke on some occasions of the pleasures he had given to women with oral sex.

Professor Hill then said, in a statement that must have hit home with huge numbers of women, "At this point, late 1982, I began to feel severe stress on the job. I began to be concerned that Clarence Thomas might take out his anger with me by degrading me or not giving me important assignments. I also thought that he might find an excuse for dismissing me. In January of 1983, I began looking for another job...."

In the remainder of her statement, Anita Hill related that she had found a teaching job at Oral Roberts University in Tulsa, informed Clarence Thomas (whose response, she said, was to say that "now I would no longer have an excuse for not going out with him. I told him I still preferred not to.") and left the government and Washington. She stated that from 1983 to 1991 she had only seen Thomas twice. She said that over the years she had told very few people about Thomas's behavior, and then only with great reluctance. She closed by stating, "...when Senate staff asked me about these matters, I felt I had a duty to report. I have no personal vendetta against Clarence Thomas. I seek only to provide the committee with information which it may regard as relevant. It would have been more comfortable to remain silent. I took no initiative to inform anyone. But when I was asked by a representative of this committee to report my experience, I felt that I had to tell the truth. I could not keep silent."

* * * *

After she had finished reading her statement, Anita Hill was questioned by members of the committee about her statement. It soon became clear to million of viewers and listeners and readers that when it came to the emotionally charged issue of sexual harassment, the United States Senate, as represented by these 14 men, in the parlance of the day, simply didn't get it. And if the Democrats were bad, the Republicans were even worse. It was not, as both Paul Simon and Howard Metzenbaum admitted in separate interviews for this book in 2001, the Senate's finest hour.

Chairman Biden's questioning of Anita Hill was not exactly a model of the art of cross-examination, but then he, unlike the Republicans who followed him, was not out to destroy the witness and thus weaken the impact of her statement. He did, however, succeed in eliciting from her the name of a porno star she said Thomas had mentioned. In fact, the name was, for obvious reasons, Long *Dong* Silver, but Hill said "Long John Silver." Nonetheless, the introduction of this name was enough to produce thousands of mentions, from newspaper columnists to late night comedians, to say nothing of the man (and some women) on the street.

Senator Specter, a former big-city prosecutor, tried hard to make Hill out as a liar because she had not told the FBI the gross specifics of Thomas's comments to her of a sexual nature. But her responses seemed quite reasonable, and after a while his questioning took on a badgering tone. He also pressed hard to get her to admit that she had been promised by a staff person for a Democratic Senator on the Judiciary Committee that just making her charges against Thomas would be enough to cause him to withdraw as a nominee for the Supreme Court. There had been a newspaper story alleging this, but Hill denied it.

Howell Heflin, the Democrat from Alabama, lightened the proceedings somewhat, by virtue of his Southern accent and his rather quaint choice of words, as when he asked her, "Now, in trying to determine whether you are telling falsehoods or not, I have got to determine what your motivation might be—are you a scorned woman?" He also asked her if she had a "martyr complex." To audible laughter, she said no.

Senator Specter had another turn, after a recess, and again he wanted to know about the newspaper account that claimed a Senate staffer had told Hill she could make her charges secretly and that would be enough to get the nominee to step down. And again she denied the account, at least the way he characterized it. When he pressed her as to whether she had told the press that Thomas's actions toward her 10 years earlier were, legally speaking, sexual harassment, she not only got in her denial, but managed to add, "It seems to me that the behavior has to be evaluated on its own with regard to the fitness of this individual to act as an Associate Justice. It seems to me that even if it does not rise to the level of sexual harassment, it is behavior that is not befitting an individual who will be a member of the Court."

Like a pit bull with its jaws locked, Specter refused to let go of his point of inquiry, and moments later, Hill was able to expand her testimony, and explain (to the satisfaction of countless women in the viewing and listening audience who had tried for years to make the same point to male bosses and workplace superiors), "I did not bring this information forward to try to establish a legal claim for sexual harassment. I brought it forward so that the committee could determine the veracity of it, the truth of it, and from there on you could evaluate the information as to whether or not it constituted sexual harassment or whether or not it went to his ability to conduct a job as an Associate Justice of the Supreme Court."

After the dinner break, Utah Republican Senator Orrin Hatch got his chance to question the witness, but he passed, for the moment, choosing instead to make a brief conciliatory statement. A few minutes later, another conservative Republican, Alan Simpson of Wyoming, had the microphone.

Picking up where Specter had left off on the issue of why she hadn't told the FBI all of the sexual specifics to which she had just testified, the senator said, in reference to the public, "Well, I think they should know that the witness did not say anything to the FBI about the described size of his penis, about the pubic hair in the Coke story, and describing giving pleasure to women with oral sex...." He then entered the FBI report, a brief document, in the record.

Several other senators from both sides of the aisle made short statements, and then Chairman Biden, noting both the late hour and the fact that Judge Thomas wanted to be heard again before the day was over, called a dinner break at 7:40 p.m. He said the committee would reconvene at 9:00. Anita Hill had testified for seven hours, and despite the tone and tenor of the Republicans' questioning, she had held firm to her story. She had done an impressive job, for herself and for the issue of sexual harassment, and against Clarence Thomas.

* * * *

Clarence Thomas, John Danforth later reported, was steaming. He said, "How can the committee believe her? When is Biden going to be fair and rule some of this stuff out of order? Why doesn't he stop this lynching?...They all allowed me to be destroyed and no one had the guts—you know what it reminded me of, Jack? It reminded me of when I was in the seminary and guys would yell racial slurs

224

and nobody would stand up. That's wrong. The way I felt about the committee was that nobody was standing up and saying no. I mean the Republicans were fighting, but Biden, the chairman of the committee, who prides himself on fairness, wasn't standing up and saying this is wrong.

"So when I went up there I was exhausted and I was not going to tolerate them. They had wronged me. They had wronged this country. They had bastardized their own process. They had distorted it, it was a joke. No one should be put through that in this country. I wasn't going to let them off the hook. They weren't going to get off the hook and make me or this country believe that what they were doing was fair....

"They wouldn't let us subpoena her, anything about her, they didn't even want us to touch her. She had to be treated with kid gloves. There were no procedures. There were no rules of evidence. There were seven people there who had voted against me."

If Thomas's team was less than sanguine about the way things were going, the same could not be said for the nominee. Despite the fact that two television networks had already reported that the White House was wavering in its support to the point of considering withdrawing the nomination, Thomas, pleased with his performance earlier in the day, was actually looking forward to another shot at the committee.

Danforth wrote, "Ken Duberstein remembers that before Clarence left my office for his second appearance of the day before the committee he said, 'If you thought I did well this morning, tonight is going to be even better.'"

* * * *

Thomas wasted not a moment getting down to business. As soon as Biden asked him if he had anything to say, he was into it: "Senator, I would like to start by saying unequivocally, uncategorically that I deny each and every single allegation against me today that suggested in any way that I had conversations of a sexual nature or about porno-graphic material with Anita Hill, that I ever attempted to date her, that I ever had any personal sexual interest in her, or that I in any way ever harassed her."

Having got their attention, he turned up the volume.

"Second, and I think a more important point, I think that this today is a travesty. I think that it is disgusting. I think that this hearing should never occur in America. This is a case in which this sleaze, this dirt, was searched for by staffers of members of this committee, was then leaked to the media, and this committee and this body validated it and displayed it in prime time over our entire nation.

"How would any member on this committee or any person in this room or any person in this country like sleaze said about him or her in this fashion or this dirt dredged up and this gossip and these lies displayed in this manner? How would any person like it?

And then he played his ace. "The Supreme Court is not worth it. No job is worth it. I am not here for that. I am here for my name, my family, my life and my integrity. I think something is dreadfully wrong with this country, when any person, any person in this free country would be subjected to this. This is not a closed room."

Professor Hill had stunned the audience with her graphic depiction of the pubic-hair-on-the-Coke charge. Now the nominee was ready with some memorable lan-guage of his own.

"...This is not an opportunity to talk about difficult matters privately or in a closed environment. This is a cir-cus. It is a national disgrace. And from my standpoint, as a black American, as far as I am concerned, it is a high-tech lynching for uppity blacks who in any way deign to speak for themselves, to do for themselves, to have different ideas, and it is a message that, unless you kowtow to an older order, this is what will happen to you—you will be lynched, destroyed, caricatured by a committee of the U.S. Senate, rather than hung from a tree."

With that having been said, the questioning began, but it was pale in comparison. Clarence Thomas had stolen the committee's fire, had all-but-literally shaken his finger in its face. He had, to use the pop psychology phrase of today, gotten his power back.

In *Resurrection*, former Senator Danforth explains how Thomas came up with his most-quoted phrase: "I remember precisely where Clarence was when he spoke what would be the most memorable words of the hearing. He was sitting in the middle of the couch on the south wall of my office, and he said, 'You know what this is, Jack? This is a lynching. This is a high-tech lynching.' The idea was his. The words were his. No person put them in his mind. I said, 'Clarence, if that is how you feel, then go upstairs and say it....'

"It was exactly what he felt, and he said it with power, even in my office. He had heard tales of lynching as a boy in rural Georgia. He had read a book on lynching while in law school. He knew that claims of sexual misdeeds by black men gave rise to lynchings. This was not a hanging out in the woods; this was on national television. It was, indeed, a high-tech lynching."

Of all the people on Clarence Thomas's side, the one most pleased about his outburst and his choice of words was his mother. "Now *that*," she said most emphatically, "is the Clarence I know!"

* * * *

A heightened emotional state was also evident among Thomas's detractors. Carl Rowan, who Thomas often singled out as an "enemy," wrote:

The nominee was...brilliant...[but] What a bitter twist of fate. This black man who had, in hustling the favors of Bush and the right-wingers who currently controlled America, and who disparaged and ridi-

227

culed Thurgood Marshall, James Weldon Johnson, Roy Wilkins, and others who wiped out lynching, was now crying 'lynching' to justify his confirmation. This child of Georgia poverty who had, in modest success, exhorted blacks never to fall back on cries of 'racism,' was shouting 'racist lynching' in the most galling of ways.

Black Americans who considered Thomas a consummate con man knew that they were right....

The [Anita] Hill appearance provoked most members of the Judiciary committee to behave like sexist asses, who rushed to initiate a stupid, then half-abandoned Senate probe to try to find out who leaked the existence of the Hill charges that turned the Thomas hearings into such an agonizing test of their characters...[and] one of the wildest television spectacles, one of the nastiest plunges into sexual prurience in the nation's history...."

* * * *

There was another entire day to the hearings, also fully televised, during which a parade of witnesses, both pro and con, appeared before the committee. But for all intents and purposes, it was already over. To this day, anti-Thomas people such as former Senator Metzenbaum believe that if only the final two women witnesses, Rose Jourdain and Angela Wright, statements had been allowed to testify in person instead of submitting, the margin of victory would have been a margin of defeat. That is not, however, a widely-held belief.

On Tuesday, October 15, the Senate voted to 52-48 to approve the nomination of Clarence Thomas as the 106th Justice of the United States Supreme Court. In her Georgia kitchen, Leola Thomas, filled with pride for the singular accomplishment of her son, sang a hymn. Three days later, in a White House ceremony, President Bush said, "Celebrate this day. See what this son of Pin Point has made of himself."

Chapter Eleven
The United States Supreme Court

Clarence Thomas is going to surprise a lot of people.
He is going to be the people's justice.

–Senator John Danforth
October, 1991

My husband isn't going to owe anything to the groups
that opposed him.

–Virginia Lamp Thomas
October, 1991

To the delight of some and the astonishment and anger of many, the November 11, 1991, issue of *People* magazine bore, on its cover, a cheek-to-cheek, arms-around-each-other color photograph of Justice and Mrs. Clarence Thomas. Labeled an "exclusive," it was entitled, in huge letters, "How We Survived." The caption read: "The wife of Clarence Thomas describes the 'hell' of the hearings, her own experience with sexual harassment and her belief that Anita Hill 'was probably in love with my husband.'"

"Frankly, the confirmation process was hell," wrote 34-year-old Virginia Thomas. "We didn't have many good days, except maybe that first day, July 1, at Kennebunkport, when Bush announced the nomination. Clarence called me before he and the President went out to the press conference. We were in shock. I just said, 'Wow!' We never imagined what lay ahead. If we had, we never would have gone through it." She continued:

> We expected differences over political views but never imagined people would dig so low. At first there was this marijuana charge that evolved into a wild rumor he was doing drugs. That didn't stick, so people made up a crazy charge that he beat his wife. Then Clarence was attacked by the black leadership for his conservative political views. That was particularly painful. But by the end of September we thought the worst was over. Wrong. It was just beginning.
>
> I was at work at the Labor Department Sept. 25, the day Clarence got a call from the White House. 'There's been a new charge leveled,' someone told him, and then said they were sending the FBI over to the house to question him. When the two agents came, they said a charge of sexual harassment had been made against him by Anita Hill. He couldn't believe it. When I got home Clarence told me his heart sank when he heard that. It was just so devastating that this person he had always helped at every turn had said this. I told him it was so outrageous it would blow over, like the other charges that had come out of the shadows. But I could tell he was killing himself inside, searching to figure out why she would do this.
>
> What makes this whole Anita Hill thing so bizarre is that I was once sexually harassed at work—before I met Clarence. And for what that man did to me, I think Clarence could have killed him. It wasn't verbal harassment, it was physical. ...

Mrs. Thomas, who declined to provide any specifics, went on to explain how wonderfully supportive her husband had been ("He gave me the courage to go forward."), and asked, "How could all this [Hill's allegations] happen to a man who is so intolerant of sexual harassment?"...My case was also different from Hill's because what she did was so obviously political, as opposed to trying to resolve the problem. And what's scary about her allegations is that they remind me of the movie *Fatal Attraction* or, in her case, what I call the fatal assistant. In my heart, I always believed that she was probably someone in love with my husband and never got what she wanted."

She then takes the reader through the dark days before, during, and after the famous hearings, chronicling her and her husband's disappointment at Senator Biden for reneging on his promise of support, her husband's outrage and threat to withdraw his nomination when he heard Anita Hill was going to hold a press conference, and his befuddlement at the motives of his opponents. At one point she writes, "The Clarence Thomas I had married was nowhere to be found. He was just debilitated beyond anything I had seen in my life."

She described how they turned to prayer: "Clarence knew the next round hearings to begin that day was not the normal political battle. It was a spiritual warfare. Good versus evil. We were fighting something we didn't understand, and we needed prayerful people in our lives. We needed God.

"So the next morning, Wednesday, we started having these two couples in our home to pray for two or three hours every day. They brought over prayer tapes, and we would read parts of the Bible. We held hands and prayed. What got us through the next six days was God. We shut the kitchen blinds and turned on Christian praise music to survive the worst."

The extent to which their religious beliefs enabled them to get through this "hell" is evident throughout the article. Referring to the morning of October 11, when he would have to give the statement he'd written in the middle of the night, she says, "Later, after two hours of sleep, we walked into the hearing room, and people were lining the hallways, urging him on. 'Who are these people?' Clarence asked me, and I said, 'I think they are angels.'" And: "By the time the final Senate vote came, on Tuesday, Oct. 15, it was like we were riding on this magic carpet. We had put ourselves in a different world, listening to our Christian music at home and praying. Honestly, it could have gone either way, and it would have been okay.... He kept saying, 'Maybe I'm not supposed to be on the Supreme Court, and God has another purpose in mind.'"

As to why Anita Hill had leveled these charges against her husband, Virginia Thomas wrote, "I have my theories, but I don't have evidence. I believe the charges were politically motivated. You can tell because of the timing. We were hit with all of these charges, but they didn't get him. So his opponents had to keep digging deeper and deeper. Something about Clarence, a conservative black man, must threaten an important segment of our society."

The article ended with these two paragraphs:

> What hurts most in all this is that there are people out there who still might believe Anita Hill. My only prayer is that the truth comes out as fast as possible. I think Anita Hill was used in the sense that she never wanted her story to be public. She wanted to be one of the shadow people.
>
> I'm coming forward to thank everyone who believed in Clarence. I hope no one else has to go through what we went through. I also hope we have set a new low, that Americans in their outrage can say, 'No, there is a level at which it is disgusting, horrible and wrong.' And if the Senate's not going to stand up for what is right and wrong, then the American people have to. Enough is enough.

* * * *

The American people, at least the segment that reads *People* magazine, responded in great numbers. But it was not, statistically speaking, the response for which Virginia Thomas had hoped. Several issues later, the magazine ran a larger than usual Letters-to-the-Editor section, which it prefaced with this statement: "Virginia Thomas's account of what she and her husband, Supreme Court Justice Clarence Thomas, went through during the Senate confirmation hearings brought more letters than any other story this year. Overwhelmingly, correspondents condemned her decision to be interviewed and the Thomases to be photographed. Many were angry about Mrs. Thomas's suggestion that Anita Hill's charges of sexual harassment grew out of thwarted love for Justice Thomas."

Of the 15 letters the magazine printed, three were pro-Virginia Thomas and the remaining 12 were con. The first letter, from a woman in New York City, also took the magazine to task. Stating that she was "appalled" by the cover, the woman wrote, "To portray them as smiling heroes belies the deeply disturbing Senate confirmation process. The allegations made by Professor Hill raised very serious questions about Clarence Thomas's conduct and integrity. To then turn his struggle into something noble is beyond the pale. To elevate to cover-page material his wife's gratuitous conjectures about Anita Hill's affections shocks one's sensibilities. Many Americans, including myself, do not regard Justice Thomas's confirmation as a cause for celebration, and I, for one, would have hoped that *People* would have shown some restraint in sensationalizing this story."

A California woman wrote, "It would appear from Virginia Thomas's story that Justice Clarence Thomas should have been nominated for sainthood instead of the Supreme Court," but a Ms. Staley from Mississippi countered by saying, "Most readers will scoff at Virginia Thomas's declaration that the fiasco she and her husband were thrust into was 'spiritual warfare,' but many recognized it as just that. The battle ended victoriously, but the war is surely not over. We'll keep praying, Virginia. God bless!"

A brief letter from a woman in Chicago was followed by one from another woman, this one on the West Coast. The first read, "Virginia Thomas was right that the fight was 'good versus evil.' But I'm not sure that when she shut the kitchen blinds, she shut the good in and evil out." The second read, "There's a story told in law school about the counselor who, in his overeager defense of a client, stated he was so sure the man was innocent that the real culprit would come right through the door to the courtroom. The entire assemblage turned to the door except for the client. He knew no one would be coming. The jury convicted him. Thomas, by not listening to Anita Hill's testimony, showed he didn't need to watch that door either."

The Pulitzer Prize-winning novelist Alice Walker had this to say: "Black women around the country are sharing a rich chuckle at Virginia Thomas's assertion that she believes 'Anita Hill was probably in love with (her) husband.' The mistress on the plantation used to say the same thing about her female slave every time she turned up pregnant by the master. Most of us are thankful that the Goddess has seen fit to bless Virginia's life with the irresistible Clarence, who is sure to provide her with even more learning opportunities and enlightening experiences in the future, which are likely to be shared by the rest of the country and the world."

And a male attorney from Tennessee wrote that he found it "...incredible that the newest Justice on the Supreme Court would be pictured grinning and hugging his wife like the latest television celebrity—especially in light of what transpired during the confirmation hearings. I believe this is unbecoming of a justice and degrading to the court. Justice Thomas should be ashamed of himself, as should the President who appointed him."

That was not, however, the way the President who appointed him viewed the matter. In an interview with David Frost that aired on PBS two days before Christmas, 1991, George Bush made it clear that he, in fact, agreed with Mrs. Thomas.

> FROST: One of the most, hugest, controversies this year obviously was the Clarence Thomas nomination. When you used your famous words ["best-quali-fied"], would you rewrite those words at all now, picking the best man for the job on the merits?

> PRESIDENT: I think he proved to come out of that with enough support around this country that others agree with me. I think it was a very good choice. I think he'll make a superb justice, and he went through hell to get there.

* * * *

On taking his seat—the farthest to the right—the newest Justice of the United States Supreme Court had to play catch-up ball, to borrow an analogy from basketball, one of Clarence Thomas's favorite sports. He'd missed the first 17 days of the fall term, and had a great deal of official court reading to do, as well as hiring his first set of four law clerks. He later admitted that when he drove into the court's underground garage on his very first day as an associate justice, he said to himself, *What am I doing here?*

"The pace was a lot faster than I expected," he said in an early speech. "We review more than 7,000 requests to be heard each year. We have to read the briefs of the cases we are going to hear. The cases we hear on Monday, we have to vote on on Wednesday. Those we hear on Tuesday and Wednesday, we have to vote on on Friday. So you can't say, 'Oh, I'll get around to reading this later.' At the same time, you are either writing opinions or reviewing opinions written by the other eight justices. The work is more analysis of the law than philosophical; there is little time to sit and think about things on the job."

Thomas's civics class explications notwithstanding, his addition to the court was not an easy fit. As many court-watchers pointed out, he had been appointed and con-firmed (if barely) because he was a partisan, and the Pres-ident of the United States had wanted to send a message to both friends and enemies—"Take that!" As a result of the confirmation process, the public had not been educated in the beliefs and legal philosophies of Clarence Thomas, and thus had no real idea of how much intellectual firepower he might bring to the court—on which he could well sit for three or even four *decades*, given the longevity of many jus-tices. By supplying the committee with copies of his speeches and writings on such subjects as natural law, privacy (i.e., abortion), affirmative action, and civil rights in general, his opponents hoped to ignite a debate that would show he was too far outside the mainstream of contemporary American thought and action to be given a lifelong position, and vote, on the highest court in the land. But the nominee foiled their efforts by following the White House's suggestion and employing "the Pin Point strategy," and also by passing off his earlier statements as somehow irrelevant.

One commentator said, "The Thomas affair powerfully reinforced the idea that Supreme Court confirmations were not occasions for seriously evaluating the nominee's legal thinking and qualifications but rather election campaigns for political control of the Court, to be waged by any means necessary."

That commentator, attorney Edward Lazarus, has some intriguing qualifications himself. Now a federal prosecutor in Los Angeles, and a former clerk to Justice William Brennan, several years ago Lazarus surprised the legal world in general and stunned the small world of the Supreme Court specifically by publishing a tell-almost-all book about the Court. Entitled *Closed Chambers: The Rise, Fall, and Future of the Modern Supreme Court*, that book was aptly described in *Newsday* as "ambitious, opinionated, scholarly, gossipy...." Former Supreme Court clerks do not, as a rule, speak out or write about the inner workings of the court after they leave, and they most certainly do not do so with the candor found in this book, for which the author was roundly criticized. In fact, following the publication of, and furor over, *Closed Chambers*, Chief Justice Rehnquist instituted a policy change: instead of being barred from writing or speaking about the court while serving as clerks, they were now to be barred from writing about them *forever.*

Lazarus, who was a Supreme Court clerk three years before Thomas became a justice, makes some thought-provoking observations.

From the moment Thomas crossed the Court's threshold, he carried an aura of partisanship as well as indifference to the institutional culture to which he had ascended. Some of this was a matter of style or taste. For example, Thomas offended some Justices with an unusually political guest list for his installation [such as baseball great Reggie Jackson and Sylvester Stallone of Hollywood and "Rocky" fame], and shocked almost everyone by posing for the cover of *People* magazine with his wife and a Bible.

More substantively, at oral argument, Thomas not only remained unvaryingly silent but looked uninterested, often not even bothering to remove the rubber band from his stack of briefs. He also surrounded himself with uniformly archconservative clerks— including Chris Landau, a hand-me-down from Scalia who had found even his first boss insufficiently pure ideologically. Thomas gave these clerks enormous latitude, and they, with typical narrow-gauged zeal, crafted drafts remarkably provocative in result and

237

dismissive of any point of view other than their own.

Thomas's chambers exuded a sense of score settling. His wife spoke ominously about the Justice feeling that he "doesn't owe any of the groups who opposed him anything." Thomas himself reveled in distinguishing himself from prior appointees, such as Blackmun, who disappointed their political patrons by moderating their views once on the Court. As Thomas likes to tell his clerks, "I ain't evolving." And, as if to prove the point, he flouted convention (and the Code of Judicial Conduct, from which the Justices exempt themselves) by making public appearances on behalf of right-wing organizations that had backed his nomination. All in all, he presented a figure very different from the one who had assured the Senate, almost meekly, that "I have no agenda."

While it should be kept in mind that Edward Lazarus clerked for Harry Blackmun, who was hardly a conservative Justice, his observations of Thomas in the early months of his service on the court are not greatly at odds with those of other commentators and writers on the court. For example, the writings of historian and essayist Gary Wills on Clarence Thomas make Lazarus's work seem pale in comparison.

If there was one case that brought attention to Thomas—and howls of protest from his critics—in the first years it was *Hudson v. McMillian*, a case involving the issue of police brutality brought under the Eighth Amendment's cruel and unusual punishment clause. Keith Hudson, a prisoner in a state penitentiary in Louisiana sued three guards, claiming that while they were moving him—handcuffed and shackled—from one cell to another, they beat him severely. Among his injuries were a cracked dental plate, several loosened teeth, and facial bruises and swelling. He charged that one of the officers, a supervisor, refused to stop the other two from beating him, but did admonish them "not to have too much fun." A federal magistrate in Louisiana found for Hudson, but his finding that his injuries were minor proved to be an important point.

On appeal, the Fifth Circuit ruled against Hudson, holding, among other things, that Hudson had to have had a "significant" injury. Hudson's lawyers appealed to the Supreme Court which eventually ruled, 7-2, that the lower court had not applied the correct test, and that a prisoner's injury need not always be significant in order to be cruel and unusual punishment. The two dissenters, in one of the first of what would be a sizable number of cases over the next decade, were Antonin Scalia and Clarence Thomas. (In fact, Thomas wrote the opinion and Scalia joined him.) In his dissent, Thomas said that while "punching a prisoner in the face," as Justice Sandra Day O'Connor phrased it in her opinion for the majority, was wrong under other legal pre-scriptions, it was not cruel and unusual punishment as he read the findings of the prevailing cases on the subject.

The reaction to Clarence Thomas's dissent in the Hudson case was not just harsh, it was the harshest he would receive in his decade on the Supreme Court. *The New York Times* called him, editorially, "the youngest, cruelest justice." In Washington, the *Post* said, "mind-boggling." Its generally liberal black columnist William Raspberry was incensed. Speaking directly to the Justice, he closed his col-umn by writing, "Of course I don't expect that you will always do what strikes the rest of us as 'the right thing.' But why go out of your way to do the wrong?"

In a 1994 lecture, Federal Judge A. Leon Higginbotham, author of a famous open letter to Thomas shortly after his confirmation taking him to task for turning his back on his African-American heritage, labeled Thomas's views and legal theories as the 20th-century equivalent of *Plessy v. Ferguson* and *Dred Scott*. At about that same time, however, Thomas was praised by former Judge Robert Bork, who wrote in the *National Review*, that Clarence Thomas was "a tough-minded judge who cares about law more than popular results." He was, said Bork, "a bright spot" on the court.

(In a footnote to his treatment of Thomas's dissent in *Hudson*, Edward Lazarus wrote: "Critics noted that Thomas's view seemed to conflict with his poignant confirmation hearing testimony about watching busloads of prisoners from his window and saying to himself 'almost every day, there but for the grace of God go I.' Less remarked on is the fact that Thomas's opinion not only was drafted by Landau but was nothing more than a warmed-over version of a memo Landau had written for his former boss, Scalia.")

In 1996, law professor and legal scholar Jeffrey Rosen (who teaches law at the George Washington University and is legal affairs editor of *The New Republic*) wrote what amounted to a defense, or at least a partial one, of Thomas in the "Annals of the Law" section of *The New Yorker*, which is hardly a conservative organ. Entitled "Moving On," its explanatory subtitle is, "In his latest incarnation, Justice Clarence Thomas takes his text from Booker T. Washington." The article presents an interesting picture of what its author seems to view as at a partial coming-of-age for Thomas.

After noting Thomas's penchant for silence ("Alone among his colleagues, Thomas rarely asks questions from the bench...."), Rosen pointed out that in two recent court conferences—the regular twice-weekly sessions in which all nine justices sit around a huge conference table and discuss the case or cases at hand, Thomas spoke up to add *personal* notes. In one he said, according to Rosen, that he was the only justice at the table who had attended a segregated school, and later to recount some of the travails of his grandfather, Myers Anderson. His point, particularly in regard to the latter story, was that his grandfather had made it without affirmative action, and that was the way things should be because the Constitution should be "color-blind."

"The idea of Clarence Thomas passionately engaged by questions of racial justice is not easy to reconcile," wrote Jeffrey Rosen, "with images that have been frozen in the public eye. In the aftermath of his tumultuous confirmation hearings...the youngest justice seemed traumatized, and consumed by rage.... Over the past year or so, however, a less bitter and more influential Thomas has begun to emerge, both inside and outside the Court."

He travels around the country, preaching a muscular message of self-help and ethnic pride. According to his clerks, he receives a great deal of mail, and he replies to each letter, on the ground that anyone whose character is strong enough to defy black opinion-makers deserves a response. And Thomas continues to have long conversations about race with some of the black conservatives he first encountered in the nineteen-eighties. This group includes Thomas Sowell and Shelby Steele of the Hoover Institution, Walter Williams of George Mason University, and Glenn Loury of Boston University. To them, he has revealed a racially compassionate side that has not been visible to outsiders.

According to Rosen, all this stems from the fact that Thomas has "an unlikely intellectual hero, Booker T. Washington," the champion of black self-sufficiency. "Yet," he writes, "Justice Thomas still finds himself a social and political pariah. Among members of the civil rights establishment in particular, Thomas is vilified in terms that would be inconceivable for other black officials, let alone other Supreme Court Justices." For example, says Rosen, "At the NAACP's annual convention in July, Thomas was denounced as a 'pimp' and a 'traitor.'"

At the end of the chapter of *Closed Chambers* in which he treats Justice Clarence Thomas, former Supreme Court clerk Edward Lazarus writes:

Thomas was chosen because of his sharp-edged politics, an edge since tempered in the flame of public trial. According to his own mentor, Senator Danforth, during the confirmation nightmare, Thomas was reduced to uncontrollable fits of weeping, vomiting, hyperventilating, and writhing on the floor. Even before Anita Hill, he suffered visions of people trying to kill him. After, he envisioned his guts being pulled out and his life and family destroyed [In a footnote, Lazarus gives his source—a December 19, 1994 *New Republic* article by Jeffrey Rosen]. What such man wouldn't be bitter, wouldn't surround himself with aggressive and loyal foot soldiers, wouldn't try to help out those who stood by him in his hour of need. If Anita Hill told the truth, Thomas's enemies had humiliated him, exposed him, forced him into lying. If she lied, all the worse.

Either way, the cost to the Court was substantial. To an institution already desperately short on mutual trust, self-restraint, and intellectual integrity, Thomas brought not only ideology but an inner rage, a willingness to sacrifice every inch of his personal dignity to satisfy his own ambition, and the deep scars of one who thinks himself grievously wronged. These are not ingredients that make for balanced, impartial, collegial judgment, and they ensured that Thomas's wounds would only add to those the Court had already inflicted on itself.

So who is right? Lazarus? Or Rosen, who says that just a few years later Clarence Thomas had become, in fact if not in appearance, a much more collegial justice? The answer, quite possibly, and strange as it may sound, may be: both of them. Even if, as seems to be the case, Thomas *is* a more collegial justice and one who has carved out for himself a respectable legal position that he applies consistently, he may still be, because of his continuing political partisanship and his ongoing sense of victimization, a divisive and therefore harmful presence on the highest court of the land.

As legal scholar and law professor George Anastaplo put it in an article for the University of South Dakota Law Review in 1998, "Both Clarence Thomas and various of his key defenders regarded the challenge they faced," in getting him through the confirmation process and onto the Court, "as warlike—and by so doing they contributed further to the violence which we already have too much of in our society. They reinforce thereby the influence of those who believe that all differences of opinion come down to a struggle for power, not to a search for truth."

* * * *

One of the problems, at least as far as the general public is concerned, is that to the layman reading accounts of Supreme Court decisions in the popular press or hearing of them on television or radio, Thomas's position often seems to be that of the heavy. He sounds the way he appeared the last time they saw him on television—on his second appearance before the Senate Judiciary Committee—angry and even mean. The image projected by the accounts of his (and Scalia's) dissent in *Hudson*, the prisoner-beating case, that of Mr. Insensitive, has been projected anew in a number of other cases.

For example, in a voting rights case in 1994 (*Holder v. Hall*), Thomas didn't just vote with the majority (Rehnquist, O'Connor, Scalia and Kennedy) to overturn a win for the black plaintiffs, he wrote a very lengthy concurring opinion in which he stated this belief that this type of action was not covered by the Voting Rights Act (or the 14th or 15th Amendments to the Constitution). In a pamphlet ("Courting Disaster") put out for use during the presidential campaign of 2000 to alert voters as to what they might encounter if George Bush were elected and fulfilled his promise to name more judges like Scalia and Thomas to the Supreme Court, the liberal activist group People For the American Way stated that if the position advocated by Thomas and Scalia in *Holder* had been adopted by the majority, it "...would have done great damage to the nation's progress toward ensuring all Americans an equal opportunity to participate and be heard in our democratic system."

"Not only would Thomas and Scalia's position in *Holder* sharply diminish the protections provided by the Voting Rights Act of 1965 (VRA)," it continued, "it would also overturn 30 years of Supreme Court precedent and at least three congressional reauthorizations of the Act.... The Thomas-Scalia position ignores the legislative history that shows Congress intended the Voting Rights Act to be interpreted broadly as a powerful tool to root out discriminatory election practices. Justices Stevens, Blackmun, Souter and Ginsburg criticized the Thomas-Scalia opinion, calling their position 'radical' and estimating that it would have required the overturning or reconsideration of at least 28 previous Supreme Court decisions holding that the Voting Rights Act of 1965 should be interpreted broadly to prohibit racial discrimination in all aspects of voting."

Of Thomas's reasoning in the Hudson case, George Anastaplo wrote, "The artificiality of the Thomas argument in Hudson is part and parcel of his generally mechanical approach to legal issues. This is symptomatic, I suspect, of his limitations as a student of the law. Also symptomatic here is how Justice Thomas talks about precedents: sometimes he makes too much of them, at other times he can be cavalier about them. He does not yet seem to appreciate that *he* is on the Supreme Court. Perhaps that will come in time."

One of the earliest cases in Thomas's service, *Lee v. Weisman*, also drew quite a bit of popular attention. In this, a First Amendment case involving school prayer, the high court ruled 5-4 that a mandatory prayer at a Rhode Island public high school graduation ceremony was unconstitutional. According to Thomas (and Scalia and Rehnquist and White) in dissent, there was no Constitutional problem with a state-imposed prayer at an official public event.

* * * *

In March of 2000, the Black Law Students' Association of American University's Washington College of Law sponsored a panel discussion entitled, "Clarence Thomas After 10 Years." The participants were: Nancie Marzulla, founder and president of Defenders of Property Rights; Scott D. Gerber, professor of law at Roger Williams Law School in Rhode Island and the author of *First Principles: The Jurisprudence of Clarence Thomas*; and two member of AU's law school faculty, Mark Niles, who'd been in private practice (with Hogan & Hartson) and spent four years as an appellate lawyer with the Department of Justice, and Stephen Wermiel, associate director of the law school's Program on Law and Government, and for 12 years a correspondent for *The Wall Street Journal*. The discussion was moderated by NBC television anchor Joe Johns, who is also a law student at American University.

In their wide-ranging remarks, the four speakers managed to cover the landscape of opinions regarding the 106th Justice of the United States Supreme Court, from his judicial philosophy as seen in specific cases to the diversity of public opinion from the perspective of 10 years on the bench—and 10 years after his most contentious confirmation hearing.

Ms. Marzulla mentioned that when she, then an attorney with the Civil Rights Division of the Justice Department, met Clarence Thomas in the mid-1980s, she was "...even then, struck by his ability to cut through complexity to get to the heart of an issue." As proof, she recalled that he once asked her, without any preamble, to name what she thought was the most important civil rights issue facing the nation. When she answered "voting rights," he immediately answered, in what she called typical Clarence Thomas fashion, "No, that's not right. The answer is discrimination. We have not in this nation, rooted out invidious discrimination, and until we do this will remain our number-one problem in the civil rights arena." Marzulla characterized that answer as being quintessentially Clarence Thomas," adding, "Whereas I had focused on hair-splitting and the inadequacies of the regulatory regime, he, instead, had leapt immediately to the heart of the issue, the crux of civil rights protection, and I think this approach to decision-making is evident in his decision-making today."

Stating that in her area of the law, property rights and the protection or lack of protection thereof, Thomas's judicial opinions reflected "a strong fidelity to textualism," she suggested that in that respect "Justice Thomas can almost be seen as a modern-day Justice Hugo Black. Justice Black used to say that because the First Amendment very plainly says that Congress shall make no law abridging the freedom of speech, it means just that: Congress shall make no law. I can very easily imagine Justice Thomas today saying something very similar. However, that is not to suggest that Justice Thomas's philosophy is in any way hampered or burdened by an artificial emphasis on structuralism or a wooden formulaic approach to decision-making, certainly not with respect to constitutional interpretations. Rather, his decisions are animated by his strong commitment to the founding principles upon which this country was formed."

She said that in his decade on the high court, Justice Thomas has emerged as "a sturdy and reliable column that supports the 5-4 majority so often seen in key decisions involving the just compensation and due process clauses of the Fifth Amendment, as well as decisions in a number of important environmental law cases."

The next speaker was Professor Gerber, whose most recent book, *First Principles*, covers Justice Thomas's first five years on the Supreme Court. He recalled that when the book came out he was asked to speak to a similar group about it, and the law student who'd invited him sent him an e-mail message that said, "Please provide me information concerning the substance of your talk. Are you supporting Clarence Thomas? Are you against him?" Gerber said his answer to that was neither: "I simply started following Mr. Thomas because of work I had been doing on the relationship between the Declaration of Independence and the Constitution."

In his Introduction, Gerber said his research convinced him that Thomas was both "articulate enough and prolific enough" to warrant a book-length study after just his first five years on the Court. That, he said, and the fact that Thomas "has fascinated the American people like no other Supreme Court justice ever has." He told the audience at American University that in *First Principles* he had tried to "move beyond Anita Hill" to study those first five years to see what he had done on the court and what reactions that received, and in doing so he had found, essentially, that "People judge Justice Thomas as they judged *nominee* Thomas—in almost purely partisan terms. The left strongly dislikes his jurisprudence and the right strongly approves of it." The same was true, he said, of the reviews of his book. The left liked the book until he agreed with Justice Thomas, and the right liked it until he *dis*agreed. The other major conclusion he came to was that "Justice Thomas is *not* simply Justice Scalia's loyal apprentice. He has written many provocative opinions, separate opinions primarily, and many with which Justice Scalia declined to join, such as the dissenting opinion in the Lopez case."

Gerber made an interesting distinction when he said, "On civil rights questions, he's what I term a *liberal* originalist, and on civil liberties and federalism questions, he's a *conservative* originalist. He appeals in race questions to the principle of inherent equality at the heart of the Declaration of Independence—'the natural law thing,' to quote Senator Biden from the hearings—and with regard to civil liberties and federalism, he does what Robert Bork would have done had he been confirmed, and that is ask how James Madison would have decided the question." His final conclusion in regard to Thomas's first five years on the Court, said Gerber, was that Justice Thomas, "…like everyone else on the Court, seems to write judicial opinions that read very much like his prior policy speeches, especially in civil rights, the area in which he has the most prior experience."

As for the second five years, the post-acclimation period, Gerber pointed out that the justice himself had said that his "rookie years were over, and you would see a difference," but, Gerber noted that he also said, in response to criticism, that he was "not evolving." As for recent decisions, Gerber said Thomas's jurisprudential framework was unchanged: he was still very "individualistic" on civil rights questions, and still very "Borkian" on civil liberties and federalism.

Gerber said that Thomas's influence was "still limited primarily to separate opinions, i.e., concurring opinions or dissenting opinions," as opposed to majority opinions. He expanded this idea by pointing out that in these non-majority opinions of the post-acclimation period, Thomas the originalist often goes out of his way to suggest that certain well-established areas of the law should be, to use Gerber's word, "rethought."

The last two speakers, Mark Niles and Stephen Wermeil, both AU law professors, were not as favorably inclined toward Justice Thomas as the first two had been. Mark Niles, who identified himself as a "dyed-in-the-wool, left-leaning Democrat," said he'd had misgivings when he learned of Clarence Thomas's nomination, but not terribly serious ones, because he didn't happen to believe that all African-Americans should have the same views. He said he'd prefer to see more of them as "free agents," politically speaking.

In fact, he said, he originally thought that having a conservative black American on the Supreme Court might "invigorate the political dynamic." After a while, however, that view began to change. It wasn't so much Thomas's politics, Niles said, but what he called "a glowing set of inconsistencies that began to arise between some of his beliefs and some of his other beliefs and actions. And, with all due respect to a man who was highly accomplished before he became a Supreme Court Justice," he continues to have "serious concerns about these inconsistencies to this day."

His first concern was that Thomas (and others like Robert Bork) who stressed interpreting the law, not making it, were, in fact, and especially over the last 10 years, doing the latter, not the former. "If this court, and these five justices including Justice Thomas, are willing to ignore the language of the Constitution and precedent when they see fit, then what really was their problem with the decisions of the Warren Court?" What so worries him about Justice Thomas, he told the assemblage, was Thomas's "enthusiastic participation in this mission."

His other concerns were that during the highly contentious confirmation hearing, Thomas had said he believed Anita Hill's charges to be "racially motivated." Niles said he was "particularly bothered" by Thomas's use of the phrase "high-tech lynching for uppity blacks," in light of the nominee's history of being "extremely willing to reject allegations of discrimination raised by others." Another concern was Thomas's lengthy history of having opposed affirmative action after having accepted it in his own case—and then later trying to split hairs and call it something other than what it actually was. Finally, Professor Niles said he was bothered by Thomas's accepting President Bush's description of him as being the "best-qualified" person for the nomination, and also agreeing, in public statements, with Bush's comment that race had played no part in his selection.

Mark Niles closed by saying that he is sure Justice Thomas is a "good and honorable man" who could become, he believes, just like the man he replaced on the court, "a role model for a segment of the nation in need of one.

"I was in my five-year-old daughter's classroom yesterday and saw a picture of Thurgood Marshall on the wall for Black History Month, and wondered if, no, hoped that, some day Clarence Thomas's picture might also be on that wall."

Professor Wermiel, the former *Wall Street Journal* reporter, said the reading he did in preparation for the panel had caused him to be struck by a number of things, one being that "Clarence Thomas would have been more comfortable as a Justice nominated in 1791, or even 1891, instead of 1991, because what he seems to hold most dear is the original intent of the Constitution."

Wermiel took issues with several conceptions regarding Thomas that he feels are wrong, one being that Thomas does not care deeply about anything. Wermiel says Clarence Thomas cares deeply about *the state*, in fact it is the thing about which he cares most deeply, and he does so at the expense of the individual. He cited Thomas's dissent in the prison-beating case (*Hudson*) as one in which he cared more about the importance of the state being allowed to set the standard, not the federal government, rather than what had happened to the prisoner. He said this same observation could be made of Thomas's positions in cases involving school desegregation, term limits, partial-birth abortion, and the Gun Free School Act and the Violence Against Women Act.

Having noted that, Wermiel said, "One searches in vain in his opinions for any evidence that Thomas is also concerned about the jurisprudence of the last 50 years, which has been about valuing humanity and individual rights and individual dignity. You get a sense from reading these opinions [in the prisoner-beating case and the partial-birth abortion case] that Thomas's view of the Constitution, at least as to individual rights, is just plain stingy."

Wermiel then flipped the coin and mentioned examples of instances in which he thought Thomas has been treated unfairly. One was the idea that he is a Scalia clone: "Most people say that because he and Scalia vote together exceedingly often, and it is true that they do, but consider this: over the last eight terms, their level of agreement was about 87%, which is very high by the Court's standards. *But*, in the last eight years that they were on the court together, William Brennan and Thurgood Marshall averaged agreement of 94.3%."

He closed by talking about Thomas's refusal to ask questions. "I would just urge him to get over it! To be perfectly honest, and I say this as a compliment, if you've ever heard Clarence Thomas's voice it's as eloquent and commanding a deep baritone as I've ever heard. I'd be more concerned, not that people wouldn't understand him, but that he might scare the hell out of them because his voice is so overpowering."

Finally, echoing several of the other speakers, Wermiel stated that he was bothered by Thomas's "engaging in his own brand of judicial activism. One of my images of a justice who is *not* an activist is that he or she sticks to the cases before them and does not go roaming across the Constitutional landscape. Clarence Thomas is building up a remarkable record, in separate opinions, of extending open invitations to litigants to bring the next case forward. That's not my idea of a conservative justice. A conservative justice ought to be deciding the cases before him, and not extending engraved invitations across the constitutional landscape."

* * * *

If law professors and legal scholars are, at least to a certain extent, reassessing their views of Clarence Thomas, how

251

about the American public? Has its opinion of the 106th justice, the Silent Justice, changed over the last 10 years? When they think of Clarence Thomas, do they still see, in their mind's eye, the angry defiant figure who dared the Senate Judiciary Committee to push him so much as an inch further? Or do they see the smiling, accessible, noticeably grayhaired Clarence Thomas who met with a group of high school students on the day after the Court decided the fate of the 2000 election in *Bush v. Gore*, and told them, among other things, that politics had played no role in the Court's deliberations? Do they see the Clarence Thomas of the *Hudson* case, or the Clarence Thomas who remembers to acknowledge, in a roomful of dignitaries, "my buddy Mark?"

One way of answering that is to see how the media portrayed him as his first decade on the Court—a court on which he himself has said he may serve until the year 2034—drew to a close. Quite possibly the best of the Thomas-watchers, and a reporter who may well write her own book on the Justice one day, Joan Biskupic has been covering Thomas for as long as he's been on the high court, first for *The Washington Post* and since 2000 for *USA Today*. In late January 2001, she began a long piece about him with this sentence: "With the world hanging on the U.S. Supreme Court's every word, he was, as always, the silent justice." But that image, she writes, has begun to change. "Now in his 10th year, Thomas is a bolder, more assured jurist—outside the court, at least.

"More than any other justice, he has become a commentator on society, striking out at liberalism and the way the media affect contemporary culture and making the case for religion in public life. Lacing his public speeches with references to 'the battle' and telling his mostly conservative audiences to 'never give in,' Thomas is embracing ideals he distanced himself from during his confirmation hearings, when supporters cast him as more moderate."

"At 52, he also continues to express bitterness about how he was treated during the hearings and seems to relish delivering a pointed message to critics: I'm still here.

"I am very comfortable being alone in my views," he said last fall in a speech.... "They think they can bully me. They've got the wrong guy. I will not be bullied."

While Biskupic reports that even such liberal court-watchers as Cass Sunstein of the University of Chicago Law School now speak much more respectfully of Thomas, she suggests that he does not really care all that much about such things. But he still *does* care, and quite a bit, about what happened to him in that U.S. Senate hearing room in 1991. She closed her article with these sentences: "'I blame people in leadership positions,' he said of the U.S. Senate, which was held by Democrats at the time of his confirmation. 'I can assure you of this: I will do my job as a member of the court a hell of a lot better than they did theirs.'"

Lest there be any doubt about the matter, Clarence Thomas, for all his silence, is here to tell friend and foe alike that he is in *this* battle for the long haul.

Afterword

Evolution and Evaluation

At the beginning of this effort, I described Clarence Thomas as an enigma. Now, many months and many hundreds of research hours later, I still feel the same way. I also wrote at that point that his friends loved him, his enemies hated him, and those in the middle were few and far between. That, too, has not changed. Nor, as indicated at the end of the last chapter, has his attitude. He is open and giving on the one hand, and uptight and defiant on the other, and thus he remains, as the King of Siam would say to Anna, "a puzzlement."

The following comments were elicited for this book from people chosen specifically because of their different connections to Justice Thomas. It is hoped that by seeing these varying views the reader may get a glimpse of the whole man.

* * * *

One attorney who has been watching Clarence Thomas with special interest ever since his name first surfaced in the late 1980s as an outside possibility for the Supreme Court is Sarah Weddington, the lawyer who "won" *Roe v. Wade* back in 1973 (when she was 26 years old). Today, Weddington, who provided an exclusive interview for this book, teaches law to undergraduates at the University of Texas in Austin, where she also has a law office. As a fierce protector of the right she worked so hard—at such a young age—to win for all American women, Ms. Weddington has kept a close eye on the Court and its make-up, both actual and potential, for nearly three decades.

In preparation for this interview, I looked back over my testimony before the Senate Judiciary Committee on September 19, 1991, which was after Clarence Thomas had appeared and been questioned by the Committee, but before the news broke about Anita Hill's allegations. The following are parts of a few key statements. "I have followed these hearings with great interest, but Judge Thomas's testimony here has been frustrating and *un*enlightening. What we have learned is that he has had wonderful and careful coaching about how to avoid political pitfalls. What we have seen is a nominee who was willing to answer questions only on issues that are politically safe, and who has been deliberately evasive on the critical issue of a woman's fundamental right to privacy.... This panel should demand the same certainty and clarity of Judge Thomas, given his fundamental endorsement of an extreme position that would abolish the fundamental right to choose. To vote to confirm Judge Thomas, when he has responded with only evasion would be to treat the right to choose abortion as a second-class right...."

Then I point out how he had said things in various contexts that indicate he was opposed to abortion, and then at the hearings he was saying, well, I didn't really mean that.

Never, until these confirmation hearings, did Judge Thomas seek to clarify his views or to distance himself from that highly-publicized controversial report. He referred to the Republican Party's opposition to abortion as likely to attract African-Americans to the Republican Party. Every sign from his record points in one direction: Judge Thomas, if confirmed, would vote to overturn *Roe v. Wade*. Judge Thomas's repeated references to the issue of abortion, at a minimum, undercuts the credibility of his statement that he has no opinion on *Roe v. Wade* and has never debated the contents.... In particular, a careful reading of the transcript reveals that in his responses to Senator Biden's deliberate and repeated questions, Judge Thomas avoided saying even that an individual has *any* fundamental right to privacy, including the right to use contraception, that is based on the liberty, due process clause of the 14th Amendment. "

When I look back, there are several things that strike me for this ten year period. First is the tragedy, in my mind, of Clarence Thomas being appointed to, and having been for these years, the only black justice. Many of us who have worked hard to support diversity and the principles of affirmative action so admired Justice Marshall, particularly for his sensitivity to people, and so to have him replaced with Clarence Thomas is almost an insult to the chair that Justice Marshall occupied. What was clear in the hearings was that Clarence Thomas was trying to avoid even owning up to things he had said, things he clearly believed in, and we can look back after ten years and see that what I had said at those hearings about abortion is absolutely correct.

257

Based on what he had said and written before those hearings, I had predicted that he would vote against *Roe v. Wade* every opportunity he had, and that is exactly what has happened. If you look at the three people who consistently vote to overturn *Roe v. Wade*, it is Scalia, Thomas and Rehnquist, Rehnquist being the only one who was on the bench at the time *Roe v. Wade* was heard.

Sarah Weddington's two other points are, first, that when she and the other women on her panel (Faye Waddleton of Planned Parenthood, Kate Michelman of NARAL, and former Maine governor Maxine Kunin), "...said at the time what his positions would be, the senators on the Committee said, 'Oh, not really.' But, *yes*, really. He's done exactly what we predicted."

Her other point involved Clarence Thomas as a member of the Court.

There are a number of decisions of Sandra Day O'Connor's that I disagree with, nonetheless I respect her as a member of the United States Supreme Court because she is someone who participates in the discussions during the hearings, asks very good questions, and writes opinions that are well-substantiated. The sad part is that Clarence Thomas is somebody who almost never asks questions. The problem is not quite that he's uninterested, but that he certainly is not a pivotal point on the court, not someone who you as an attorney would reach out to as a leader in terms of the Court's philosophy. Some people have referred to him as "Scalia's shadow," because whatever Scalia does, Thomas seems to be right there saying, "Me too." So I think the disappointment is partly his lack of impact on the court other than as a back-up for Scalia and Rehnquist.

When it comes to his work on the Supreme Court over the past ten years, the phrase that comes to my mind is "Missing in Action."

As for the nominee's famous answer that he had never discussed *Roe v. Wade*, the lawyer who won the case says, simply, "I don't believe that—didn't believe it then, don't believe it now."

* * * *

Eliot Minceberg, chief counsel for the liberal activist group People for the American Way, is another lawyer who believes that Clarence Thomas should not have been appointed or confirmed. Nor does he see anything positive in the Justice's decade of service on the high court. Whereas Sarah Weddington still gets worked up about Clarence Thomas 10 years after his confirmation, Eliot Minceberg talks about him quietly, in measured tones and respectful terms. Yet his views are equally negative.

Do I see Justice Thomas changing? You never can tell, it's a lifetime job, so who knows. But I think he's gotten into a pattern. He continues to get tremendous reinforcement from this society of right-wing folks he talks before and associates with, and I don't expect at this point any significant change in his jurisprudence. I hate to say we told you so, but this is pretty much what we, and many other critics of his, thought we'd see from a Justice Clarence Thomas. In some cases he may have been even a little worse than we predicted, but I think what we have seen along these lines is what we were expecting.

As to the question of whether or not, in his opinion, Thomas has "grown" on the court in the sense of jurisprudential or judicial development, Minceberg says, "I think the only change has been that he has found, more, his own

259

voice. In the early days, he generally would simply go along with Scalia and write not much of his own opinion, but now he's found his own voice, and sometimes he's to the right of Scalia—if it's possible to believe that—on issues like the limited power of Congress and things of that nature.

"I don't think there is any moderation whatsoever in his points of view. I heard parts of his AEI speech and read others, and I think it reflects, unfortunately, his attitude. He remains quite embittered by the confirmation controversy. He sees a lot of things in an 'us versus them' format, and I think he now feels that with Republicans in the White House and in the Congress that he can, as he did, come out a little bit, and say, 'Let's go get 'em.' I think that's very unfortunate. One of the whole purposes of lifetime tenure is in some way to take Supreme Court justices out of politics and let them step back and look more broadly at what's going on, and I don't have a sense that Thomas is there.

"And that anger is not going away. Part of that is that over the last ten years the criticism of him from what I would consider the mainstream bar of African-Americans and other minority lawyers has, if anything, become more pronounced. I went to an NAACP lawyers' committee group a couple of years ago, and someone was doing a review of the Supreme Court, and when the fellow said, "Now let's talk about some of Thomas's opinions," there were snickers and moans in the crowd.... And, in addition to his continuing to try to please the people who appointed him, there's no question that he is activist in the sense that he would like to shift the law very dramatically in a number of areas."

As to whether or not Justice Thomas is carving out and putting his own stamp on a particular judicial philosophy, attorney Minceberg says, "There are some aspects of a judicial philosophy, although frankly I believe that both he and Scalia, to a very large extent, are very results oriented, and you can easily find contradictions. For example, the whole emphasis that they usually give on states' rights is flatly contradicted by the opinions in *Bush v. Gore*. Overriding his judicial philosophy is, for both him and Scalia, a clear interest in particular kinds of results, justified on political or other grounds. But in most of the cases, the philosophy certainly reflects a profound disregard for and distrust of Congress as a coordinate branch, a veneration of states' rights and states' prerogatives, an interest certainly in natural law (although that is such a vague and nebulous concept that it's hard to know exactly where it goes), and an interest in his version of original intent, though, again, as people like Justice Souter have pointed out, original intent can mean very dramatically different things to different people. Those are certainly aspects of his judicial philosophy that run through a lot of his opinions, but I think they are overlaying a very strong sense of results orientation."

Summing up, Minceberg says, "In the sense that one defines 'growth' in a positive way, I have not seen anything that I would regard as that. There are a *few* aspects. If there is any growth in a positive direction, it would be in those occasional situations where he, along with Scalia, will reflect a certain libertarian bent.

"When it comes to actions by government imposed directly on individuals, occasionally there'll be a joining on a First Amendment issue, though what he and Scalia do is to narrowly constrict the scope of the First Amendment. But once it's within the scope of the First Amendment, he can be reasonably protective of it, and maybe that is a certain amount of growth, but I don't know that it reflects any major changes."

* * * *

Two former United States Senators who were members of Clarence Thomas's "jury," the Senate Judiciary Committee, and who retain strong opinions about the Justice 10 years later are former Senators Paul Simon and Howard

261

Metzenbaum. In separate interviews for this book in the spring of 2001, both spoke freely about their feelings, then and now.

Howard Metzenbaum, who has been heading the Consumer Federation of America since 1996, a year after he retired, by his own choice not the voters', from the U.S. Senate, says there's not a day goes by he doesn't miss the action on Capitol Hill ("If I'd known my son-in-law was going to lose, I'd have never stepped down!"). Of the fall 1991 hearings, he said, "There was a greater sense of excitement and emotion than I'd ever seen before. Perhaps there were others that were more tense, but this was extremely tense. I suspect that these were more tense and exciting than the Bork hearings because here, of course, you had a female factor."

As for Clarence Thomas the person, Metzenbaum minces few words. "I think he's a very insecure man, and that's evident in his service on the Supreme Court. Most of the time it's Scalia, and Thomas votes with him. As for those people who say how smart he is, in my experience with him I never had the feeling he was that smart. I don't *study* what the Supreme Court does, but I certainly pay attention to what they do, and I almost never see an opinion by Clarence Thomas, and I don't think I've ever seen an instance in which he voted differently than Justice Scalia.

"I'll be blunt about it: he never should have been confirmed. To this day, it's my opinion that if those two other witnesses [Angela Wright and Rose Jourdain] who wanted to be heard had testified, it's not at all impossible he would not have been confirmed. Simpson and Hatch urged Biden just to take their statements and put them in the record. I consider it one of my big defeats that I was not successful in defeating him. I would have performed a service to America if we had defeated him.

"He hasn't made a great justice, and when the incumbent President says the two members of the Supreme Court for whom he has the greatest respect are Scalia and Thomas,

I sort of look askance. Scalia is a very smart guy, but Thomas is not a great credit to the Supreme Court. Putting aside his political philosophy and his conservative credo, Justice Thomas doesn't deserve to be on the Supreme Court. He doesn't have the intellect to be a member of the Court, and that's the reason, in my opinion, that you see Thomas voting with Scalia so often."

As for whom he believed, Clarence Thomas or Anita Hill, former Senator Metzenbaum says, "I think we didn't know the whole story of their relationship, but I think she was telling the truth." And he was not? "I'm inclined to think that, but I have no proof of that, and that's why I wouldn't want to make that charge."

Reading the transcript of Metzenbaum's questioning of nominee Thomas, it seems, even a decade later, that he was angry at the witness. Asked if that were in fact the case, he says, "No, I think I was angry at myself, because I was being pushed in two different directions by different persons, and as a consequence I feel in retrospect that I didn't do as good a job as I could or should have done."

Paul Simon, Howard Metzenbaum's former ally in the Senate and on the Judiciary Committee, feels much the same way about Clarence Thomas. "When he was up for EEOC head, I voted against him. When you chair something you have to believe in its mission, and he clearly didn't believe in its mission. Then he was up for the appellate court, and I voted for him...but I said I probably would not vote for him if he were nominated for the Supreme Court, because there was a little bit of talk of that even at that point."

Simon does not give Thomas particularly high marks for his first 10 years on the Court. "Look at the *Hudson* case," the beating of the shackled and handcuffed prisoner, cruel and unusual punishment case. "It's pretty hard to get farther out than that, but if you recall the hearings, when Howell Helfin asked him if he was going to be sympathetic to prisoners and people who are less fortunate, he said, 'Every time

I'm sitting in my office and see that bus [filled with prisoners] go by, I think there but for the grace of God go I.' But clearly that hasn't come across in his decisions."

Simon makes the point, from personal experience, that Clarence Thomas is "a personally gracious guy, and I like Scalia personally too, but they are too far off to the right and want to push the country in a direction I don't think we ought to be going."

Paul Simon says he fears former President Bush may have been, relatively speaking, "indifferent" to the quality of his nominees to the highest court because he did not "scour the landscape the way Gerald Ford had had his Attorney General, Edward Levi, did when they came up with John Paul Stevens." As for the current President Bush, Paul Simon was one of the six Democrats George W. Bush invited to the White House on his very first day in office. When Simon got his chance to offer some advice, he suggested the new President think long and hard about his Supreme Court nominees, saying, "'This is going to live long after your presidency.' He made some notes, but all he said was, 'That's an interesting suggestion,' and what that means, who knows?"

As for Thomas's performance on the Court, using a plus-or-minus scale, the former Illinois Senator said, "I think it's a minus, which is not a *total* surprise, but I thought he would be a little more moderate. At his confirmation hearings, I said to him, because of my observation that some people who rise up from humble beginnings and make it big forget where they came from, that I hoped he would not do that, and he said, 'Let me assure you that's going to be in my mind all the time.' Well, if it is on his mind, he's been translating it in unusual ways."

Unlike Metzenbaum, Simon has no hesitation in saying he believes Clarence Thomas did not tell the truth at his confirmation hearings. "I think, frankly, that he was lying. When you lay out all the facts, including the woman from North Carolina who was not called to testify [Angela

Wright], I think it is clear that he lied. Now some people say, well then he's a perjurer and he ought to be impeached, but there's no point in that—you'd never get a two-thirds vote in the Senate to impeach him. He was under great pressure. Here's a job that any lawyer would yearn for, and it looks like it's blowing up in his face, so he ended up lying. And, if Anita Hill were going to make up a story, she would have made up a better story than that. She would have had him physically touching her, that sort of thing. I think that, basically, what she said was correct."

While Simon believes the Judiciary Committee could "certainly have handled things better," and that it should have heard Anita Hill's charges in executive session first, he also feels that because she was "a substantial person," her charges would have had to have been made public eventually. (He says that at one early point in the proceedings, Hill had asked him, through an intermediary, if her FBI report could be read confidentially, first by the members of the committee and then by the full Senate, and he replied, "You might just as well give it to the Associated Press.")

Continuing to reflect on the historic hearings, Simon mentioned that he believed, "And I may be completely wrong on this, that Joe [Biden] originally told Danforth and Thomas, 'I'll do my best to get you through,' and then when he saw how things were going, kind of reversed field." As for Republican Senator Arlen Specter, whom he says he believes to be a straightforward person, "I do remember him saying at one point that Anita Hill should be indicted for perjury, and when I appeared on the 'Larry King Show' that night with Arlen I said there wouldn't be a prosecutor in the country who would indict her for perjury, and Arlen had no defense whatsoever. I think, as to why he questioned her the way he did, I think he was concerned about a right-wing challenge in Pennsylvania. He had voted against Robert Bork, and got a lot of criticism from the right wing of the Republican party, and he was facing an election, and I think this was an attempt to placate that wing of the party—at the expense, unfortunately, of the Supreme Court. But Arlen overall is a good legislator and an ameliorating factor on the Republican side, but he just found himself in an awkward political situation. ...

"We had no idea how much this had captured public attention, particularly the attention of women. We held the hearings over a weekend, and slowly it dawned on us, because of the phone calls our offices were getting, that there was just massive interest in this. I remember that a woman in Carbondale, where I live, said she and her husband were listening to it, and suddenly she broke down crying. When her husband said what's the matter, she said 'I told him for the first time about how I was harassed when I was 18 years old.' Clearly, the hearing brought out that aspect, and was a massive public education in the whole question of sexual harassment. It was not the Senate's finest hour, but it did do something very constructive for the nation in terms of sexual harassment."

* * * *

As might be expected, the people who support Clarence Thomas and his record are every bit as strong in their opinions as those who oppose him. He brings that out in people.

The following people are all defenders of Supreme Court Justice Clarence Thomas: Prof. Robert Destro, Catholic University of America Law School (and former commissioner, U.S. Civil Rights Commission); Judith Hope, partner, Paul, Hastings, Janovsky & Walker; Clint Bolick, vice president and director of litigation for the Institute for Justice; and (in Final Arguments) former Senator John C. Danforth, now a partner in the law firm Bryan Cave, St. Louis, Missouri.

* * * *

Professor Robert Destro got to know Clarence Thomas

266

during the first Reagan administration when he served on the U.S. Civil Rights Commission. He recalls that the presidential personnel people who interviewed him for the post did not ask his opinion about such things as quotas and affirmative action, but rather wanted to know if he was independent of or beholden to any of the special interest groups. When he and the other two commissioners were named— Clarence Pendleton and Morris Abrams, as well as staff director Linda Chavez—"even though the three of us were generally unknown, the reaction of the civil rights community, generally, was overtly in-your-face hostile. Even though we, individually, had good relations with them, collectively we represented a threat."

Destro said that because of this attitude he had an experience similar to what would happen to Clarence Thomas some years later. "My father came to my first set of Senate confirmation hearings, and was fascinated watching the preliminary hearing, which involved federal circuit court judges. It was very cordial—maybe a couple of questions about their judicial philosophy—and then, we got up there they really let us have it. My father said, 'I don't understand it. These judges, with just their signature can make troops move and can send buses into school districts, but you guys hardly have any real power at all!' I explained to him that it was symbolic.

"And that's why this is important in regard to Clarence Thomas. There is a symbolism involved in the civil rights apparatus in the federal government that far transcends any of the authority that these positions have—if we can't rely on the federal government, who is going to protect us? To me, that's a two-edged sword. As far as African-Americans are concerned, if it hadn't been for the federal government from the '50s to the present, existing civil rights protections just wouldn't be what they are. If you look at it in the longer term, and in more practical terms, it hasn't been as successful as we'd like it to be, but nothing ever really is.

"I started hearing about Clarence Thomas when he was over at the Department of Education. I didn't really know who he was, but I was hearing that he was a really smart guy, a go-getter, and a lot of other good things, but that a lot of people in the civil rights community didn't particularly like the way he did things. And my reaction to all that was that he sounded like a really interesting guy."

Destro says he met Thomas when Clarence Pendleton, the African-American who headed the Civil Rights Commission, introduced them at lunch.

"I did not become a close personal confidante of his, or a good friend, like say Clint Bolick at the Institute for Justice. But over the years I have come to respect and admire him. During the time I was on the Civil Rights Commission, a lot of the discussions we had were mirrored over at EEOC, especially in regard to remedies such as quotas, etc.

"The approach during the Reagan Administration was, how do you apply the same rule to civil rights remedies that you apply to the base line in other areas – i.e., is there an offense? If Title VI says you're not allowed to use race in any programs receiving federal assistance, then why wouldn't that be true in federal remedies too? If it says you're not supposed to do it, then you're not supposed to do it. But the response from the civil rights community generally speaking is: how else are you going to do it? Because the general idea was that they would see remedies as kind of redistributing the spoils, and while in some respects that's true, in other very important respects it's not true. And this shows up later in Clarence Thomas's jurisprudence."

Destro recalls a time when there was a "huge outcry" from civil rights groups because the EEOC, under Thomas, settled a large number of discrimination cases for money. "At the time, Thomas was quoted as saying, 'It's time to get people money and to cut the lawyers out of it.' And I think he did something similar at the Department of Education where he talked about using the money that would go to the lawyers to help the kids and the teachers directly.

"And while we need the lawyers to open it up, people in the civil rights community tend to think not in terms of settling the case, but in terms of ongoing supervision. My recollection of why he got savaged in the EEOC matter is that it was because he was saying that people who get discriminated against in the workplace need to get paid. Getting paid and getting re-established are real remedies. So what Clarence Thomas represented in those days was that the Reagan Administration was saying, 'Isn't there another way? Can't we accomplish the same goals? And if you look at some of Clarence Thomas's Supreme Court opinions, you're going to see that coming out of them."

As far as opinions go, Robert Destro has some pretty strong ones of his own: "If you look at the late William Brennan as the patron saint of the liberals, I think people are afraid that Thomas has that same capability. As for the statement someone made that were it not for the Anita Hill controversy he'd be the most powerful African-American in the country, well, I think he probably is anyway! It's said that he can't go anywhere without causing a demonstration. But what has the man done wrong? He hasn't done anything wrong. What is it that threatens people about Clarence Thomas? It's that he's got all the characteristics of a leader. He's got the brains to lead, he's got a great liberal arts education and he knows how to put it together. But he's been hammered.

"And unlike a politician like Bill Clinton, because he's on the Supreme Court he can't come out and defend himself. So in a way he's kind of a prisoner in a gilded cage."

* * * *

Attorney Judith Richards Hope has a rather special perspective on Clarence Thomas: he ended up with the job she almost got. To clarify that statement, in 1988 President Reagan nominated her for the seat on the same court of appeals to which he would nominate Thomas a year later. In fact, she was to fill the vacancy left by Robert Bork, after his failed nomination to the Supreme Court. There was a common feeling at the time that no matter which party ended up in the White House, it was highly likely that the next vacant seat on the Supreme Court would go to a woman who was already sitting on the Circuit Court of Appeals in Washington, because that court was known to be a "stepping-stone" to the highest court in the land. But, as the story goes, Democratic presidential candidate Michael Dukakis wanted to name his campaign manager, Harvard Law professor Susan Estrich to the Court if he won, so he worked out a deal with then-Judiciary Committee chairman Patrick Leahy of Vermont to keep Richards' nomination bottled up.

"You never know if lightning is going to strike twice, but there were people urging me to do it, both during President Reagan's administration and the beginning of the Bush administration. People said that it was certainly a place to be observed and considered for the Supreme Court, but I had made my promise to Harvard which I kept. And then Clarence Thomas was named to that seat, and because of the background I just mentioned and the conversations I'd just had, I thought that Clarence Thomas would be moving up, not necessarily picked but that he would be considered because they were looking to have a group of people in the D.C. Circuit, and other circuits, who could be in a position to be nominated to the Supreme Court, a broad and diverse group of people should a vacancy occur. The "group" was Boyden Gray, Attorney General Thornburg, and, I think, President Bush himself, as well as some lawyers in the Justice Department and the White House. But by then I was no longer a candidate as I had taken myself out...."

While one might expect, human nature being what it is,

that Ms. Hope might harbor a bit of resentment toward the man who got the job she could very well have been in line for, in an interview for this book in May, 2001, she expressed nothing but praise and support for Clarence Thomas.

"I could have had that seat on the Court of Appeals [that eventually went to Thomas] because I was offered it a second time, this time by Attorney General Thornburgh, but I had given Harvard my word. So, while I watched what happened with interest, it was never personal with me.

"In terms of Justice Thomas, I had known him a bit when he was at EEOC, and had known of his work there, and knew it was well-respected. And I also knew of his work for Senator Danforth, who was very impressed with Clarence Thomas and the quality of his mind and the clarity of his mind. Plus, at the time he was nominated for the Court of Appeals, I knew the administration was looking to get as diverse a group as possible, diverse in every way, in position who could then be possible selections for the Supreme Court."

Hope says that while she doesn't know anybody she agrees with 100 percent, "...and I am sure nobody agrees with me 100 percent, I think he is a man of integrity and conviction. I don't know in detail about his affirmative action views, but I do believe, being a woman who was discriminated against, leaving aside the racial issue, many times over my career, that I have been accused of getting somewhere because of my talents, and I resent that. As does he, I'm sure."

Hope says the Clarence Thomas she knows is a sincere person and in no sense an opportunist, as some have alleged. "Look," she says, with a small laugh, "I too started out, in college, as a Democrat—as was Ronald Reagan— which I guess shows you get better judgement as you get older."

* * * *

As the 2000 election drew near, People For the American Way was not the only interest group to prepare a document ("Courting Disaster") meant to alert voters to the potential impact their choice would have on the Supreme Court. Several blocks away, the Institute for Justice, a conservative group, put out "State of the Supreme Court 2000," an equally cautionary tale subtitled "The Justices' Record on Individual Liberties." One of the chief architects of that document is Clint Bolick, the Institute's Vice President and Director of Litigation—and a good friend, former employee, and unabashed (and unashamed to admit it) fan of Clarence Thomas, the man and the Justice. Of his judicial stature, Bolick says, simply, "Clarence Thomas, over the course of his tenure on the Supreme Court, has developed the most pro-individual liberties record of any justice."

Why did I work so hard to get Clarence Thomas confirmed? He was my first boss here in Washington, at the EEOC, and I knew him as a person and felt he was a man with tremendous integrity. In fact, compared with almost anyone I had known in my life I would put him very very much at the top in terms of his own personal integrity. He served as a mentor to me, which I greatly appreciated. Also, I thought that Thomas's views of the proper role of government and on the rights that are embodied in our Constitution were very congenial to my own.

This is not just an esoteric concern for him. Having grown up in the segregated South obviously hammered home the importance of restraints on government power and the importance of individual sovereignty. So, combining his jurisprudential beliefs with the courage of his convictions, I just thought he would be a magnificent Supreme Court Justice. And I now believe that the only error I made was that I underestimated how good he would be. He's the greatest Justice, certainly of this generation.

Clint Bolick says it used to make him laugh when he would read and hear people say that Thomas was in "lock-step" with Justice Scalia. "Thomas," his former aide says unhesitatingly, "is no one's follower on earth. It just so happens that they agree on a number of issues, but Thomas has always been a person who is willing to follow his own convictions. He's happy to be the lone dissenter when the situation calls for it." What about the charge that Thomas has been, as far as his career is concerned, an opportunist? "Certainly, the Court was not his intended career trajectory, but, like any bright person, he's made the most of the opportunities he's found availing."

Bolick says that he does not think Thomas, as a Justice on the Supreme Court, has as yet carved out a special legal niche for himself. Instead, he avers, "Generally speaking, I think he is probably the most enamored of attempting to divine original intent and to adhere the court to original constitutional intent, and of course that permeates everything that the court does. As for a true distinctiveness, he is the most willing among the justices to reconsider past precedent in order to make sure that the Court had not veered either from original Constitutional intent or statutory intent."

Asked if that doesn't make him an activist judge, Clint Bolick says, "Absolutely! 'Activism' is typically considered a pejorative, but if you look at the Federalist No. 78, the founders intended for us to have an active judiciary in safe-guarding individual rights. Only the judiciary is capable, among our three branches of government, of vindicating individual rights, so in that regard he is an activist in the way that judges were intended to be activists." Bolick says that "…both liberals and libertarians alike should be cheered by the fact that Thomas views the Constitution first and foremost as a limit on government power, not as an exhaustive

273

compendium of rights."

Clint Bolick offers an explanation as to why others don't see the same Clarence Thomas he sees:

> Thomas is a true individualist. My historical hero is Tom Paine, and they are similar in a lot of regards. Paine is not revered by a lot of conservatives either, because he really was willing to upset the apple cart, and so too is Thomas. I think that some of Thomas's civil libertarian leanings on certain issues do not enamor him to all conservatives, but if your conception of an ideal justice is one who will safeguard individual rights rigorously, whether they are considered liberal rights or conservative rights, then Thomas is your man.

This same individualistic attitude is what accounts, according to Bolick, for the fact that Thomas is not better-liked among the American populace. Could it be that when it comes to promoting himself he is, in fact, his own worst enemy?

Bolick says the answer is simple: "He doesn't care what people think about him. He's an intensely private person, and he really doesn't care about his public persona. As long as he lives up to his own very high standards, he's satisfied at the end of the day. History will ultimately be the judge, and I am confident that history will judge him very well. We're still living in the reflected experience of the confirmation hearings, and I think that a lot of people view Thomas through that prism. The wounds are still too fresh.

"Objectivity, when it comes to Clarence Thomas, is a difficult thing to obtain. Nonetheless, I really believe that if you were to go to an American Civil Liberties Union meeting ten years from now, you're going to hear some grudging respect for Clarence Thomas. History will treat him as a very very serious Constitutional scholar. He probably already is the most powerful African-American in the country today.

He could schmooze people and temper his views by hewing to the middle, but he'd rather be true to his vision. As for his personal sense of contentment, I have every reason to believe that he is a very happy guy."

* * * *

What then does all this mean? Can the same man wearing the same robe be both devil and savior at the same time? It hardly seems likely. As he himself has indicated, Clarence Thomas could well serve on the Court until 2034, and perhaps longer. The potential impact of such a lengthy tenure is very great. The seismic shift in the United States Senate caused by Vermont Senator James Jeffords' leaving the Republican Party to become an Independent will make it harder for President Bush to get his Supreme Court nominees through the Judiciary Committee. But that does not mean that the Court's swing to the right will be halted, or even slowed. Thomas's power will only increase.

Anyone in doubt about the extent of that power need only look to December, 2000 and the Court's decision in the epochal case of *Bush v. Gore*, which decided the election for—some would say "gave it to"—George Bush. One of the best cracks made at the time, and often attributed to comedian and political savant Mark Russell, was "The people have spoken—all five of them." That was as much a commentary as a comment, and perhaps also a warning.

Anita Hill has had her hour on the stage, whether she wanted it or not, and has retreated into a world of academic semi-anonymity. She has not written *Speaking Truth to Power, II*, and does not appear likely to do so. Nonetheless, she continues to stand, in the minds of many many Americans, for the principle of speaking up against oppression, in particular sexual harassment, and this represents a not inconsiderable amount of power. But it is power with certain inherent limitations. Clarence Thomas, on the other hand, is in what financial people call a growth position. And

275

how he grows is entirely up to him

If we had a better idea of who Clarence Thomas is then we might well have a better idea of what to expect from him, what he might do and how he might rule in cases that will be argued in future terms of the Supreme Court. But like Ronald Reagan before him, he keeps his own counsel, and only his wife knows him best.

Thus we can only wait, and hope that as time passes and the trauma of his confirmation hearings fades even further into the past, he will decide that, as he once put it, enough is enough, and he will no longer feel the need to be the Silent Justice.

Final Arguments

ust as the 2000-2001 term of the United States Supreme
Court came to its end, so did this book. Granted, the relative importance of these two events is decidedly
unequal, but that common occurrence was helpful to me for
a number of reasons. Not the least of these reasons was that
the people whose profession it is to follow the Supreme
Court—for the benefit of readers, viewers, listeners, or students—traditionally produce an end-of-term evaluation that
includes some historical perspective. Two of the earliest
responses were those that appeared in *The Washington Post*
and *The New York Times*; the first was by a law professor and
the second by the newspaper's chief Supreme Court reporter.

In the *Post*, Notre Dame law professor Richard W.
Garnett wrote, in part, "This Supreme Court term revealed

that our justices are neither easy to pigeon-hole nor easy to predict. Their dispositions are not merely 'restrained' or 'activist.' Their decisions aren't predetermined by the ideological labels slapped on by partisan animators. Over this past year, they did what they always do: they worked hard to decide difficult cases. And in numerous instances, the results were far removed from what the 'law and order versus bleeding heart' paradigm would lead us to expect." As a prime example, he offered the case of *Kyllo v. United States* in which the supposed law-and-order judges Rehnquist, Scalia, and Thomas helped form the 5-4 majority that ruled police use of a thermal imaging device to "search" a house for marijuana was a violation of the Fourth Amendment. He also cited Thomas's majority opinion in *Good News Club v. Milford Central School* which held that "the first amendment does not permit a public school to discriminate against a student group on the basis of its religious activities...."

Linda Greenhouse opened her account in *The New York Times* by writing, "There is a paradox that the recent Supreme Court term—the term that saw the court decide a presidential election—cast into high relief: rarely has the Supreme Court been as deeply embroiled in the political life of the country and rarely, if ever, have the justices themselves been so removed from the craft of politics." Citing the fact that no justice on today's court ever held an elective office on the federal level, "or even a high appointed one" (Sandra Day O'Connor had been a state legislator), she says that while this has produced "a fluidity with legal doctrine in its many nuances...something vital had been lost—a framework for seeing the world in all its gritty reality from inside the marble cocoon. It is hard to imagine, for example, that justices with substantial political experience would blithely assume that defending against the Paula Corbin Jones sexual harassment suit would not be a burden for Bill Clinton."

She provides an interesting quote from former acting

Solicitor General Walter E. Dellinger: "I said when Thurgood Marshall retired that the court had lost its only..., and people expected me to say 'black justice.' But what I said was 'national figure.' The present court could use one, someone with real-life experience."

At about the same time, several events which occurred almost simultaneously indicated that the passage of a decade has not appreciably lowered Clarence Thomas's controversy quotient. One was the news out of Hawaii that three black members of its American Civil Liberties Union (ACLU) chapter had moved to block an invitation to Justice Thomas to speak at a conference on the First Amendment. In what would have been, to my knowledge, a first, Thomas was to have debated national ACLU president Nadine Strossen. One of the objecting members was quoted as saying, "Bringing Clarence Thomas sends a message that the Hawaii ACLU promotes and honors black Uncle Toms who turn their back on civil rights." According to *The Washington Times*, "To bolster the case against Justice Thomas, his opponents presented a letter solicited from the members of the Hawaii Civil Rights Commission. 'We are appalled at the thought that the ACLU of Hawaii may invite Justice Clarence Thomas to speak,' the commission's letter stated. The board voted 12-3 against inviting Thomas during a meeting that included a barrage of personal insults aimed at the justice.... The Hawaii ACLU members were derided by their national colleagues in New York. Miss Strossen has written a letter to the Hawaii chapter, urging it to reconsider. A spokeswoman in the ACLU's New York office called the incident 'unfortunate and embarrassing. We're now trying to reacquaint them with what the First Amendment means,' she said."

The other event that reminded anyone who may have forgotten that Thomas is a figure of controversy was an excerpt in *Talk* magazine from *Blinded by the Right*, the upcoming book by Thomas-defender (and Conservative

279

Quisling) David Brock. In it he says he lied and badgered potential witnesses in order to suppress the fact that Thomas had been a "consumer" of adult videos. As Howard Kurtz, the *Washington Post*'s media maven put it, "David Brock, who made his name trashing Anita Hill after the Clarence Thomas confirmation hearings, now says he lied—and he's sorry.

"The formerly right-wing author...says he 'lost my soul' in printing allegations he knew to be untrue. Brock writes that he was 'dumping virtually every derogatory—and often contradictory—allegation I had collected on Hill into the vituperative mix.' Brock now charges that Supreme Court Justice Thomas used him to spread derogatory information about one of Thomas's critics—an allegation strongly denied yesterday by the man who Brock says was the intermediary between them. 'Thomas was complicit in an effort to discredit another witness against him with negative personal information, which is exactly what he claimed the Anita Hill forces had done to him,' Brock said in an inter-view. Thomas declined to comment through a court spokeswoman." [author's note: As interesting as some of Brock's charges are, in light of his admission that he has already lied in print, I see no justification for reprinting them here.]

Finally, there was the publication of a new book on the Supreme Court by Alan M. Dershowitz, Harvard Law professor, appellate lawyer, prolific author, and (very) frequent media commentator on matters legal. In the book, Professor Dershowitz, a known liberal, has some unusually harsh things to say about the court in general and the five pro-George Bush justices in particular.

The first paragraph sets the book's consistently dominant tone.

> The five justices who ended Election 2000 by stopping the Florida hand recount have damaged the credibility of the U.S. Supreme Court, and their lawless decision in *Bush v. Gore* promised to have a more

enduring impact on Americans than the outcome of the election itself. The nation has accepted the election of George W. Bush, as it must under the rule of law. But the unprecedented decision of the five justices to substitute their political judgment for that of the people threatens to undermine the moral authority of the high court for generations to come.

Unsurprisingly, Clarence Thomas receives his share of scathing criticism. As one example of what he termed Thomas's "glaring and dramatic inconsistencies," Dershowitz cites his joining Rehnquist's concurring opinion stopping the hand count on Article II grounds. After pointing out what he terms clearly contradictory language in Thomas's opinion in a 1992 case (*New York v. The United States*), he then writes, "But in *Bush v. Gore* Thomas ignored these principles of federalism...which, for purposes of a presidential election, treated the Supreme Court of Florida as if it were a lower federal court that had erred in interpreting a federal statute." Just after that, he writes: "Indeed, Justice Thomas explicitly referred, in his opinion in *U.S. Term Limits v. Thornton*, to 'even the selection of the President—surely the most national of national figures' as being accomplished by electors 'chosen by the various States.' But in *Bush v. Gore*, Thomas joined an opinion that would forbid the state of Florida to allocate to its own supreme court the power to interpret and apply its own election laws in a manner consistent with what it has been doing for generations."

Just in case there were any readers who by page 174 of this 206 page book did not fully grasp its author's main thesis, Dershowitz writes:

> ...the decision in the Florida election case may be ranked as the single most corrupt decision in Supreme Court history, because it is the only one that

I know of where the majority justices decided as they did because of the personal identity and political affiliation of the litigants. This was cheating, and a violation of the judicial oath. The other dreadful Supreme Court decisions, dangerous as they were, do not deserve to be placed into this special category of judicial misconduct, though their impact on history may have been more serious and enduring.

It is the uniquely corrupt nature of the decision in *Bush v. Gore* that explains the extraordinary vituperativeness of the language employed by so many unusually cautious critics of the high court. In the nearly half a century I have been following the Supreme Court, I have never seen or heard such strong negative language used about the justices by responsible critics."

Lastly, just before the Court and this book were closing their doors, I was able to conduct two interviews I had been seeking for a long time. The first was with Rosser Barrett ("Bary") Maddox, owner of Graffiti, the five-store chain of stereo and electronics stores that Clarence Thomas patronized in the mid-1980s. By the end of this lengthy interview and several shorter follow-up interviews, it was clear to me that over the years Maddox has given a lot of thought to the subject of Clarence Thomas. Having come to see him as more than simply a good customer, he felt a degree of friendliness toward him, and thus was pleased and rather excited when Thomas was nominated to the Supreme Court. But when Thomas, in Maddox's opinion, evaded the central question of whether or not he had rented and watched adult videos, the store owner was surprised and, ultimately, very disappointed. In listening to Bary Maddox, what came across was that he'd been let down by someone from whom he'd expected much more, someone who was not quite a personal friend, but close to that.

"I knew him as a regular customer who worked at EEOC," Maddox told me at the beginning of the longest and most candid interview he has ever given on the subject, "and when I read in the paper that he got the first judgeship, I congratulated him, and we talked. We knew each other well enough. If I saw him on the street he would recognize me and I would recognize him, and we'd say hello. He was a nice guy, absolutely. Quiet, and nice, but not the kind of guy you'd call smooth with women, that sort of thing."

Asked for an example of what he meant by his last comment, Maddox replied, "He would make inappropriate comments, statements that were out of context, and that were sexual when they shouldn't have been sexual. I remember that he'd be in a group of people and he would say something that was kind of icky and inappropriate. It made you feel ill at ease, and I recall being more careful around him because of that. He was a guy you wouldn't mention certain things in front of for fear of what he might say, and a guy you would definitely not portray as one who got along easily with women."

Bary Maddox says that as far as adult video rentals were concerned, Thomas was an average customer. "He rented all kinds of videos, not just adult. About one-third adult and two-thirds regular. That's what everybody did."

When Anita Hill's charges became public, Maddox says he had no difficulty connecting Clarence Thomas with such rentals because he recalled the titles. "There was one title, Long *Jean* Silver, that in its own way was more notorious than Long *Dong* Silver. Those were two different titles, and I think he rented them both. They were what we now call 'gonzo' films, which means that rather than just sex stories, they were a little freakish. They were unusual in some manner. For example, Bad Mama Jamma, the adult movie with the 450 pound woman, was another popular rental. It was a party film, just something different. You'd put it on and say, "Hey, check this out!"

Graffiti's owner says that to be fair to Clarence Thomas or any of his other customers who regularly rented adult videos in the mid-1980s, people should keep in mind that, "It was a different time, and that's what people did. It was the disco years, and it was common for people to talk casually about cocaine and smoking marijuana, and watching X-rated movies. It has more of a stigma now than it did then; today, if you still do those things you don't admit it."

As for the central did he or didn't he question, did Maddox get the impression from watching the hearings that Thomas denied having rented those videos? "Absolutely. I was astounded at his 'non-denial denial.' He said, I'm insulted or amazed that you would ask me such a question, but he never went beyond that. When they got to that question, "Did you rent those movies?" I don't know what his phrase was, but it was I'm astounded, or insulted, or amazed that you would even ask me such a question, which of course struck me as very humorous because I knew half a dozen people who knew otherwise."

But didn't both Senator Danforth and Evan Kemp, Thomas's friend and successor at EEOC, deny he ever did such things? "I might say the same thing if I were defending a friend of mine, but the fact is he rented adult movies. Let me put it this way—at this stage, ten years later, there's no question in my mind that he rented adult porno videos. I know that to be a fact. I know he rented adult movies because he would ask me for advice about them. 'Is this one any good? Is that one any good? What does this one have? What's this like?' The *adult* ones. "He would ask me specifically for advice.

"I was the person who recommended movies to him, so this is not, 'I kinda remember him renting movies,' *I helped him pick them out.* He would hear about them and I would go and buy them. I might not have had a couple of the titles that are in question had not he or some other customer asked for them. Different people wanted different things, and you wanted to learn peoples' tastes. I didn't push anything I thought was beyond somebody's tastes. They would have to ask me, 'Do you have anything that's a little weirder?'"

In the early Summer of 2001, when "journalist" David Brock made his startling confession, in the pages of *Talk* magazine, that he'd purposely lied in print to cover up Thomas's history of renting adult movies, the name Graffiti was back in the news, with almost every account describing it as a "porno video store." In fact, though, Graffiti was never that type of store. It was a standard electronics, stereo, video commercial outlet, much like Circuit City in the Washington area, though much smaller. For several years in the 1980s, Graffiti carried movies for rent as an added feature. Displayed in bins at the rear of the store, they were a small-scale version of what stores like Blockbuster, which were just coming on to the scene, would do exclusively and on a huge scale. While it turned out to be a profitable sideline, that part of Graffiti's business eventually was eliminated.

Maddox explains, "We got out of the video rental business because we wanted to stay in business. We're a family business, and during that decade there were rumors of snuff films and things like that. I never saw any of that, probably because the side of the industry we were in was home movies for video rental. We had a wide-ranging collection— 2,000 adult titles and about 8,000 regular titles—and many of our customers came to us specifically because we had titles nobody else had. People would seek us out because we had 'depth of titles!' But the big stores that did nothing but rent videos were opening up, and in order to compete with them we would have had to stay open seven days a week and later at night and get rid of all the stereo equipment and television sets to make room for more bins. But that wasn't the type of business we were in, and that wasn't why I'd gone into business. So we got out of it. If I'd stayed in it, I'd probably be retired today, because that became a huge business. But so be it."

Asked if he were aware that college friends of Thomas's have said on the record that he always had a "trashy mouth," Maddox replied, "Oh, he's no innocent. You asked if he were socially graceful or adept with women, but that's a different issue. He could talk the talk if he wanted to talk guy-to-guy. In that situation he was a different individual."

As Bary Maddox sees it, Clarence Thomas was downright lucky that his "non-denial denial" worked. "He said he was 'shocked' that they would ask him such a question, but he never said I never did it, either. He was shocked, he was outraged, and the senators all said, 'Of course, you should be, we're sorry we asked,' and that was the end of that and the only time they asked him directly. What they needed was a good prosecutor to ask the core question: Did you rent those movies? Yes or no? But instead of giving a direct answer, he said I'm insulted, I'm outraged that you would ask, and he wormed his way out of it."

Maddox says he was surprised to learn from the media that his former customer was such a religious person. "I don't want to say he doesn't have an inner religious belief, but he didn't come off as a religious, saintly type of guy. In fact, if he actually is as his wife portrayed him in that *People* magazine article that would have been a complete, chameleon-type of change. Now that's *Danforth*, that's the way *he* is—but not Clarence Thomas. The new Clarence Thomas, maybe."

For Bary Maddox, the experience of getting swept up in the whirlwind of a media feeding frenzy very quickly lost whatever appeal it may have had initially. And not only was his life (and that of his wife) disrupted and aggravated, so was that of his mother, a long-time employee of the White House.

"Here I was all of a sudden being called by reporters,

being *hounded* by reporters, everybody calling on the phone, wanting to know my comments, wanting to know what I could show them, tell them, give them. My mom worked for the Bush administration in the office of correspondence. She had worked there for previous presidents and stayed well into the Clinton years. When she retired in 1997—as director of correspondence—she had worked in the White House for six presidents. She felt that while her job wasn't considered a political post, it had become very political, and she was sure that if I was called to testify, or anything like that, she would lose her job. There was no doubt in her mind. The end result would be that she would lose her job. And she was getting close to retirement, and she didn't want anything to do with that, and I agreed with her. Fortunately, her name never came out, and no one knew of the connection. My mother was afraid that if I testified I would have the FBI and the IRS on me and they would arrest me. She believed that, and she's not a conspiracy person. Fortunately, her name never came out, and no one knew of the connection."

Maddox, who left the University of Maryland 16 credits short of a degree in journalism, says he found it ironic to be the story and not the storyteller. "One reporter was, to put it kindly, 'overzealous.' That was Nina Totenberg of NPR. She was tenacious. She said, in essence, that the future of the country was on my shoulders and I *had* to come forward. But I told her what I told everybody else: that Clarence Thomas was a customer whom I believe did rent adult videos. I went as far as I could go, but 'on advice of counsel' I went no further. The titles that were mentioned in the media were not made-up titles, but I was called a liar and whatever else by several right-wing writers, in particular David Brock, who just took my words and twisted them to give them the opposite meaning. His article in *The Spectator* was a real hatchet job. And then Rush Limbaugh took it and read it on his program, over and over, for one whole day, during which he referred to me continuously as a liar and a pornographer.

"The point was that if people believe that Clarence Thomas did in fact rent that type of movie and thus there's this connection to Anita Hill, then he's a liar. And I *know* he's a liar because I know what I know, and people that I know know. When he said I won't dignify that with an answer, that was where they had him penned. You could see him start to sweat on TV. In the whole thing, that was the moment of truth that I recall watching. I'm saying, 'Go ahead, tell the truth, you can't lie about this.' And no one asked the question, no one pressed the point, and they let it go. But, come on, what junior attorney doesn't come back and ask the obvious question, '*Why* won't you dignify it with an answer?'"

For Bary Maddox, who'd always enjoyed a cordial relationship with Clarence Thomas, the whole experience was bittersweet. "I was excited that somebody I knew was nominated to be a Supreme Court Justice. *And*, I felt he deserved some privacy. So I had a dilemma. Part of me said, putting aside all the politics involved, you don't deserve to be exposed. But it got nastier and nastier, and it kept blowing up, and people started lying and saying that couldn't happen and she's a liar, or, she's not a liar." And was she, in Maddox's opinion, a liar? He thinks not. "She was pretty accurate."

"When I first heard he was nominated, I thought, wow, that's great. I actually know somebody who's going to be on the Supreme Court of the United States, and what I knew about his viewing habits didn't mean anything to me. So he rents adult videos, so what? Who cares? It shouldn't be anybody else's business. So, I did what my attorneys told me to do, which was to give the media very little of what I knew, and I think in hindsight it was the only thing I could do. If anyone was disappointed with my not being called, that's unfortunate. But it was the only fair way to go. Funny thing, I heard later that the reason the Democrats on the Judiciary

Committee didn't call me as a witness was that they made a deal with the Republicans. If the Democrats wouldn't call me, then the Republicans wouldn't call a particular witness against Anita Hill. I've always wondered, if that were true, then what did that person have—or claim to have—on Anita Hill?"

Rosser Bary Maddox says his frustration over the way things worked out has definitely diminished the respect and admiration he had for Clarence Thomas. "Come to find out the 'lynching' wasn't a lynching at all. But calling it one worked. It was a brilliant strategy. When he used it, I thought, 'That's not going to fly,' and then suddenly it was all over. It was theater, grand theater.

"The information was there, but they kept harping on other things—he said, she said, and all this other stuff. And then when the leeringly ugly stuff about watching *adult movies* came in, then the Senators on the committee said, well that's unseemly.

"But what Anita Hill said about being harassed and all that, it all fit. It all was there, because half the stuff she'd said he talked about was out of the movies, like Long John Silver, and Long *Jean* Silver. Long *Jean* was a woman who'd had a car accident and lost her leg, and she had her leg shaped into the shape of a penis on a stump, and she would use the stump...talk about outer edge! That's weirder than just over-sized sexual organs, but that was the sort of thing he would rent. Can you imagine the furor if the Senators had started talking about *that* movie? They were confusing Long Jean with Long John, which is a whole series of six or seven kind of soft core tapes, and he would get those. He was inclined toward the softer core rather than the hard core, but Thomas really was kind of off-the-wall."

So, to sum up, is it fair to say that by avoiding a direct answer to the question of whether or not—as Anita Hill claimed—he watched adult videos, Clarence Thomas proved himself to have feet of clay? Bary Maddox says, simply, "There's no doubt in my mind."

Maddox says that on the advice of his attorney Fred Cooke he resisted reporters' efforts (especially those of PBS's Nina Totenberg) to come forward and "give them more." Had he been so inclined, or allowed, one of the more intriguing items he could have given them was the fact that during his video-renting days Clarence Thomas shared his Graffiti rental card with a woman friend. "It was his card," Bary Maddox told me in one of our last interviews. "The charges went to his credit card, but the names on the card were 'Clarence Thomas/and then the name of this woman.'" Maddox says he does not remember the woman's name, though he recalls she was a fairly light-skinned black woman *and* that she never took out any of the adult-rated videos.

I told Maddox I'd like to know the woman's name, and he promised to look for the card, which he said he has "in storage." But as this book went to press, and despite his having spent several hours searching, he had not found the right cardboard carton.

As several sources have reported that Thomas had a "relationship" at that time, I suspect it was with this woman. But whoever she is, or was, speaking with her might have been very interesting. I can't help but wonder about—and feel a certain amount of relief for—this woman. Had her name surfaced at that frenzied time, she would undoubtedly have been the object of a media stakeout of unprecedented proportions. And, had she been found and had she testified before the Judiciary Committee (or, for that matter, had Bary Maddox testified), and gave added credence to Anita Hills' claim that the nominee had regularly watched soft core porno videos, it is not just possible, but I would say probable that Clarence Thomas would not be a member of the United States Supreme Court today.

* * * *

If the nomination of Clarence Thomas of Pin Point, Georgia to the Supreme Court of the United States of America had failed, no one would have been more distraught than John C. Danforth, the former U.S. Senator, who declined to run for re-election in 1994. Six years later he won praise from both sides of the political aisle for the even-handed way he conducted, as a special prosecutor appointed by Democratic Attorney General Janet Reno, the probe of the FBI's conduct at Waco, Texas. Today he practices law with his old firm, Bryan Cave, in the home office in St. Louis. A man who gives full meaning to the word commitment, Senator Danforth is as fierce a supporter of Clarence Thomas today as he was when he first came forward on his behalf, over ten years ago.

"It was terrible, it was just awful." In a telephone interview in late June, 2001 for the exclusive purposes of this book, that is how Jack Danforth began to describe his current recollection of Clarence Thomas's confirmation hearings ten years ago. "It was watching a terrible thing happen to somebody I cared about, and care about, and it was just dreadful to see somebody go through that experience. It was almost gruesome. And then to have somebody just to be publicly humiliated in that way—awful." A few moments later he said that he thought Thomas had put the whole ordeal behind him, but when I mentioned that the Justice himself keeps bringing it up in his speeches and writings, indicating it must still to be on his mind, Danforth snapped, "How could it not be?"

My next question had to do with the comment I'd heard from a Washington lawyer who'd said the time had come for Thomas to just "get over it." There was a brief pause during which I could almost hear the former Senator shaking his head. "I can't imagine somebody saying that about somebody else," he said, finally, and then added, "Let's say somebody had some just awful war experience or something of that magnitude, and somebody said 'get over it.' I mean how do you say that to somebody?" Clearly, John Danforth's faith in Clarence Thomas rests on a bedrock of friendship.

Asked if he'd kept up with "the literature" on Clarence Thomas and Anita Hill, he said he had read some of the books—and candidly admitted he was less than enthusiastic about talking to me.

"I read the Brock book, which was very negative about Anita Hill" [our interview took place before Brock's confessional article appeared in *Talk* magazine] "but not all of it, and I skimmed the book by the two *Wall Street Journal* reporters, and I must say I was a little bit gun-shy when I was told you wanted to talk to me. I thought, am I going to lend myself to another job being done on my friend? However I decided I would take that risk."

The former senator says that he and Thomas talked extensively about the whole experience of the hearings while Danforth was researching and writing *Resurrection*, but it is not a subject that occupies their time these days. "When I am talking to him now, it is as a friend, and we talk about life, about what's happening in his life and what he is doing—his nephew, his bus, and the other things he's doing."

Asked if he thought the ordeal of the confirmation hearings had scarred Clarence Thomas so badly that—as some critics have suggested—it made him a negative and perhaps secretly unhappy person, Danforth answered quickly and emphatically, "I think he's a *very* happy person. If I had gone through what he went through I'm not sure I would have been a whole and happy person, but I really believe he is. He's a person who likes his job, and he likes his life, and he likes his wife, and he likes his little nephew who's living with them. He likes to be Clarence Thomas."

Throughout the course of the interview, the former senator kept coming back to the "ordeal" of the hearings and to what a terrible toll it took on Thomas and the people around him.

"I still get asked about him quite a bit. Most people who ask me about it are like you, somebody who's writing about it, or a reporter who asks about it for one reason or another, or, it's people who admire Clarence who thank me for supporting him, and that sort of thing. I don't have many people who are badgering me, in my face arguing about it. I used to get boxes of mail, and it was pretty much in favor of Clarence, though there was some on the other side for sure. But don't you think people are seeing him as a Supreme Court Justice now, as a human being, and not just that caricature of him? I think so anyhow. I think people remember that awful episode, but memory sort of gets blurred, and I don't know that many people are harping on the Anita Hill story. Maybe they are, but I would doubt it. I think it was such a vivid thing when it did happen that people remember, hey, that was a big deal at the time. I was in a taxi cab in Washington this week, and when the cab driver saw me he said, 'Oh, yeah, Clarence Thomas.'"

As for Thomas's performance on the highest court, Danforth says he's not the person to ask: "I don't hold myself out as a Supreme Court scholar, and I really have thought from the time that Clarence went on the bench that I was not going to be the sort of running commentator of what he's done on the Supreme Court. Having said that, I can say that I am very proud of knowing Clarence Thomas. I think that he is a really fine person, and that he has established an excellent reputation as a Supreme Court justice, as somebody who's hard working and productive and thoughtful and somebody who writes interesting opinions." Therefore no second thoughts about having put him forward? "No. I think that he is a really good person and a really good Supreme Court justice. As I say, I'm not purporting to be a person who critiques Supreme Court opinions, because to tell you the truth, the amount of time I spend reading them is very small."

Danforth clearly did not agree with my suggestion that, like his hero Ronald Reagan, Clarence Thomas keeps his "real self" hidden, to the extent that even his close personal friends do not know him that well.

"I think people who know Clarence *do* know him very well. One of the really interesting things about this ordeal was the number of people who knew him who rallied to his side, and who *really* felt strongly about it. I mean very very strongly about it, especially women who'd worked with him, and thought it was just so unfair. We had those women—I think there was about 10 or 12 of them—who insisted on testifying on his behalf, and waited until one in the morning until like Monday morning. They were in my office and they were *insisting* on an opportunity to be heard, and Nancy Altman said she was thinking of getting *placards* and marching into the room. They were really adamant about expressing themselves on behalf of Clarence. And that's one thing about him. He generates enormous affection and loyalty from people who have known him and worked for him. I know a young man who was one of his Supreme Court clerks, and he just radiates admiration for and devotion to Clarence."

When asked if he was familiar with the story of Clarence Thomas showing up at the hospital in his "sweats" to be there for one of his clerks whose wife was fatally ill, Danforth said he was not, but commented, "That's Clarence. That is the human being he is, and that's why this was so hard for people who care about him. Do you remember 'To Kill a Mockingbird?' That's what it was, that was the way it seemed, and I think to people close to Clarence, it was just a kind person, and a decent, humane person being attacked in this way. That's why I think people really wanted to help him out and were sick about what was happening to him.

To me, and to people who care about Clarence, political and legal philosophy didn't have anything to do with this. And that was the point. It wasn't, 'What's your political or legal philosophy?', it's that this is a *person,* it's a person we knew, a person we cared about, and a person is more than political or legal philosophy, and it's not right to destroy a person because that person does not share your political or legal philosophy. It's just not right."

John Danforth says that while he's aware some commentators have said the attempts of Republicans over the last few years to "get" President Clinton were a form of payback for what the Democrats did to his friend Clarence Thomas, and to Judge Robert Bork before him, it is not a theory he takes seriously.

"I don't think that's the case, but we do now have this new word in our vocabulary, to 'bork' somebody, and that has become a tried-and-true way to destroy a person. But I think for people who felt strongly about the Clinton situation it was different. At least to me it was different. That was a question of, should we redefine our moral standards in order to fit the needs of the President, and I don't think that was the same as the Thomas thing at all. To me, it didn't have anything to do with political philosophy, it didn't have anything to do with paybacks. It was just that I knew Clarence Thomas—had known him for quite a while when this happened—and I knew what kind of person he was, and it just wasn't right. And my hope is that even if it was somebody whose political or legal philosophy I couldn't bear, I would have felt the same way."

In *Capitol Games,* Timothy Phelps and Helen Winternitz say that on the day Clarence Thomas was sworn in, Senator John Danforth predicted that he would "…surprise many people on the United States Supreme Court. He is going to be a good and competent and decent and fair justice. He is going to be the people's justice on the United States Supreme Court."

I asked former Senator Danforth if he thought that in his first ten years on the Court, Clarence Thomas had surprised people and had become the peoples' justice. He replied, "I think that was in my book, and, I think, I was either quoting him or Orrin Hatch." Then, after a pause, he added, "I don't know that I ever said that, but I think that may be in the book, and that I may have attributed it to somebody else, but I don't know. That book is seven years old, and, I don't re-read it. I am not, as I've mentioned, an analyst of Clarence's Supreme Court opinions, one way or another. However, I do believe from what I do know about them that he has a judicial philosophy and he expresses it consistently, and that it's basically a position that, regardless of ones personal political ideology, the role of the courts should be to interpret the law and interpret the Constitution, rather than embellishing it to achieve a result, and I think that's basically what his legal philosophy is, and from what I understand, he expresses it well and he expresses it clearly, but I'm not the person to ask about that."

What about Clarence Thomas's famous, or infamous, silence, his practice of asking so very few questions during oral argument before the Court?

"I think that what happens, and I've only had one Supreme Court argument, so I'm no great expert, but what happens when you're a lawyer in the Supreme Court, it's generally the biggest case you've ever had in your life, and you have prepared for it for a *long* time, and you polished your brief, and you've gone over the points you want to make in oral argument, and you're trying your best to do the finest job you can possibly do, and you want an opportunity to do that. You understand that Justices can ask you questions if they want, but you really want to do your best to put forth your best arguments to the best of your ability. If a justice genuinely has a question to clarify a point, that's one thing, but I think that sometimes justices are more interested in the gamesmanship of sparring with the lawyers, as opposed to helping the lawyers clarify the points that are relevant to the case. So my own view is that unless it's really necessary to clarify the points, the justices shouldn't themselves sort of hog the limelight in the oral arguments. My preference would be for a Supreme Court Justice who is not given to asking a lot of questions. Is that the latest line of attack on Clarence Thomas—that he doesn't ask enough questions from the bench? If it is, then that would seem to me to be a frivolous criticism."

Nearing the end of the interview, I told Danforth that my few remaining questions represented a mixed bag. The first had to do with pornography, the second with his current view of Thomas's chief accuser, and the third with religion.

Asked if he believed that Clarence Thomas had *never* rented or watched adult videos, Danforth replied, "I don't think I ever said one thing or another about that. I don't know that he ever expressed a view on it himself, one way or another. I just don't know."

As for his present-day feelings about Anita Hill, did he still believe as he did then that she was lying?

"I don't know. I don't think I ever said that she was lying, and that's why I was groping around for some explanation other than somebody who is just lying. I thought [what she'd alleged] didn't happen. But if somebody said something happened, and you don't think it did, that doesn't necessarily mean somebody's lying. And that's why I was, at the time, groping around for some explanation."

Does the explanation put forward by Republican Senators Orrin Hatch and Arlen Specter, among others, that some of her charges came from the book *The Exorcist* and the *Long Dong Silver* video, that still ring true as a plausible explanation?

"I believe in Clarence Thomas. I was certainly interested at the time in whatever might have been an explanation for this happening, and how could this story be there, and, particularly when what was said about him was so contrary to the person that I knew, and that everybody else knew. So I don't know. Orrin Hatch was actually the one who dropped that in the hearing, I think. But to me, anything that explained it, that explained—gee, I mean, what somebody said as to what could be the possible origin of it, to me that sounded reasonably plausible at the time."

As a quick follow-up, I asked him if he now thought it would have been better for Senator Hatch to ask those video-watching questions of Anita Hill, rather than of Clarence Thomas. "I don't know," he said. "Look, I was there as Clarence's friend. My *role* was as Clarence's friend, and to be there for him, and to try my best to be a source of strength for him. It was purely a matter of my being there for a friend."

My last question had to do with the amount of religious imagery and theologically evocative language in his book. I prefaced it by asking if Thomas is as religious as he, John Danforth, clearly is.

"He's a former seminarian, and, I think he goes to daily Mass," Danforth replied instantly. "He certainly is a person to whom his religious faith is very important. And there was a lot of praying going on at that time. It was an effort to destroy somebody, to destroy a human being, and the fact of the matter is that the Clarence Thomas I saw, through all of this, was destroyed. It had worked. He was, in a sense, dead. It was an effort to kill him, which was, I think what one of the leaders of one of the groups said, 'We're going to bork him, we're going to kill him,' and so on. But, I think it was very successful. It was the total taking of everything that's dear to a human being, and taking it away from him and destroying him. And yet, he lives. That *is* a religious theme, and it does have to do with death, and it does have to do with resurrection. And for a person in the Christian tradition, those are themes that certainly resonate."

When we'd finished, I thanked Mr. Danforth, who then said, his tone shifting from wary to weary, "I just hope you're fair, and that it's not another one of these hatchet jobs." Attempting to reassure him that it was not, I made John Danforth the same offer my publisher had made his friend Justice Thomas. I asked him if he'd like to read the finished manuscript for factual errors. At this, he sounded *truly* weary. "Oh, no," he said. "Thanks a lot, but no thanks."

* * * *

If my research represents an accurate picture, then— former Senator Danforth's wishes to the contrary—people do not yet see Clarence Thomas as a Supreme Court Justice, but continue to view him through the prism of the hearings, to borrow Clint Bolick's phrase. The blame for this, if blame is the right word, is on both sides. The fair thing to do would be to look at Clarence Thomas solely on his record, as it exists in the tabulation of his votes and the words of his opinions, plus what he has said and done in his public appearances over the last decade. But part of the problem is that the justice himself makes that hard for people to do because *he* doesn't do it. As a prime example, his Boyer lecture to the American Enterprise Institute in March of 2001 is laced with the language of confrontation—us-versus-them, reference to his "enemies," and talk of "the limits of civility."

When I called Martha Fitz, John Danforth's secretary, to thank her for helping arrange my telephone interview with her boss, who'd been reluctant to talk to me initially, I said I wished Justice Thomas would have agreed to an interview, and her immediate response was to say, "Oh, I'm sure he's still too hurt." I believe anyone who heard his AEI lecture, or saw it on C-SPAN, can understand the basis of her remark, can see "where she's coming from."

To reiterate, what makes being fair to Clarence Thomas difficult for many people is Clarence Thomas himself. For example, while the U.S. Supreme Court is famous for being cloistered to the point of reclusivity, Thomas, by nature the most outgoing of all the justices, seems to build additional walls around himself. When he agrees to take questions following a speech at a school, something he is very good about doing and which brings him considerable praise, he specifies that only students be allowed to ask questions and that the media be barred from doing so. In his excellent three-part series on Thomas that ran in early July, 2001, Ken Foskett of *The Atlanta Journal-Constitution* wrote, "Thomas' friends offer another explanation for his affinity for young people: Unlike grown-ups, children don't give him too much attitude. 'Their minds are more open,' said Dave Kautter, one of Thomas' friends. 'I think he finds them more intellectually honest than some of the adults he talks to.' In Washington, Thomas generally shuns the social circuit, preferring to spend free time at home or working on his bus."

That bus, which former Senator Danforth said Thomas talks about quite often, is an intriguing subject for speculation. Granted that one could carry the idea to unfair lengths, I find the type of bus it is to be interesting. According to Foskett's account, the bus, which the justice has had for over two years, is a 1992 Prevost "...with a custom Marathon interior. Powered by 500-horsepower diesel engines, the Prevost is built to travel 1,000 miles or more between fuel stops and 1 million miles between major overhauls. Luxury Prevosts can cost well over $1 million, depending on interior features such as satellite television, marble trim and leather upholstery." A Prevost website lists several Prevosts of about the same vintage, all of them priced at considerably more than $200,000.

What I find intriguing about this vehicle is not its price but its character. Again, without going off the deep end, this sounds like a near-perfect mode of travel for someone who wants as little contact with other people as possible. Now that may have nothing to do with why Justice Thomas purchased, and is so enamored of, this particular bus, (he has always been a "car guy")but it does seem a somewhat odd choice for a person who is said to be gregarious, outgoing, and friendly. The bus sounds like a splendid isolation booth on wheels in which he and his family can travel coast to coast almost non-stop and with the absolute minimum of human contact.

Phil Cooper of Cooper Motorhomes in Urbana Illinois, whom I found via the Internet, told me he was Thomas's first contact (also via the Internet and then the telephone) with the wonderful world of Prevost. Clearly, Cooper said, the vehicle, which is a motor home custom-built on a bus chassis, is the ne plus ultra of motor homes. "You get down to Nashville," he says, "and it's wall-to-wall Prevosts. Clarence has a 45 foot model, which had to have cost him between $200,000 and $250,000." Although Thomas ultimately bought his bus from someone else, Cooper feels proud of having talked to him first. "He's a real cool guy," said Phil Cooper. "He does his own thing."

Another possible explanation for the justice's selective silences is offered by Washington lawyer Frederick Douglass Cooke, Jr. It is not, I must say up front, one that any of the pro-Thomas people I've interviewed buys into.

Cooke says, "In his book, *The Miseducation of the Negro*, Carter G. Woods in essence says that the most insidious thing about racism is that if you educate a man to know his place, he will find it. You don't need chains, you don't need cells, you don't need guards. If he has been educated, he will find it without any help from anybody else. And part of the problem with guys like Clarence is that they buy into this inferiority thing, and believe that somehow they are inferior, and so they need to find a role, a secondary role in life. What's interesting is that a lot of guys and ladies who grew up in the South in the maw of discrimination have this sort of intuitive inferiority complex that is such an essential part of their behavior. It is learned behavior. And it's hard for them to overcome it."

By contrast, Cooke says that growing up where he did, Washington, D.C., "I never took on the idea that somehow because I was a minority student in a majority community that there were some things that I couldn't do, that I was limited. But if you come from a small, sheltered, minority community and you move into a majority community, if you don't have a very well-developed sense of self—who you are, what you are, what your capabilities are—that incipient feeling of inferiority creeps in and you have this self-doubt, this negative sense of can I, am I, good enough? And I think, now this may be way too psychological, because I'm not a mental health professional, that a lot of Clarence's behavior is a function of that sense, that lack of true belief in himself. And that if he were to embrace the notions of affirmative action or champion some of the things that Thurgood Marshall championed, he would somehow be exposing himself to charges that he was there only because he was black and not because he was good enough, because he still has a big cloud of doubt about himself. I think that if he got to a point of extreme self-confidence, he wouldn't have some of these worries."

True as that all may or may not be, what does Fred Cooke, and by extension the majority of black America, want? Did they want him to say no to George Bush, to have turned down the job of Supreme Court justice?

"Of course not," says Cooke, laughing, "When they're making you one of nine on the planet, you don't say no. But I talk to a lot of my black friends about this, friends who are really successful, and a lot of them say they have this insecurity thing going. So, I think on one level it's got to be very hard, and a difficult life for Clarence, because in a lot of ways, the court as an institution cloisters you, and forces you to withdraw from a great many normal human interactions. That's the nature of the beast. But then to know that you are reviled in so many quarters—not just passively disliked, but almost hated—by people who don't even know you, who never ever met you, but who feel as though they hate you, has got to be very very difficult."

Obviously, it is not fair to evaluate or even to describe Clarence Thomas using a template stamped out by Thurgood Marshall. Indeed, to do so would be clearly unfair. But that does not mean one cannot or should not talk about Clarence Thomas in terms of the type of man he is, and how his humanity, his innate sense of human decency and friendliness and his willingness to do and to be there for others that all of his friends cite, could stamp his record on the court. But again, too often the man himself makes that difficult because he so often throws down gauntlets, aggrieves about those who seek to destroy him, and issues defiant statements, as he did in December, and then again shortly after the last Court term ended, about the decision in *Bush v. Gore* having absolutely nothing to do with "partisan politics." For Clarence Thomas, given all the different facets of his personality, and his obvious love for spreading all sorts of gospels, would seem the justice most likely to connect with the greatest number of American citizens and thus help to restore some of the damage done to the body politic by the extreme partisanship, in all three branches of government, that we have lived through in recent years.

If Justice Thomas were to break that famous silence and take his message—whether one agrees with it or not—to a wider audience, then he would certainly be less of an enigma. And we might all be better off for it.

* * * *

303

Index

Acknowledgments

First and foremost I thank my wife, Denise Del Priore, for putting up with me during the shorter-than-usual, and therefore quite intense, period of time in which this book was written. I'll never do that again (I hope). Next comes Joseph C. Goulden, *il miglior fabbro*, who passed this challenging opportunity on to me. Our friendship is now in its fifth decade. I thank my publisher Lyle Stuart for believing I could do this, and for charging me with the yoke of fairness. Extra-special thanks go to Jeff Nordstedt, vice-president of Barricade Books, who is not only wise beyond his years but unusually talented as well.

I thank all of the people mentioned in the text who gave me their time and the permission to quote them. I also thank those who felt they could not go on the record but still gave me time and guidance. As for those people who would not speak with me, or return my call, and I encountered more of them on this project than in any other over the last 30-plus years, I wish you had agreed to be interviewed because if you had then Justice Thomas would have been better served.

Special thanks to the following people: Larry Berman, Gerald P.Boyle Stan Brand, Plato Cacheris, Prof. James Chen, John Florescu, Sir David Frost, Prof. Michael Mello (and his third year law student Ted Sweet), Alan Morrison, Ramin Oskoui, MD, Prof. Jamin Raskin, Tony Romano, Sam Simon, Thomas Smeeton, Jacob Stein, Brendan Sullivan, and Steven Urbanczyk, Les Whitten.

Finally a most heartfelt thank you to Dr. Dennis Kraus and all the people who work for and with him at Memorial Sloan-Kettering in New York City. You made resolving a life-threatening situation feel even less scary than writing a book.

John Greenya
Washington, D.C.
July, 2001